Nothingness
and
Emptiness

Nothingness and Emptiness

A Buddhist Engagement with the
Ontology of Jean-Paul Sartre

Steven W. Laycock

State University of New York Press, Albany

Published by
State University of New York Press, Albany
© 2001 State University of New York

For information, address State University of New York Press,
90 State Street, Suite 700, Albany, NY 12207

Production by Michael Haggett
Marketing by Anne M. Valentine

Library of Congress Cataloging-in-Publication Data

Laycock, Steven William
  Nothingness and emptiness : A Buddhist engagement with the ontology
of Jean-Paul Sartre / Steven W. Laycock.
    p. cm.
  ISBN 0-7914-4909-2 (alk. paper) — ISBN 0-7914-4910-6 (pbk. : alk.
paper)
  1. Sartre, Jean Paul, 1905–   2. Sunyata. 3. Nothingness (Philosophy)
I. Title.

B22430.S34 N64 2001
111'.092—dc21
                                                            00-056275

10 9 8 7 6 5 4 3 2 1

Contents

Acknowledgments

The author is gratefully indebted to the following publishers for permission to reproduce copyrighted material:

Passages from *Against Ethics: Contributions to a Poetics of Obligation with Constant Reference to Deconstruction,* copyright © 1993, by John D. Caputo. Used by permission of Indiana University Press.

Passages from *The Fundamental Wisdom of the Middle Way: Nagarjuna's Mulamadhyamakakarika* by Nagarjuna, translation copyright © 1995 by Jay L. Garfield. Used by permission of Oxford University Press, Inc.

Passage from *Out in the Open,* copyright © 1985, 1986, 1987, 1988, 1989, by Margaret Gibson. Reprinted by permission of Louisiana State University Press.

Passages from *Zen: Poems, Prayers, Sermons, Anecdotes,* translation copyright © 1963, by Lucien Stryk and Takashi Ikemoto. Used by permission of Doubleday Press.

The Radiance of the Lotus

The lotus, resplendent symbol of the awakened mind, exfoliates in enigma. Is it an explosion, a cosmic detonation, flinging its energy outward? Toward what? From what center? Do we rather see, not dynamism, but quiescent serenity, loveliness eternally distilled, a vision disturbed only by the gentle lapping of the waves? Or is it that "[t]he film suddenly stopped, and the picture on the screen remained fixed—but alive" (Sekida 1992, 201). Have we somehow surprised the detonation in a moment beyond time, disclosing its dynamism in "a breathtaking continuum of the present" (201)? What we *see* of the lotus, what appears, is presented as an enigmatically silent burst of color and light, quiet uproar, motionless explosion, occurring upon, within, as an expression or manifestation of, the supporting waters of the pond. It is as if the stillness and motionlessness of the pond, mating with the savage dynamism and biting beauty of the sun, gave birth to a being of few days, yet, in its presence, eternal. And it is as if the event of parturition, though never completed, were always complete: the salience of the lotus not repudiating its expressiveness. In its wild radiance, the lotus evinces the serenity of the pond.

Nor is the pond free from enigma. Its quiescence is both a glass and a mirror. The ingenuous settling of stones at the bottom, the effortless grace of the savvy koi patrolling the pond, are seen *through* the waters. Yet—and at the same time—the overhanging leaves, the wisps of evanescent cloud, the idols of one's own visible presence, are cast *upon* the waters. The waters are indecisive, hesitating, ambiguous: transparent? reflective? Or does the pond play a double game? Does it, simultaneously or in succession, wear two very different masks? Or again, is it not rather indifferent to such merriment, leaving the masquerade to others? The pond keeps its secret. The answer remains undisclosed in its presentation. The blackbird, arrested in its flight, lites upon the arched wooden bridge (*merle au pont*), peering without comment at the pond below, its "mind quiet as water in the fissure

1

of Being" (Merleau-Ponty 1969, 235). And mindful of the enigma, the plucky visitor decries:

> When through the water's thickness I see that tiling at the bottom of a pool, I do not see it *despite* the water and the reflections there; I see it through them and because of them. If there were no distortions, no ripples of sunlight, if it were without this flesh that I saw the geometry of the tiles, then I would cease to see it *as* it is and where it is—which is to say, beyond any identical, specific place. I cannot say that the water itself—the aqueous power, the syrupy and shimmering element—is *in* space; all this is not somewhere else either, but it is not in the pool. It inhabits it, it materializes itself there, yet it is not contained there; and if I raise my eyes toward the screen of cypresses where the web of reflections is playing, I cannot gainsay the fact that the water visits it, too, or at least sends into it, upon it, its active and living essence. (Merleau-Ponty 1964a, 182)

Within the water, there is neither "here" nor "there." Or rather, "here" and "there" do not designate the coordinates of an absolute Cartesian grid. The waters of the pool are uncontainable, unlocalizable.

And the lotus itself shares, though differently, this refusal of containment. The quiet-exuberant lotus flings itself, flings its *self*, centrifugally beyond all bounds. Its ecstasy, its savage habit of being perpetually beyond itself, is a negation, a warning. "Do not presume that I will succumb to your snares. I am a being of pure freedom." Do not assume, with Sartre, that I am subject to "*violation by sight*," that "[w]hat is seen is possessed," that "to see is to *deflower*." Do not suppose that "[e]very investigation implies the idea of a nudity which one brings out into the open by clearing away the obstacles which cover it" (1971, 738). "You cannot grasp me, seize me, lay hold of me. To know me is to *be* what I am, to throw yourself away." In Suzuki's words, "To know the flower is to become the flower, to be the flower, to bloom as the flower, and to enjoy the sunlight as well as the rainfall. When this is done, the flower speaks to me and I know all its secrets, all its joys, all its sufferings; that is, all its life vibrating within itself" (cf. Sohl and Carr 1970, 85). Or rather, it is no longer *I*, the snarling, red-fanged, predator, ripping away the veil of appearance (the *Schleier des Seins*) from my quivering victim, who am thus informed. For the lotus speaks only to those who do not pursue, who, in Dogen's words, allow the myriad things to advance and experience themselves. With the unadorned simplicity of Gary Snyder's verse:

A flower
for nothing;
an offer;
no taker; . . .   (1991, 264)

The lotus communicates with those who are capable of authentic
Gelassenheit, releasement, letting-be, and, in Heidegger's sense, authentic
"greeting" which "bespeaks mindfulness of the differential origin of manifestation; it holds in memory (*Andenken*) the enigma of the Differing as
that which already-was (*das Gewesene*). In contrast to conceptual grasping,
the gesture of greeting releases that which presences to show itself in its essential 'whiling' " (Fóti 1992, 51). Irigary perceives that "the Buddha's gaz-
ing upon the flower is not a distracted or predatory gaze, it is not the lapse
of the speculative into the flesh, it is the at once material and spiritual contemplation that provides an already sublimated energy to thought" (1991,
171). The enlightened regard is not "incisive." It does not "penetrate"; it
does not "grasp." Though *prajñā*, etymological kin to the Greek *prognosis*,
suggests a "knowing" (*jña, gnosis*) "into" (*pra-, pro-*), the "into" does not
designate a vector of intrusion. Knowing, like our encounter with the
furtive denizens of the wild, occurs within a domain of beings who, without
threat, are allowed to advance, as we remain silent, motionless, open, practically breathless. "Buddha contemplates the flower without picking it. He
gazes upon this other than him without removing it at its roots. Moreover,
what he gazes upon is not just anything—it is a flower, which perhaps offers
us the best object for meditation on the adequacy of form to matter"
(171). The lotus communicates in its wholeness, in its organic indissocia-
bility from the turbid ooze of the reality in which it is rooted, and as an expression of all-that-is, only when we find ourselves quiet and still among
beings (*inter esse*), with an "inter/est" which is no idle curiosity, nor even the
insistent passion to "know," but an openness, a wonder, which as Burke
(1990) discerns, "is the originary question that the look addresses to the
world, but, unlike the questions of cognition, does so without expectation
or demand . . ." (93). Indeed, "[t]he philosopher's manner of question is . . .
not that of *cognition*" (Merleau-Ponty 1969, 101). We cannot wrest the secret, extract the secret. Yet, in words spoken on Merleau-Ponty's behalf, this
openness, this wonder, the authentic vitality of the question, "provides a reflective and intuitive access to Being which philosophers of intuition and reflection quickly sought to close up by trying to prove that the answer was
already contained in the question; for them the 'meaning' of Being was
prior to the question, for it was contained a priori in the mind . . ." (Burke,
88). Both intuition and reflection, as commonly understood, assume a do-

main to be dis/covered, dis/closed, un/veiled, in effect, denuded. But the repudiation of disclosure, of a presence prior to presentation (a being, in Heidegger's idiom, prior to Being), prior, in fact, to the demand for disclosure, in which "[t]he unknown object is given as immaculate, as virgin, comparable to a *whiteness*," or "like a woman whom a passerby catches unaware at her bath" (Sartre 1971, 738), is not the occasion for despair. "Today we consider it a matter of decency not to wish to see everything naked, or to be present at everything, . . . One should have more respect for the bashfulness with which nature has hidden behind riddles and multiple uncertainties. Perhaps nature is a woman who has reasons for not letting us see her reasons?" (Nietzsche 1974, 11–12). We shall not lapse into the nihilism of the question without an answer. The refusal of dis/closure "does not mean that the ontological question has no answer. On the contrary, it means that we do not know a priori what answers are forthcoming. It means that if answers come, it will be only as a result of our having recognized the interrogative space, the abyss, within which alone Being can freely and continually manifest itself" (Burke, 89). Though alien in spirit to those who would seek a "verbal substitute for the world we see" (Merleau-Ponty 1969, 4), the vision of Buddhism, no less than that of Merleau-Ponty, is no more hospitable to the nihilists, the "negative metaphysicians" who "proclaimed that 'what is essential cannot be said any longer'" (Golden and Jamison 1990, 399).

But the lotus is not only ecstatic, not only "beside itself," beyond self, empty of self, its *self* being exactly its refusal of self-coincidence, it is, in all of its glorious richness, in every fibre of its detail, exactly *such* as it is. In its brilliant outburst it remains serene, still, untroubled. Not merely to *think*, but most genuinely, to *see* is to confine oneself to a single phenomenon "that one day stands still like a star in the world's sky" (Heidegger 1971, 4). The lotus, this curiously frozen explosion, is an anchor in the heaving midst of the world's fluidity. Though it throws itself freely, without reserve, into the "interrogative space" of wonder, it is nonetheless a *response* to the wonder which it pervades. It is answer dissolving into question; question condensing into answer. In the splendid verse of Bunan (1602–1676 C.E.):

> The moon's the same old moon,
> The flowers exactly as they were,
> Yet I've become the thingness
> Of all the things I see! (Stryk and Takash 1963, 15)

The emptiness of the lotus is in no way compromised by its suchness. Bunan, standing among the flowers of this world, quietly lifts the floodgate and is inundated by their presence. Dōgen, in a wholly concordant vision, sees "flowers of emptiness." Presence and absence, suchness and emptiness, are not separate cabinets in which the world's cups and the world's saucers are kept. Nor are they incompatible manners with which the same cups and the same saucers comport themselves. They are indissoluble verities.

But a final enigma. Kelp, perhaps the earliest ancestor of the lotus, was first to master the paradox of dipolarity, driving its roots downward into the nourishing depths only to grow upward toward the empowering light, the tension between depths and heights, earth and the heavens, shadow and illumination, being integral to its very life. The lotus knows this secret and more. To be sure, dipolarity informs its *being*. But its *appearing* is no less dipolar. Buddhism has always made much of the fact that the resplendent lotus, the burst of enlightened awareness, the detonation of self flinging its fragments into the void, is nonetheless rooted in and draws deep nourishment from the lightless depths of samsāra. The lesson, however, always comes as a surprise, not because we suspect the lotus of rootlessness, but because the brilliance and salience of its exfoliation dominate the eye so thoroughly that its rootedness is overlooked. It may be that "the 'flower' of philosophy" is "the heliotrope or sunflower" (Rovatti 1988, 127), but the sunflower's visible stalk affords no astonishment at its rootedness. The contrast, however, between the radiant lotus blossom which breaks and expresses the mirror-like, glass-like surface and the murky roots is maximal. The eye, if not the mind, takes the blossom as its all. To be reminded of the roots breaks the spell of exclusive absorption in presence.

But there is our sagacious avian companion, the *merle* perched observantly *au pont*, who will not be deceived. The enigmas we have sensed—the interpenetration of temporality and the timeless, transparency and reflection, self and selflessness, presence and absence, light and dark, appearance and reality, the visible and the invisible—are patterns of reciprocity, entwinement. The lotus is the site of manifold crossings and recrossings. Its being, then, is that of the chiasm, the abyssal locus, the "interrogative space," of the chi, the *X*, the determinable indeterminate, the enigma. The pages that unfold before you are, in the spirit Merleau-Ponty's (1969) posthumous deposit, *The Visible and the Invisible*, mindful of the chiasm, and therefore unsympathetic with the dualizing tendencies, however rarified, of Sartre's thinking. And they are no less imbued with wonder at the miraculous blossoming of enlightened mindfulness, and dedicated to the Buddha's liberating and unobtrusive envisionment. I offer, at this site of wonder, a sustained meditation on Buddhist meontic phenomenology.

But our purpose is not the simple rejection of Sartrean ontology. Sartre said of his relationship with Merleau-Ponty that "[a]lone, each of us was too easily persuaded of having understood the idea of phenomenology. Together, we were, for each other, the incarnation of its ambiguity" (1965,

159). Sartre and Merleau-Ponty form of themselves a chiasm, a framework of reciprocal encroachment, or in an idiom to be cultivated, a dyad of "seemings," each (we shall assume) wholly compatible with the landscape of phenomenality, neither required by it. The strategy adopted here is rather a specification of that developed in *Mind as Mirror* (cf. Laycock 1994): namely, the effort to keep logical alternativity, the incompatibility of the two "seemings," alive while remaining mindful of their failure of adequation (untruth). Immanence thus receives into itself the wedge of inconsonance, and cracks open, rendering up the smooth identity of being and appearing and becoming thus transcendent. Paradoxically, then, the confrontation of Sartrean immanentism (consciousness *is* as it *appears* to itself to be) beside the Merleau-Pontyan view that "a sufficient reduction leads beyond the alleged transcendental 'immanence,'" that immanence explodes into the transcendence of interpenetration, "the *Ineinander* of the spontaneities . . ." (1969, 172), in full awareness of the lack of preferability between the two views, culminates in a preference for the Merleau-Pontyan vision of omni-transcendence.

The ontology of Sartre's great "essay," his magnificent assay, his extraordinary venture, *Being and Nothingness*, rests upon his phenomenology like a book upon a shelf, like a bust upon a pedestal. It offers a reconstruction, a patterning, of phenomenological intuition which "makes sense" of these insights, which transforms isolated glimmers into systemic illumination. The possibility of reconfiguring the pieces of the puzzle to form a different image argues only against the necessity, not the wisdom, of Sartre's vision. But we must, from the outset, declare a different sense of the bond uniting phenomenology and ontology. While we shall not pursue the Heideggerian path of conflating the two, it will be clear that the pedestal rests upon the bust as much as the bust upon the pedestal.

If "[o]ntology is the interrogative word of adoration in the ear of Sigé the Abyss" (Burke 1990, 83), then phenomenology is the paradoxical reply. "Paradox no longer marks a deficiency; it becomes the evident sign, that which reveals the indissoluble relation between the question and the response" (*Le paradoxe ne marque plus une déficience; il devient le signe évident, le révélateur de l'indissoluble relation entre la question et la réponse*) (Timmermans 1990, 298). Ontology—not question, but questioning—precedes the ontic: the phenomenal presence (the "thingness" in Bunan's word) of the response invoked. Response—presence, the ontic—is called forth by ontology; and phenomenology interrogates this deposition. Ontology, if you will, is the earnest, ingenuous, unsuspecting wonderment of the earth's first child at the dawn of Being. But before the first few curious beams break the horizon, there are the still and timeless hours of the night. As Bataille instructs us, "night . . . is nothing, there is nothing in IT which can be felt, not even finally darkness" (Bataille 1988, 124–5). The earth-child's capacity for boundless wonder is predicated upon another illimitable: the intimate recollection of eternal night—a night, not of terror or despair, not of nihilistic abandon, but of a maternal embrace so deeply enveloping as to dissolve the glaring, angular projections of detail into the gloaming, and finally into a nightfall of openness and unimpeded acceptance.

Phenomenology, with its epochē, its suspension of assent, is the movement of suspicion, the wariness (awareness) of a mind acquainted with error, aware that the sun's effulgence can blind no less than heal the wounds of ignorance, and unwilling to substitute enthusiasm for truth. As "[t]here is no absolute error" (Merleau-Ponty 1988, 38), there is also, on the conceptual plane, no unqualified absolution from error. Ontology marvels at presence. It communes directly, without reservation, with the splendid suchness (*tathatā*) of the lotus. Phenomenology investigates the roots of this exhibition, the "how?" of appearing, leading us thus in the direction of emptiness (*śūnyatā*). Ontology and phenomenology, the lotus and the chiasm, interpenetrate, illustrating of themselves both chiasmatic reciprocity, *Ineinandersein*, and lotus-like integrity and fullness. There is no interrogation without positive deposition, no suspicion without a moment of childlike acceptance, no suspension without commitments to suspend. But equally, there is no lotus without roots, no phenomenal display without conditions, no "thus" without a "how."

Sartre would find in this intercoupling of wondering acceptance and vigilant interrogation the very condition for self-deception. "To believe is to know that one believes, and to know that one believes is no longer to believe. Thus to believe is not to believe any longer because that is only to believe—this in the unity of one and the same non-thetic self-consciousness . . ." (1971, 114). Self-deception is grounded in the instability of a commitment permeated by the nonpositional awareness of this commitment, an awareness which, inasmuch as openness is also a questioning, tinctures the commitment with a certain "questionableness." If Sartre has, indeed, disclosed the infrastructure of self-deception, then the chiasmic embrace of ontological receptiveness and phenomenological suspicion participates in bad faith. We shall have to see, however, whether unstable conviction is the recipe for self-deception, whether the interpenetration of wonder and wariness amounts to "the inner disintegration of my being" (116), and, moreover, whether Sartre's assumption of unquestionable givenness which supports an overhanging ontology is not, in another sense, deceived.

A Buddhist phenomenological ontology would sacrifice neither the innocent nor the wary, neither the immediate resonance of com/passion nor the dispassionate clarity of wisdom, neither the tranquility (*samatha*) of absorption nor the insight (*vipassanā*) of genuine discernment—so long, that is, as they are balanced (*sammā*), and in this sense, "right." In the words of that consummate distillation of supreme wisdom (*prajñā paramitā*), the sūtra (thus, suture) of the palpating, compassionate-wise heart-mind (*hṛdaya*), "[f]orm is emptiness; emptiness is form. Emptiness is not other than form; form is not other than emptiness" (Lopez 1988, 19). And as Lopez reminds us, "[t]here is a critical difference between form being empty and form being emptiness . . ." (58). It is, finally, this fathomless insight of the Heart, the crux, the crossing, the chiasm, a Buddhist phenomenological ontology is concerned to plumb.

> He who holds that nothingness
> Is formless, flowers are visions,
> Let him enter boldly!
> —Gido (1325–1388)
> (cf. Stryk and Takash 1963, 9)

Chapter 1

Dancing with the Light

The lotus, in its salience, in its ecstasy, stands out, dominates the ground of its appearance, absorbs the mind in its presence. It is the mind thus spellbound, thus captivated, a mind like the imprudent moth entranced by the flame, incautious, unmindful of condition or consequence, that, in our present acceptation, we shall call "consciousness" (*vijñāna*). Consciousness, in this sense, is, not by contingent befallment, but trivially, by definition, unawakened. In so far as a figural salience dominates the field of consciousness, suppressing awareness of marginal presence, to that extent awareness is diminished, attenuated; and to that extent, also, the mind drifts among evanescent dream shadows, haunted by shades of presence that whisper from the dark only to vanish. Under Wittgenstein's pen: "*Our* life is like a dream. But in our better hours we wake up just enough to realize that we are dreaming" (Engelmann 1968, 7). In Fichte's arresting delineation:

> There is nowhere anything lasting, neither outside me, nor within me, but only incessant change. I nowhere know of any being not even my own. There is no being. *I myself* know nothing and am nothing. There are only *images*: they are the only thing which exists, and they know of themselves in the manner of images . . . I myself am only one of these images; indeed, I am not even this, but only a confused image of images. All reality is transformed into a wondrous dream, without a life which is dreamed about, and without a spirit which dreams; into dream which coheres in a dream of itself. (Fichte 1965, 89)

9

The title, *Buddha*, The Awakened One, is the occasion of an implicit analogy: enlightened awareness is to the flickering half-light, the drowsy play of light and darkness, presence and absence, which we here designate "consciousness," as consciousness is, in turn, to the dream-state with its gossamer phantasms. In Hayward's interesting gloss, *awakened* connotes "the dispelling of confusion, or the dissipation of disorder, entropy" and *one* designates the "dynamic blossoming of all potentialities in an individual . . ." (Hayward 1989, xi). And we can empathize with Bataille's anguished lament: "Am I awake? I doubt it and I could weep" (1988, 34). The Buddha was not, in our sense, conscious. He was awakened, fully aware: *sammā sambuddhasa*.

The marked disparagement of consciousness typical of Buddhist thought would seem perplexing without its implicit contrast with awareness. It would seem, for example, merely perverse to hold that grasping after (*upācarā*) consciousness (*vijñāna*) is one of the five ways of bringing suffering (*dukha*) down upon our heads, and that to release consciousness, to let it go, to liberate it, no longer to be lulled into a state of semisomnambulance, is, then, to ignite the lamp of awareness (*sati*). Consciousness is the fifth of the *skandhas*, the five modes of erroneous self-identification, clinging to which is given as the summary formula for all sentient suffering. The exclusive identity, the nucleus of egocentricity and selfishness, which isolates us from others, and which conditions all antipathy and all greed, is the product of our "identification" with objectual form (*rūpa*) and with the four remaining skandhas having the intentional function of "naming" or designating (*nāma*): sensations (*vedanas*), thoughts (*samjñā*), habitual dispositions (*sanskāra*), and finally, consciousness (*vijñāna*). It would seem merely wanton, as well, to regard consciousness as the third link (*nidāna*) of the twelvefold chain of contingent becoming (*bhava-chakra*). Each link of the chain is a necessary condition for its successor, the last, in turn, a condition for the first. To break *any* link is therefore to break *every* link in the chain. Elimination of the evident ills of ignorance (*āvidyā*), craving (*tṛṣṇa*), and suffering (*dukha*), spells the abolition of consciousness which, by parity, must also be regarded as an evil. Again, it is *consciousness*, not *awareness*, which is the offense.

Bataille speaks of "the disguised suffering which the astonishment at not being everything, at even having concise limits, gives us" (1988, xxxii). Oceanic assimilation, pantheistic self-identification, is not an adequate response to suffering, but merely the engorgement, the obscene distension, of the self. And so long as *ātman* retains, in our conceptual imagination, the least trace of private individuality, its identification with *Brahman* is not spared this opprobrium. The inner security and illumination which can set aside our incessant and ever-more-subtle attempts to seize upon our actions *in the act*, to grasp them "red-handed," in Husserl's (1982) idiom, in order to provide—for ourselves—a cognitive foundation for our deluded sense of ourselves as agents evaporates in the sunlight of enlightened awareness. And "since reflexivity has dissolved, the moment wherein the human mind is 'together' and, thus, capable of knowing (naming) *other things* no longer exists. The human mind cannot constitute for itself the identity of other things" (Magliola 1986, 8). The dissolution, the "emptying," of identity into difference is thus concomitant with the annulment of *nāma-rūpa*, the constellation of *skandhas* which would otherwise nourish our various modes of self-identification. The *skandhas* comprise the "concepts with which we identify ourselves as true presence . . ." (Coward 1990, 78–9), and the dep-resentation of the self, its self-liquidation, leaves nothing for our egocentric grasp. An authentic Buddhist philosophy is inaugurated with the decisive suspension of self-identification, writ small or large. And "no longer to wish oneself to be everything is to put everything into question" (Bataille 1988, xxxii). Indeed, "[m]aking oneself questionable is an important element in getting under way" (Caputo 1993, 175). The decisive step beyond a merely conceptual philosophy in the direction of liberation is "to relate oneself to all 'things' in an *empty* relationship, i.e., in total freedom" (Streng 1967, 82). In Caputo's scathing remark, "the sort of *philia* philosophy is—*amor intellectualis*—goes well enough with a cold heart . . ." (121). But if our heart lies with our treasure, then what, in our aberration, we most deeply cherish is what orients our benighted sense of limited, thus exclusive, iden-tity. We identify with what we value. And if the *skandhas* comprise the vari-ous dimensions of our narrow and restricted value-orientation, then to value consciousness is to value the mere phosphorescence of awareness, to submit to the spell of apparition. Sartre is nowhere more lucid than in his clipped identification of "the being of the self: it is *value*" (1971, 92). Yet spirituality impels "the elimination of private standpoints and values" (Murti 1987, 259).

"Even the sharpest sword cannot cut itself; the finger-tips cannot be touched by the same finger-tips. Citta does not know itself" (cf. Murti 1987, 317–8). *For* the mind there *is* no mind. Or in Dōgen's words, "Since there is no mind in me, when I hear the sound of raindrops from the eave, the raindrop is myself" (Kotoh 1987, 206). And *pace* Husserl (1982), the intentional act is not present in the act, and thus cannot enter into an atten-tive description of live perception. It may be that "the universal category of all [cognitional] teleology is the *wish to see*, and even the *wish to be seen*" (Trotignon 302). But the passion to exhibit oneself in self-presence is futile and blind. And the foreclosure of awareness inherent in the "wish to see" one thing as distinct from another is the dynamic of *avidyā*: "the blindness of all organismic striving" (Parsons 1976, 7). As the ancient Sthaviras maintained, consciousness "is like a *magic show*—because it deceives and cheats us" (Murti 1987, 224). And Mehta explains that " 'magic' is only the name of a category employed to indicate what a blind spot prevents one from seeing . . ." (1987, 28). This "blind spot," that which sees and cannot be seen, that which, in our anxiety, in our troubled attempts to found ourselves, reflectively to pull ourselves up by our own bootstraps, we seek to see, is, in a specific sense, our *self*. Reflection offers at best "a maze of speculative mirrors through which we are lured in the hope of seeing ourselves as we really are, at the source of the light by which we see ourselves" (Llewelyn 1988, 203). Yet as Sartre discerns, "the consciousness which says *I Think* is precisely not the consciousness which thinks" (1972, 45). There is a rent in the fabric of our reflective self-awareness. Self *as agent*, the agency of seeing, is precisely *not* self *as patient*, self as seen. The "self" which *knows* is precisely *not* the self which is *known*. To be sure, "[a] Cartesian does not see *himself* in the mirror; he sees . . . an 'outside' . . ." (Merleau-Ponty 1964a, 170). Dews corroborates that "there is nothing *inherent* in a reflected image which reveals to the onlooker that it is his or her *own* image, and the subject cannot appeal to any third term for knowledge of identity of the two poles, since this would involve an infinite regress" (1988, 21). And to appropriate the image, to see it as an image *of oneself*, is, as Sartre insinuates, of questionable merit: "Not all who would be are Narcissus. Many who lean over the water see only a vague human figure. Genet sees himself everywhere . . ." (1964, 7). Was Genet, then, a mystic, who "sees himself in everything and all things in himself" (Puligandla 1985, xiv)? And was Sartre? Late in his life, Sartre was able to see "himself," the "self" of consciousness, everywhere: "I find it everywhere. . . . there is no in-itself that could get away from the for-itself, nor a for-itself that should not be provided with the in-itself" (Fretz 1980, 236). But the hemorrhage which severs the medium from the matter of consciousness, the vital "no one" (awareness) from the languid "someone" (a general patterning of events of consciousness) does not import an ontological disjunction. We have no experiential warrant for positing a substantial subject, even a subject afflicted with the annoying habit of vanishing in the face of its object. In Wittgenstein's insightful deposition, "nothing *in the visual field* allows you to infer that it is seen by an eye" (1974, 57). To say that the empirical ego is an impassive *Gestalt*, an object, is not to prize a putative duality of egos apart. There are not two. Anonymous awareness may found, but does not participate in Cartesian categoreality. Paradoxically, discrimination becomes nondiscrimination. Sartre approaches the Buddhist view in his conception of a "detotalized totality," the unity of consciousness and its object, bonded by internal negation, in which consciousness is experientially absent. Still, the for-itself functions as a category of Sartre's ontology. And awareness is transcategorial. Zen speaks of the "Great Self" and the "small self." But it is important to see that the Great Self is not, in any recognizable sense, *a self*— or *an* anything. To distinguish the "small" (empirical) self, the self *seen*, from the Great Self is not, then to distinguish it *from anything*. Speaking of the blind spot in our understanding of ourselves, Bataille observes, that "it is no longer the spot which loses itself in knowledge, but knowledge which loses itself in it. In this way existence closes the circle, but it couldn't do this without including the night from which it proceeds only in order to enter it again" (1988, 110–111). Merleau-Ponty sagely signifies the supplement to visible existence, that which effects this closure, the agential self, as "one" to emphasize its ineluctable anonymity. And this chimes with Hegel's view that "the thought in question is not *someone's thought*, but pure thought, thought in itself. Yet the self *is* the thought; and this self is . . . itself a universal thinker *in general, not* a particular thinker" (Molino 1962, 7). Occhamite in its ontological sparseness, in fact ontologically abstemious in the most radical sense, Buddhism takes the *one*, the [*some*]one, to bespeak entirely too much, and replaces it by *zero*, "someone" by "no one."

The *act* of perception is not concealed off-stage only to be surprised in its effacement in the last act of reflection. Merleau-Ponty was searchingly cognizant of this truth: "I should say that there was there a thing perceived and an openness upon this thing which the reflection has neutralized and transformed into perception-reflected-on and thing-perceived-within-a-perception-reflected-on" (1969, 38). Reflection discloses *not perception*, but *perception-reflected-on*. The modification is serious, indeed. And "[t]o reduce perception to the thought of perceiving, under the pretext that immanence alone is sure, is to take out an insurance against doubt whose premiums are more onerous than the loss for which it is to indemnify us . . ." (36). Sartre sharpens the point:

> . . . the viewing of oneself by oneself, that is, the reflective consciousness which views the series of non-reflected moments of consciousness, in general merely supplies syntheses that are too simple; with parts that are ejected and crowded out, with continuities that are sharper or less sharp than in non-reflected consciousness. In brief, it provides primarily an object that is poorly constituted, that strives too much towards unity, that is too synthetic. It does not supply the truth of the non-reflected consciousness. A truth, which doesn't exist, because there is no divine consciousness which supplies the veritable synthesis, a truth which is nothing else as the unreflected consciousness itself. However the synthesis that is brought about by the reflective consciousness always contains the defect of being a *consciousness*, a synthesis by con-

sciousness which is bent on achieving a total unity. Whereas the
true unity of the non-reflected consciousness is in reality given in
the non-reflected consciousness. But this unity is not itself explicit;
it does not present itself as such, but we live it in the non-reflecting
and in the unity, so that the reflective unity is a unity of the second
degree and a unity which as such falsifies the true unity. (Fretz
1980, 231)

As Duméry observes, "philosophy always comes after life. Philosophy is a
recovery of life, but it cannot be identified with life. . . . Reflection lives on
concrete life" (1964, 5–6). If perception is "live," then perception-reflected-
on, bloodless, cold, its life now past, is assuredly dead. The perpetrator: reflection—a virulent parasite. We must, then, forsake "the temptation to
construct perception out of the perceived, to construct our contact with the
world out of what it has taught us about the world . . ." (Merleau-Ponty
1969, 156). It "dissimulates from itself its own mainspring", constituting
the world from "a notion of the world as preconstituted" (34).

     Consciousness, for Buddhism, is a *skandha*—thus, in one of its luxuri-
ant senses, a *dharma*: "the key-word of Buddhism" (Sangharakshita 1987,
118)—and for Merleau-Ponty, equivalently, an integral feature of phenomenal display. Merleau-Ponty advances an entirely noematic characterization
of consciousness. Starkly: "To be conscious = to have a figure on a ground—
one cannot go back any further" (1969, 191). This formula, repeated a few
pages hence—" 'to be conscious' = to have a figure on a ground" (197)—
identifies consciousness with the *écart*, the phenomenal estrangement, of
the dominant from the recessive internal to noematic presentation.
Consciousness is *phenomenal*. Though "contrast elicits depth" (Whitehead
1978, 114), there is no need to posit an agency "off-stage," perpendicular to
the phenomenal display. Consciousness is not, to press the suggestions of
Sartre's term, "positional." It does not stand at a distantiated *position* with
respect to its object. It does not open a dimension of depth across which
thing communicates with eye, for depth, not to be conceived as a dimension invisible *in principle* (a notion which contravenes the fidelity to lived experience intrinsic to phenomenology), is rather "the experience of the
reversibility of dimensions . . ." (Merleau-Ponty 1964a, 180). Depth is either an experiential "nothing," a line of sight which vanishes precisely
because it runs endwise from the eye "or else it is my participation in a
Being without restriction, a participation primarily in the being of space
beyond every [particular] point of view" (173). The primal contrast
which institutes consciousness is swallowed up in a spaciousness, an environing emptiness, which, though not removed from the figural object, remains, nonetheless, "the means the things have to remain distinct, to

remain things, while not being what I look at at present" (Merleau-Ponty 1969, 219).

If consciousness is, then, phenomenal, it is so, not for consciousness itself, nor for a transcendentally reflecting "ego" situated at some remove from the plane of phenomenal display, nor even, in a Sartrean vein, as the interior coloration of nonpositional interiority. The phenomenologies of the West habitually overlook the distinction between consciousness (*vijñāna*) and awareness (*sati*). The "distinction" is itself deeply problematic, since awareness, like an ideally flawless mirror, has no mark. Indeed, the Buddha depicts *nirvāṇa* as a "consciousness, without a distinguishing mark, infinite and shining everywhere . . ." (cf. Loy 1988, 213). Prescinding from empirical imperfections—the tint or glare of the glass, bubbles and lesions in the tain—the mirror (a gerund, not a nominative, the event of mirroring, not an objectivated melange of sensory presences) is devoid of intrinsic phenomenal attributes, reflecting spontaneously (better: *being* a spontaneous reflecting), without attachment or aversion, and without distortion, whatever stands before it. And if awareness is thus entirely signless, it cannot be conceived as "positional" or intentional, distantiated with respect to its object. In the query of Niu-T'ou Fa-Yung (594–657 C.E.), "[w]hen there is an image occupying a mirror-mind, where can you find mind?" (cf. Chang 1971, 21). And being devoid of intrinsic quality, it cannot, except from a position ostensibly *external* to both, be conceived as distinct from its object. The anonymity and phenomenal evanescence which Sartre claims for consciousness we reserve for awareness. Awareness cannot accommodate an external vantage point. Being devoid of intrinsic determinations, nothing distinguishes awareness from its object. And the "tension" of in[tension]ality is dissolved. The "object," as that which is hurled (*jectus*) in the face of (*ob-*) subjectivity relinquishes its objectivity. Merleau-Ponty regards as "the total philosophical error" the deluded assumption that "the visible is an *objective* presence . . ." (1969, 258). And this supposition is undermined in the lovely verse of Bunan (1602–1676 C.E.):

> The moon's the same old moon,
> The flowers exactly as they were,
> Yet I've become the thingness
> Of all the things I see!   (cf. Stryk and Takash 1963, 15)

And though not to be identified with it—awareness is not a relatum or an identical—the awareness of phenomenal consciousness is nonetheless nondifferent.

Sartre discerned that "interiority seen from the outside" is afflicted with indistinctness—the intrinsic phenomenal characteristic of the in-itself—or rather, that "indistinctness is the degraded projection of interiority" (1972, 85). In our present acceptation, consciousness (contradistinguished from awareness) is purely phenomenal, and thus has no "inside." In Hegel's view, "consciousness . . . suffers violence at its own hands . . ." (Heidegger 1970, 17). "Sciousness" (*scientia*), seeing, is accompanied by (*con-*) the perpetually failed attempt to be seen, to secure "itself" as a phenomenal presence. But the presentation of its "itself" can only displace its live functioning. Knowing-with—[con]sciousness—is actually a knowing-against: [contra]-sciousness. Granting, with Sartre, that consciousness gives itself to reflection as "an interiority closed upon itself" (1972, 84), its concealed inwardness is nonetheless merely phenomenal. It is not the manifestation or "projection" of something hidden, something deep and essential, something substantial and real. It is pure "show" (*Schau*), completely and utterly exposed. It is pristine exteriority with nothing hidden. In its "showing" of itself to awareness—even its showing of itself as a deeper reality cloaked in outer manifestation—it is not re/vealed. There is no mysterious presence behind the veil which then stands forth denuded. "We no longer believe that truth remains truth when the veils are withdrawn . . ." (Scharfstein 1993, 37). If it is "indistinct," it does not thus conceal within this penumbra a being of pure crystal.

Were consciousness essentially crystalline, the grime of its sullied exterior would be adventitious. Sartre sees that a crystalline consciousness befouled by manifest indistinctness is a "contradictory composite" since "an absolute interiority never has an outside" (1972, 84). Tsung-mi (780–841 C.E.) draws a similar inference.

> The mind . . . is like a crystal ball with no colour of its own. It is pure and perfect as it is. But as soon as it confronts the outside world it takes on all colours and forms of differentiation. This differentiation is in the outside world, and the mind, left to itself shows no change of any character. Now suppose the ball to be placed against something altogether contrary to itself, and so become a dark-coloured ball. However pure it may have been before, it is now a dark-coloured ball, and this colour is seen as belonging from the first to the nature of the ball. When shown thus to ignorant people they will at once conclude that the ball is foul, and will not be easily convinced of its essential purity. (cf. Suzuki 1981, 17)

My earlier work, *Mind as Mirror and the Mirroring of Mind* (Laycock 1994), criticized the phenomenologies of the West for abandoning presuppositionless insight and succumbing to a "metaphysics of experience" exactly by making the decision which Tsung-mi demands. Do we have here qualitative pervasion or unsullied openness to quality? Is consciousness merely translucent, retaining thus a certain phantom opacity available to reflective inspection or is it the case, in words which bespeak the transparentist strand of Sartre's early thought, that "[a]ll is clear and lucid in consciousness . . ." (1972, 40), that consciousness "is all lightness, all translucence" (42), and that the least hint of opacity "would divide consciousness . . . would slide into every consciousness like an opaque blade" would "tear consciousness from itself," and would thus be "the death of consciousness" (40)? In reflection, is there "something"—however rarified, ectoplasmic—*to see* or is it rather the case that to *see* consciousness at all is precisely to *see through* it, the leveraged surmountings which we call "reflection" thus collapsing immediately into prereflective *naïveté*. To decide the issue one way or the other is to surpass experience toward presupposition, to abandon phenomenology for metaphysics. And "the distinction between experience and reason is not given in experience or reason itself" (Puligandla 1985, 17). Phenomenological rigor binds us to the recognition that qualitative pervasion is phenomenally indistinguishable from openness to quality, a crystal intrinsically befouled is indistinguishable from pure colorless crystal offering no impedance to the darkness which it transmits.

We cannot—*qua* phenomenologists—come to Tsung-mi's decision. But then it was not as a phenomenologist, but as one who would whisper "the interrogative word of adoration in the ear of . . . the Abyss," as one, that is, whose childlike wonder was granted the response of presencing, that Tsung-mi himself came to this decision. Lines from Hölderlin's "Vom Abgrund nemlich . . ." bespeak a similar commitment:

> . . . my heart becomes
> undeceiving crystal by which
> the light is tested . . .   (cf. Fóti 1992, 60)

Without abandoning my earlier insistence on phenomenological rectitude, I wish here to salute the sagacity of ontological abandon. Transparentism, the wisdom of Tsung-mi's resolve, and of Hölderlin's, is not that of wariness, a reticence to transgress the limits of the legitimately given, but is rather transformative. It is not that awareness offers itself to an external regard, that it can be properly thematized, characterized, and distinguished from the dark presence which would otherwise naively be absorbed into its very being that Tsung-mi's transparentism is of import. For, like Sartre's consciousness, it strictly has no outside. It is rather that this way lies liberation; this way lies detachment (*virāga*); this way lies releasement (*Gelassenheit*), which, in Levin's eloquent depiction,

> . . . calls for a gaze which is relaxed, playful, gentle, caring; a
> gaze which moves freely, and with good feeling; a gaze which is

alive with awareness; a gaze at peace with itself, not moved, at the
deepest level of its motivation, by anxiety, phobia, defensiveness
and aggression; a gaze which resists falling into patterns of seeing
that are rigid, dogmatic, prejudiced, and stereotyping; a gaze which
moves into the world bringing with it peace and respect, because it
is rooted in, and issues from, a place of integrity and deep self-re-
spect. (1988, 238)

As color pervades the crystal, so, in moments of captivation and clinging, the ghostly presence, the "indistinctness," of consciousness pervades
awareness. In our delusion, consciousness seems, not thematic, but environmental, present as an enveloping mist, spectral, diffuse. Its diffuseness is
given as a quality of awareness: we have, it seems, an indistinct awareness of
the distinct, not a lucid awareness of the obscure. Immersed in *māyā*, it
would seem, then, that *this* is the way the world is: the world's dough is cut
into a thousand cookies—cookie-trees, cookie-houses, cookie-women and
cookie-men—each not only distinct but distinctive, demanding recognition
as separate, isolated, exclusive, repudiating continuity with others in virtue
of a mere gap, an interstice, a "nothingness," the mere incision of our
cookie-cutter, figure-ground consciousness. And it seems that *this* is the way
we are: selective, grasping, attached, only diffusely aware. But this is only
seeming. It is not that seeming argues in any way with being, for suffusion
and openness are not only compatible, but phenomenologically indistinguishable. Both are authentic "seemings." Tsung-mi has not somehow
plucked the reality from behind the appearance. He has learned to enjoy the
freedom afforded by the seeming of openness, a seeming which expels consciousness from awareness, permitting both the flowering forth of distinct
phenomena (including consciousness) in all their distinctive detail and the
wariness which guards the postulation of existence, both suchness and
emptiness, and, at a higher level, both ontological wonder and phenomenological interrogation.
     But this is not the end of our journey. For the mere isolation of the pure
crystal of awareness easily degenerates into the cult of purity. Hui-neng, offering a "critique of pure purity" (Caputo 1993, 65), admonished his disci-
ples "neither to cling to the notion of a mind, nor to cling to the notion of
purity . . . for these are not our meditation" (Suzuki 1981, 27). A more in-
sidious snare is laid for those who, in even the most subtle way, objectify
awareness: "Purity has no form, but, nonetheless, some people try to postulate the form of purity and consider this to be Ch'an practice. People who
hold this view obstruct their own original natures and end up by being
bound to purity" (Yampolsky 1967, 139–40). Hui-neng regards as a "confused notion" the assumption that "the greatest achievement is to sit quietly

with an emptied mind, where not a thought is to be conceived" (Suzuki 1981 26–7). And we have Nāgārjuna's dialectical corroboration:

> We provisionally assert that impurity cannot exist without being mutually dependent on purity and that, in turn, purity exists only as related to impurity. Therefore, purity per se is not possible.
>
> We provisionally assert that purity cannot exist without being mutually dependent on impurity and that, in turn, impurity exists only as related to purity. Therefore, impurity per se does not exist. (1995,10–11; Inada 1970, 139)

Thus, while liberation pursues the seeming of openness—the expulsion of consciousness and its phenomena from awareness—bondage paradoxically pursues this very divergence. For distinction objectifies the distinguished. Liberation is not, then, as in the classical Samkhya theory, the simple isolation of *purusa*. Though "[t]he mind . . . is pure and perfect as it is," its ostensible segregation from quality is immediately equivalent to the abolition of its crystalline transparency, and thus its very *being* as pure crystal. It "is" as that which can *seem* a beclouded discernment of the cloudless and can equally *seem* a pellucid discernment of the clouds.

What Merleau-Ponty's abstract, if also perspicacious, delineation of consciousness as saliency, the emergence of figure upon ground, leaves tacit, or incompletely expressed, is the asymmetry, the vectoriality, of consciousness. Consciousness is absorbed in its figural object in a way which, to a greater or lesser extent, exiles the background. And to the precise degree of this exclusion, the figure cannot be seen *as* horizonally informed, *as* relevantly similar to other objects of the same type, or *as* an exemplification of the same form, structure or quality. And in Wittgenstein's depiction, the ground also becomes "mysterious." "Perhaps what is inexpressible (what I find mysterious and am not able to express) is the background against which whatever I could express has meaning" (1980, 10e). "*Māyā* is inexpressible, because language has its basis in it" (Puligandla 1985, 90). Consciousness may be the *écart* by which the dominant is detached from the recessive—or rather, the event whereby this very discrimination is instituted—but in its enactment, it is the figure which dominates the scene, steals the show. Saliency effaces itself before the salient, prominence before the prominent. In Heidegger's startling formulation, " '[c]onsciousness' is violence done against itself . . ." (1970, 17). The *écart* has no "self" to offer. In its functioning, it "itself" has evaporated. But this does not prevent the attempt or mitigate its futility. [Con]sciousness is the perpetual failure to grasp itself, to stand itself upon itself, to be unto itself its own pedestal, its own support, its own buttress, and illustrates that "heteronomic difference" that "loves invisibility, infinite recesses, recessed infinity . . . It loves what cannot make a show at all, what is embarrassed at its impoverished appearance. It is taciturn, sincere, with a bowed head, without dissemblance, *honnête*"(Caputo 1993, 61).

As argued in *Mind as Mirror* (Laycock 1994), the standpoint of engaged awareness is indifferent to the (quasi-) realist construal that, though inaccessible in the immediacy of the event, nonetheless, *there are* horizontal determinants of figural saliency; that, though evanescent, there nonetheless *is* an *écart* which wrenches figure from ground; and that, starkly, though awareness nowhere appears in the appearing of the world, it nonetheless *exists*. The standpoint of awareness is equally indifferent to the (quasi-) idealist supposition that "what you see is what you get"; that if horizonal determination is unavailable to experience, it is simply not "there"; and that, with evident paradox, awareness, which annuls its "own" presence in favor of the world, *does not exist*. For Heidegger, *Dasein* (being-on-the-scene) is exactly that being for which its own being is in question. Awareness, on the contrary, is exactly that for which, in the immediacy of its enactment, there is, and can be, no question of its own existence or nonexistence. The ontological questions put to it are not its own. And it cannot, for this reason, be charged with *naïveté*. It would rather be naive to expect the question to have any significance for engaged awareness, and *a fortiori* it would be absurd to await a determinate answer. We would seem to violate phenomenological strictures (and good sense) by insisting upon the existence of that which, in principle, cannot appear, that for which we could have no evidence and no warrant. And we would seem to transgress logical cogency, also, by first assuming an intrinsically self-effacing awareness only to repudiate its existence on the grounds of this very self-effacement. But there is a breach between the horns. Buddhist momentarism familiarizes us with evanescence, that for which *to be* is precisely to *cease* to be. And Sartrean ontology habituates a conception of consciousness for which *to be* is to be *nothing* at all. Awareness is precisely that which an ontological survey of the world cannot disclose, that which cannot appear in any appearing, that which has no "self" to offer, for its *self* is its very selflessness. For Sartre, however, the for-itself submits to "the absolute law of consciousness for which no distinction is possible between appearance and being . . ." (1972, 63). It is the "identity of appearance and existence" (1971, 17). If this meant that its being is the very appearing *of the world*, we would have no quarrel. But it is clear that consciousness "is pure 'appearance' in the sense that it exists only to the degree to which it [i.e., consciousness] appears" (17). Yet Sartre lapses here into inconsonance. Sartrean consciousness, a descendent of Descartes' conception, is also heir to Fichte's profession that "there is a consciousness in which the subjective and the objective are in no way to be separated, but are absolutely one and the same" (1975, 107). For Buddhism, consciousness, like every other phenomenon (*dharma*), is "empty" (*śūnya*). To be is to defer its own being, its own-being (*svabhāvatā*), to its conditions. Its "self" is drained away only to reappear among the manifold factors which sustain its being. To be is not only to be conditioned, but, re-flexively, to exist as an immediate reflux. Like the moon which borrows its light from the sun, and is visible only in virtue of the reflex of solar illumi-nation which it occasions, consciousness is exactly the reversal, the return, of being to that which sustains it in being. There is nothing "more" to con-sciousness than this ontological arc, the flux and reflux of being. Awareness, on the other hand, is profoundly anti-Berkeleyan in the sense that, for it, *to be* is exactly *not* to appear. Authentic subjectivity is comprised exactly in its being in no way objective. To *be* itself is precisely to *have* no self. "Vision, as Merleau-Ponty attests, "is the means given me for being absent from my-self . . ." (1964a, 186). "I am," he writes, "a self-presence that is an absence from self" (1969, 250). Pressing this claim into its most radical construal, this represents the searching insight of Buddhist wisdom.

In a qualified sense, Sartre recognizes worldly being, being-in-itself, and its objectual modes as supporting consciousness, the privation of being, in its being. The in-itself "is the foundation of itself in so far as it is *al-ready no longer* in-itself . . ." (1971, 130). Thus, to the extent that conscious-ness offers content either to the condescending gaze of reflection or to "itself" in its very enactment, there is "more" to consciousness than the turning point of a reversal. The "more" is ectoplasm, a density, a nebulosity, which, directly counter to Sartre's theoretical desideratum, effects the intro-duction of a darkness, an obscurity, into the absolute lucidity of conscious-ness, lacerating consciousness "like an opaque blade." Still, Sartre repudiates the "abrupt interpolation of an opaque element" which would divide con-sciousness "in the way that a knife blade cuts a piece of fruit in two . . ." (64).

Rather than effecting its unequivocal demise, the bisection of con-sciousness, occasioned by the blade of opacity, might stimulate a certain on-tological mitosis. And though an original identity is abrogated in cellular division, nothing really dies. The introjection of obscurity would then occa-sion, not the abolishment, but the multiplication of consciousness. The for-mation of an interior wall constitutive of a new duality is entirely consonant with Sartre's early view that there is nothing *in* consciousness. The two new "cells" would be as vacuous as their parent. This, at least, remains a possibil-ity if the "opaque element" is imaged as a *blade*. If the opacity is pervasive, however, if it is conceived as positivity saturating negativity, density perme-ating vacuity, then consciousness—a "hole of being at the heart of Being" (1971, 786)—would be swamped and destroyed by the ectoplasmic haze which imbues it. Or else, should the "haze" permit some diffuse and inhibited illumination, should consciousness be only semi-opaque, it would, of course, fail to be "all lightness," and we would have no way to account for a limited translucence in Sartrean terms. The in-itself and for-itself do not "mix." The latter contests the former. Speaking Foucaultian semiotese, "[w]hen the relation between sign and signified lost its transparency, man appeared as the one in whom knowledge is made possible" (Hiley 1988, 102). Semi-, quasi-, improper opacity, vaporous presence, gossamer materialization is a condition for the possibility of Sartrean ontology—and also a condition of its impossibility.

The disavowal of an intruding trenchant opacity which would render the apple of consciousness in twain appears in the context of Sartre's theory of temporality. Opacity does not "separate prior from subsequent . . ." (1971, 64). Significantly, what *does* is "exactly *nothing*" (64). Offering an illustration from geometry, Sartre claims that "what separates . . . two curves at the very spot of their tangency is *nothing*, not even a distance . . ."—a nothingness here conceived as "pure identity" (248). And Sartre's concordant description of nothing as "impassable" (296) suggests a curious density or solidity.

Though Sartre's iconography suggests a ghostly fog of presence nuzzling in the open valley of consciousness, and thus the disjunction of consciousness and the fog of presence which is "itself," it is clear that consciousness is not inhabited by a wraithlike spirituality but rather *is* its own ectoplasm. Consciousness is not haunted. It is a ghost. Nothingness *appears*. It displays itself—its *self*. And this ethereal presence is the surplus, the pale tatter of selfhood, which consciousness clutches to itself after all else has been drained away into the experienced world. If consciousness *is* its own presence to itself, however, then Sartre has decided the undecidable. *Mind as Mirror* (1994) cultivates the discernment, in Klee's attestation, that "I cannot be caught in immanence," (cf. Merleau-Ponty 1964a, 188) that immanent experience fissures into transcendence in virtue of two ever-ready construals: that the quality thus manifest appears *through*, and that it appears *in*, the purported immanence; that immanence is an inapprehensible opening upon apprehensible quality and that quality saturates immanence, dyes the fabric of its being. Both renderings are wholly concordant with experience, representing the modes of givenness whereby the dehiscence of immanence, its eruption into transcendence, is effected. Transcendence is the difference between seemings of the same. Both the transparentist and the translucentist views, the seeming of openness and the seeming of suffusion, stand perpetually ready to claim any item of immanence, thus conjointly infusing the difference required by transcendence. Neither view is compelled by a faithful attentiveness to experience. To subscribe to one, then, in preference to the other, is to lapse into "metaphysics" and "presupposition." The issue is rather undecidable. "Undecidability recognizes the wavering be-tween the disjuncta in any either/or and the lack of a clean break (*de-cidere*) between them" (Caputo 1993, 63). Sartre with his "*maudite lucidité*" (Merleau-Ponty 1964c, 33) is incisive, cutting (*cidere*) where there is noth-ing to cut, upholding a clear-cut position when nothing enforces a decision in favor of one view or another.

For Sartre, "[w]hat can properly be called subjectivity is consciousness (of) consciousness" (1971, 23), the parenthesized "of" designating, not the distantiation of intentional (Sartre's "positional") consciousness, but the immediate, undistanced, nonpositional awareness of the intentional act as a preobjective, "environmental" presence felt at the moment of enactment like a mood, like the delicate atmospheric modulation which thrills all things at the breaking of day. In non-thetic consciousness (of) self, "the self's awareness of itself is the denial of making itself other than what it is. When it becomes other, it is no longer the self. When the self refuses to be other—a self outside consciousness—it must be non-thetic" (Silverman 1980, 88), not a "thesis," not the target of positional directedness, but a non-objective presence. If "intentionality is itself an answer to the question, 'How can there be an object in itself for me?' " (Lyotard 1991b, 55), non-positional awareness is the answer to a related query: setting aside the ele-vated survey provided by reflection which can only reclaim a phase of our conscious life already elapsed, and which, in principle, cannot reproduce the experience as it was originally lived, how can the act of consciousness it-self be experienced concurrently with its enactment? Though there are hints of a transparentist strand in Sartre's early writing—consciousness as pure vacancy, utterly evacuated of intrinsic determination or qualitative color-ing—the vacillation between a conception of consciousness as a window flung open to the world and consciousness as a distinctively tinted pane of glass seems to have stabilized around the latter conception by the writing of *Being and Nothingness* (1971). A barely sensible incandescence has infused Sartrean consciousness. This is not the indistinctness of "interiority seen from the outside"—in reflection—but the qualitative pervasion which en-sures, for Sartre, that in its immediate, its most intimate, presence to itself, there is "something," if only a diffuse and non-objectified presence, to dis-cern. To be sure, "[a]ll reflecting consciousness is . . . in itself unreflected" (1972, 45), and is, we must add, positional. In reflection, Sartre tells us, "we are in the presence of a synthesis of two consciousnesses, one of which is consciousness *of* the other" (44). Reflection institutes a "phantom dyad," the terms of which—reflecting and reflected consciousness—"support their two nothingnesses on each other, conjointly annihilating themselves" (1971, 241). But reciprocal "annihilation" is oddly insufficient to annihi-late. For the patina of consciousness, the indistinctness of its "outside," the surface it displays to reflection, is indispensable. "It is necessary that the reflecting reflect *something* in order that the ensemble should not dissolve into nothing" (241). Transparentism, to the contrary, would happily witness the dissolution. Reflectively to *see* consciousness at all is to see *through* it. Reflection is indiscernible from prereflective disclosure. But for Sartre, the pale flush of interior self-presence is not the epidermis, but the life-blood of that nothingness which is consciousness. Transparentism deprives consciousness of both skin and tissue, surface and interior substance. But nonpositional awareness preserves the ectoplasmic mist of presence which, while no isolable *thing*, denies a more radical sense of "nothingness" to subjectivity. Cartesian self-lucidity imports the immediate objectification of subjectivity to itself. The subject is both subject and object. (For the transparentist, it is neither.) And whatever holds, objectively, for consciousness, whatever determinate, structural truth informs it, is immediately known. To be conscious, then, is to be consciousness *of* one's being conscious. And Sartre is prepared to grant whatever insight this rationalist deposition might harbor. After all, it would seem dissonant to announce "I am conscious of the table before me" and in the same breath rescind this report with the disclaimer, "but I am not *conscious* of being conscious of this table." Still, what one can be in a position to *say* is not a reliable guide to truth. I can never be in a position to *say* "I am now mute," "I am now unconscious," "I am now asleep," "I am now dead." But pragmatically paradoxical pronouncements such as these may well find their fulfillment in muteness, unconsciousness, sleep and death. And though such things could never be truly *said*, they may nonetheless be *true*. Truth overspills the sayable and undermines the Cartesian (and Sartrean) assumption that whatever is true *of me* is also representable *by me* to myself. The Sartrean position that "the imagination is the locus of possibility . . ." (Flynn 1980, 106) falters in the face of unimaginable possibilities. I may well die. But I cannot imagine *my own* death: *my* not being around to imagine anything at all. Imagination cannot, in all cases, be the engine of the possible.

Descartes did not, of course, have the conceptual resources to discriminate the self-objectification of subjectivity typical of reflection from the self-presence operative in nonreflective modes cognition which occupy themselves with the furniture of the world. And the formula for self-lucidity—to know is to know one's knowing—falls straightaway into *aporia*. For applied without restriction, Cartesian self-lucidity would generate a runaway regress of knowings of knowings of knowings . . . without end. And we would be compelled to affirm "the necessity of an infinite regress (*idea ideae ideae*, etc.) . . ." which Sartre considers "absurd" (1971, 12). Otherwise, should the series simply terminate at a primal event of knowing—a "non-self-conscious reflection"—"the totality of the phenomenon falls into the unknown"

(12). It is "ectoplasm" which delivers Sartre from the horns of the dilemma. For him, to be conscious is to be a *nonpositional* consciousness of our *positional* consciousness of the world. Sartre claims that "if my consciousness were not consciousness of being consciousness of the table, it would then be consciousness of that table without consciousness of being so. In other words, it would be a consciousness ignorant of itself, an unconscious— which is absurd" (11). But one wonders just where the absurdity lies. We could not succeed in knowing the first thing were this to attend the completion of an incompletable succession of knowings, each a necessary condition for the iteration that follows. To be impaled on this horn of the dilemma would be fatal. But it is not clear just what brief can be brought to bear against a "consciousness ignorant of itself." Positional consciousness devotes itself to the foreground, to the ecstatic burst of saliency which captivates its at/tention, its tension-in-presence. Positional consciousness discloses the ex/sistent, that which "stands out," which dominates, and with the free consent of subjectivity, renders subjectivity captive. In its at/tention to prominence, positional consciousness is actively passive, cooperating in its own enthrallment. Nonpositional consciousness is a diffuse awareness of the recessive. If positional consciousness is spellbound by exfoliating saliency, nonpositional consciousness is an atmospheric sensitivity to the ground from which the blossom springs. Nonpositional consciousness is background awareness. To say, then, that subjectivity is (nonpositional) consciousness (of) consciousness, that, for consciousness, being and nonpositional self-presence are identical, is to confine Sartre's "ectoplasm" to the background. The act "itself" stands back. Its object stands forth. But the "self" of self-presence, though deprived of objectivity, nonetheless announces itself in the indiscriminate haze which haunts the background. Loy speaks disparagingly of "Husserl's attempt to analyze that horizon phenomenologically, which . . . would amount to bringing that background into the foreground, a feat no less extraordinary than levitating by pulling on one's shoelaces" (1988, 86). And the parity suggests itself immediately. Phenomenological reflection accords to nonpositional consciousness its proper province only if this dim domain is flooded with the harsh, unremitting light of focal investigation. And this, in turn, is possible only by a transformation of background into foreground. To be warranted phenomenologically, ectoplasmic self-presence would have to be distilled from the background and objectified. And contrary to Sartre's intention, this would leave an unconscious consciousness. To say that consciousness is "unconscious," however, is to deprive it, not of its world, but of itself. "Consciousness" expresses the fact that *there is* a world. "Unconsciousness" expresses the fact that *there being a world* does not itself appear in the world. Transparentism affirms "the paradox that to grasp the unconscious is, at the same time, to fail to grasp it" (Dews 1988, 84). The very *being* of consciousness is a deferring of presence. And Merleau-Ponty speaks congruently of the unconscious as "an original of the *elsewhere*, a *Selbst* that is an Other . . ." (1969, 254). It is not, then, "a *positive that is elsewhere*," but rather, "a true negative" (254). Consciousness is *nothing but* the presence of its object. It has no self, no self-presence. There is nothing of consciousness to be apprehended but the *being-known* (*Bewusstsein*) of its object.

Transparentism, the seeming of openness, is an optional modality within the dyad of construals which fractures the integrity of all purported immanence, a "blade," of sorts, which divides every consciousness, every pellicle of immanence, and reverses the fission of being and appearing. Phenomenologically, it carries no greater warrant than the alternative seeming which would restore to consciousness its "self," the subtle presence whereby consciousness "itself" is given in the giving of the world. At the same time, however, transparentism is an inescapable entailment of the emptiness (*śūnyatā*) of consciousness. To deny transparentism is thereby to deny the universal scope of emptiness. And it is thus evident that this conception, central and indispensable to the Buddhist outlook, is, from a phenomenological point of view, undecidably optional. Buddhism, then, is undecidably optional. In Hui-neng's counsel, "separate yourselves from views" (Yampolsky 1967, 136). And we might add: "Even Buddhism." "Ch'an takes no sides" (Chang 1971, 11). Zen (and Buddhism more generally) does not insist upon "Buddhist" tenets or dogmas. There *are* none. Empty, like all other phenomena, Buddhism does not insist upon "itself." The Buddha was not "Buddhist." And " 'emptiness' is not a viewpoint . . ." (Streng 1967, 90), but a detonation, the explosion of viewpoints. "Right" (*sammā*) view, the primal factor of the Noble Eightfold Path, is not a position or a theory which faithfully mirrors the reality which it confronts. There is no need for the reduplication which even the most accurate conceptual mapping can provide when the landscape of reality is present. Rather, a viewing which is *sammā* (etymological ancestor of our "same") is even, balanced, poised between alternatives. "Right" viewing is free from the instability which would pitch one sidewards into one theoretical commitment or another. In this instance, Buddhism aligns itself with Rorty's criticism of "edifying" philosophy in "decry[ing] the very notion of having a view" (1979, 371). Thus, in the teaching of Huang-Po, "[t]he fundamental dharma of the dharma is that there are no dharmas, yet that this dharma of no-dharma is in itself a dharma; and now that the no-dharma dharma has been transmitted, how can the dharma of the dharma be a dharma?" (Blofeld 1958, 64–5). Sprung remarks that the Middle Way, the way of equilibrium, is "the end of socratizing . . ." (1978 136). In fact, to the extent that Socratic wisdom represents an authentic introspective knowing of unknowing, to the extent that the expression of this wisdom is more than ironic posturing, and to the extent that the Socratic *elenchus* is not merely an "apogogic device" (Inada 1970, 9), the negation of one view presuming the affirmation of its negate, "socratizing" may, with some qualification, be regarded as a continuation in spirit of the Middle Way. In the declaration of Fa-yen Wên-I (885–958 C.E.), "[n]ot knowing most closely approaches the Truth" (Chang, 239). Aside from the scant handful of teachings which exceeded the common convictions of his day (*para/doxa*), Socrates left us little but questions. And Buddhism teaches that "[p]erfect wisdom . . . does not assert a teaching; the only 'answer' one can receive from wisdom (*prajñā*) is silence" (Streng 1967, 89)—a conception entirely removed from that of Rorty for whom wisdom consists in "the ability to sustain a conversation" (377–8). "Primeval wisdom" is not, for Buddhism, merely "the counter-image of 'primeval stupidity' " (Gadamer 1984, 243), but is the nondiscriminative intuition which plumbs infinitely deeper than the distinction between wisdom and stupidity. The volubility exhibited in Socrates' love of disputation, no less than the immensity of the corpus of Buddhist scriptures, may simply illustrate the "freedom from the alternatives of words or silence" (Chang, 90) of which the Zen tradition speaks.

But if the seeming of openness is a pure *phenomenological* option—or better, if the tension between transparentism and translucentism is phenomenologically irresolvable—it nonetheless conspires with its alternative to establish an *ontology* of emptiness. An ostensible item of immanence, an event of consciousness, as our prime example, can always be *seen* as pellucid, vacuous, a pure revelation of the world which exhausts "itself" in the world it reveals. Its "self-presence" would thus be extruded from consciousness and would belong, with all else, to the world. Consciousness would thus become awareness (*sati*). For transparentism, "self-presence" is not the presence of consciousness "itself," but a peculiar modality of transcendence. At the same time, and with no lapse of faithfulness to experience, self-presence can be *seen* as immanent to consciousness. Neither seeming represents the way things *are*. Neither appearance coincides with the reality. Neither is phenomenologically *true*. The "truth" rather lies in the absence of truth: the unrestricted failure of fusion which perpetually disjoins the being and the appearing of consciousness. *Pace* Sartre (and Husserl), consciousness cannot be immanent. It cannot simply *be* as it appears, for it appears, always, in two entirely incompatible ways. And the consequent transcendence of consciousness is displayed in its perpetual remission of self-presence to the world which conditions it. Phenomenology does not witness the rupture of immanence, for nothing on the part of experience compels transparentism as opposed to translucentism. Phenomenology rather assumes the transcendence of consciousness as a (quasi-transcendental) condition of the faithfulness of its investigation. The avowal of one seeming in preference to the other is a fall from phenomenological grace, an unbalanced plunge into "metaphysics." And it is our stereoscopic ability to see—indifferently, undecidably—from both points of view, and to do so without attachment, without the assumption that one or the other is *true*, that the "truth" of their common default of truth is attested. In this way, then, a rigorous and conscientious phenomenology, a phenomenology which refuses to posit more than is given, entails an ontology of universal transcendence, an ontology of emptiness.

To be sure, the two seemings are not enframed by a relativism of respect. They are not equally, though equivocally, valid. It is not that each is true from its own vantage point. If "[r]elativism is the absence of truth conditions" (Magliola 1986, 81), the Buddhist rejoinder is that nothing—not even the relative truth of our common experience (*saṁvṛti*)—is without condition, that emptiness therefore revokes relativism. Buddhism takes to heart Davidson's dismissal of the duality of conceptual scheme and its content. Buddhist antisubstantialism denies an underlying invariant which, according to this "third dogma" of empiricism, would sub-stand the profusion of constructions which we place on it. Dogmatism, scepticism and relativism are equally invested in the scheme/content distinction, differing primarily in their distinctive apportionment of truth and falsity, and in their views of the warrantability of this allocation, to the multiplicity of schemes. There is a trivial sense in which the abolition of scheme/content dualism would, as Davidson believes, reestablish "unmediated touch with the familiar objects whose antics make our sentences and opinions true or false" (1973–74, 20). In Danto's explication of Nietzschean perspectivism,

> There is no way the world really is in contrast with our modes of interpreting it. There are *only* rival interpretations . . . And accordingly no *world in itself* apart from some interpretation . . . We cannot even speak of these interpretations as "distorting" reality, for there is nothing that counts as a reality, for there is nothing that counts as a veridical interpretation relative to which a given interpretation could distort: or *every* interpretation is a distortion, except that there *is* nothing for it to be a distortion of. (1965, 76–7)

Nothing is true or false independent of a given construal. Veridicality is intrinsic to the conceptual framework. And we must inquire, with Uchiyama Roshi, "[t]hen where is the absolute reality that departs completely from our point of view as a yardstick?" (1988, 191). Or in the words of Montaigne, "[t]o judge the appearances that we receive of objects, we should need a judicatory instrument; to verify this instrument we need a demonstration, an instrument: thus we are in a circle" (1965, 454). As Puligandla comments, "neither the physical nor the mental comes to us with labels such as 'real,' 'illusory,' or 'unreal' " (1985, 41). We have "unmediated touch" with the denizens of our world and their "antics" because there is no gap between scheme and content, no room for mediation, nothing to be mediated separable from our categorial scheme. It is, then, the indissoluble unit comprised of schematized content, objects *as* given, *as* conceptually informed—not a separable order of "familiar objects," an independent *Inhalt* awaiting *Auffassung*, a disjoinable hyletic stratum attending morphic transmutation—which is the measure of verity. "[N]othing exists unless I give it a form" (Lispector 1988, 6). And it is misleading to import the idiom of the "third dogma" in speaking of objects which *make* our opinions true or false. The suggestion, if not the implication, of this language is that there exists a domain of independent entities to which our constructions either con[form] or fail to con[form], and that conformity, correspondence, *adequatio intellectus et res*, is truth. But this assumes that, detached from our conceptual scheme, the object *has* a form. And we would have no way of knowing this, no "yardstick," independent of a conceptual scheme. If the "absence of truth conditions" implies that there is nothing—no invariant and variously interpretable substratum—beyond our construals which could, in this sense, *make* our construals true, then the absence of truth conditions will simply undermine relativism, and with it dogmatism and scepticism as well.

The two seemings, transparentism and translucentism, are not, then, equally *true*, though they assuredly enjoy a certain minimal "adequacy": they do not, and cannot, conflict with the experience which they construe. Experience welcomes both—not because they in any way con[form], but because they do not de[form]. Or rather, because mind is "pure as the Void, without form" (Chang 1971, 97), and nothing con[forms] to the formless. The formless is the womb of form, the ambience, the medium, in which form arises and into which it dissolves. In Prufer's provocative declamation, the matrix (derivative of *māter*, mother) "is by anticipation the matrix of the differents, but as matrix it itself is different from them by its indifference" (1973, 226). We must, however, distinguish between the formless, the indifferent, and *concept* of formlessness. Within our conceptual economy, the term, "formless," participates in bipolar contrast with "formed," and differs from the formed in its determinate absence of form. Absence of form is its *differentium*. Like the term "inconceivable," "formless" functions within the lacework of our conceptuality as a quiet, but ruthlessly effective, solvent: the *concept* of inconceivability, the *form* of the formless. At the heart of our conceptual system there pulses the dark and boiling blood of contradiction, a rebellion of reason, a surdity which threatens to infect the entire organism. The *concept* of the inconceivable features that which is devoid, in principle, of an inner contest of principles, that which is entirely coherent and incapable coming into conflict. Ironically, this very concept—because it is a concept—menaces the overall consistency of our conceptual framework. But the formless (as distinguished from the *concept* of formlessness), the indifferent (distinguished from the *concept* of indifference) is devoid of any attribute which could differentiate it from the formed, the differentiated. The indifferent is *not* different from the differents. It is indifferent to the differents—but not in virtue of the quality of indifference. And by application, we see that self-effacing (self-deferring) consciousness is *not different* from the dyad of seemings which respectively posit the transcendence and the immanence of qualitative presence.

But as "minimal adequation"—mere absence of friction—is clearly not truth, the failure of complete con[form]ation is not (exactly) falsehood. Only in the ethereal realm of floating abstraction, "the land where there are all and only Capitals, . . . the world where German nouns come true . . ." (Caputo 1993, 33), does representation mirror reality with perfect adequacy, and then not without paradox. Though demurring from Royce's conclusion, we might nonetheless consider his provocative illustration:

> let us suppose . . . that a portion of the surface of England is very precisely levelled and smoothed, and is then devoted to the production of our precise map of England . . . the map, in order to be complete, according to the rule given, will have to contain, as a part of itself, a representation of its own contour and contents. In order that this representation should be constructed, the representation itself will have to contain once more, as a part of itself, a representation of its own contour and contents; and this representation, in order to be exact, will have once more to contain an image of itself; and so on without limit. (1976, 504–5)

A "self-representational system" leads immediately to the *aporia* of infinite regress—not, as Royce supposed, to the endlessly iterative cognitive wealth of the Absolute. Assuming perfect adequacy, a map could not *map* without mapping "itself." And this "self," the impress of its "own" presence upon the terrain, could not be mapped without, once again, mapping "itself." And thus, regressively, without limit. The Buddhist revocation of the self and of the "itself" requires the abandonment of perfect conceptual adequacy. And Royce unwittingly provides the argument. The "self" represented always suffers a diminution of presence. Something is always lost. In the optical analogue, that of the *mise-en-abîme* generated by the confrontation of two mirrors, the loss is in the extent and distinctness of the image. The bottom-less iteration of images within images . . . converges to a vanishing point. And phenomenologically, the singularity which appears to lure all concentric, conformal forms into "itself" is more evident than the infinity of their iteration. Curiously, the vanishing of images, their absorption and disappearance at the infinitesimal, is a genuine phenomenon. We "witness" the site of this extraordinary arrested implosion as a point of reference which is not "there." And though, in virtue of these incessant references, we can speak of the vanishing point "itself," it has no self, no presence, at all. Its "presence" is the occasion of a relinquishment of presence. It is a present absence. Yet this "presence," which can be thought as evanescence, is more clearly manifest by far than the positive infinity of inclusions which it devours. The eye does, of course, catch the "*und so weiter*" of nested images. But the center dominates the scene to the extent that the infinity of concentricities seems a mere inference. And from a phenomenological point of view, the interminable regression of images is an airy fabrication wafting in logical space. The vanishing is apodictic. The interminability of the regression is merely presumptive.

Our reticular system of conceptual representations suffers a similar diminution, there is always something "excluded." And as Puligandla discerns, there is always a "tension between the included and the excluded" which "sustains the framework." Thus, "[r]emove the tension by total inclusion or total exclusion, and there can be no categorial framework" (1985, 32). The grand compendium of all possible concepts constitutes a cataclysmic contradiction. This immense cacophony is not unlike the running-together of all the paints in the paint box—a horrific mess. To the degree that a conceptual scheme is internally coherent, it is unavoidably exclusive. Binary contrasts have been truncated, dissonant voices silenced. Yet the excluded is not without vengeance. And exclusion only appears to abate the force of contrast. We have spoken of the logical mutiny of the *concept* of inconceivability, the *form* of the formless, which transmit their instability to the surrounding web of concepts, causing them to tremble with inconsistency. But the more general stimulus of conceptual revolt is our misguided efforts to apply to the regal domain of the real the necessarily impoverished resources of conceptual [re]presentation. And "the breakdown of a categorial framework is testimony to the tension between the included and excluded" (Puligandla, 32). To apply to the province of presence what pertains only to one of its warring municipalities courts incongruity. To frame reality as, for example, "infinite" is to invite implicit contrast with the finite. The excluded conception of finity gains surreptitious entry through the "not" required to understand the [in]finite. The infinite is that which is *not* finite. That which is *excluded* to effect coherent attribution must now be *included* to enable intelligibility. Finitude cannot, ultimately, be exiled from the conceptual scheme which frames reality as infinite. "[I]t is none other than inquiry into the included, through the instrumentality of a given categorial framework, that leads—nay, compels—the inquirer to a consideration of the excluded" (32). To perform its dual task of framing and rendering intelligible, the scheme must, then, be incoherent.

Perfect adequation is not the hallmark of truth. It is conceptually and phenomenologically impossible. And an adequation of imperfect degree is not a consummate falsehood, but at best, a relative truth. Nietzsche's inversion of Plato is at the same time an inversion of relativism. Frozen, immutable, timeless, our conceptions are inescapably disloyal to a fluid reality. Our positions, our theories, our systems are not, then, equally true, but for Nietzsche, equally *false*. With evident paradox, the Nietzschean *truth* is that "truths are illusions about which one has forgotten that this is what they are" (1980, 47), that truth is at best a vital lie. And while it may be "true" of relative truth (*saṁvṛti*) that " 'the true,' 'truth' in the traditional metaphysical sense, is a *fixation* of an apparition" and that "it clings to a perspective" (Krell 1979, 237), that, in other words, truth is intrinsic to our outlook, this is not the case for the truth that exceeds all conceptual understanding: Absolute Truth (*paramārtha*). In Foucault's view, "Kant's awakening from his dogmatic slumber was just the beginning of the 'anthropological sleep' " (Hiley 1988, 103). "Anthropological sleep" is induced by the lullaby of the *for us*, or the *for me*, the presumption, the arrogance, of position-taking. Absolute Truth is awakening (Buddha). While Absolute Truth does not swim in the bright waters of Nietzsche's thought, there is much insight in the notion that "[t]ruthfulness is all that is left when one sees that Truth is the will-to-truth . . ." (Caputo 1993, 190). Absolute Truth is not a final answer to our deepest question, a place of final rest for our restless cognitive mind. Like truthfulness, it is more like receptivity than something received, more like openness than content. Truth, Lyotard tells us, "is not an object but a movement . . ." (1991b, 63). Absolute Truth is not an acquisition, but a loss. "There is nothing gained only something [language] to be removed" (Loy 1984, 442). In Benoit's admonition, "[s]earch not for the truth; only cease to cherish opinions" (cf. Sohl and Carr 1970, 49).

Relativism, once again, is the absence of truth conditions—not, of course, in the sense that independent features of the landscape fail to "make" for the accuracy of the map—for there *are* no such features—but in the sense that (relative) truth is intrinsic to our outlook, and thus, that falsehood can be pronounced only from a competing vantage point. Absolute Truth (*paramārtha*) shares is formal conception with relativism: its truth is beyond condition, as also beyond conception. As Blofeld comments, in Hui-hai's teaching, there is not "a hairsbreadth of difference" between "relativity and ultimate truth" (1972, 32). Were we to understand this term as "the common postulate of dogmatism and scepticism," we must concur with Lyotard that "[t]here is not . . . an absolute truth" (1982, 38). But what is shared by dogmatism and scepticism is the assumption of objective, not absolute, truth. And if we think of objectivity as "the capacity on the part of investigators to set aside their own prejudices and predilections from distorting the framework from within which they produce knowledge-claims and determine their truth" (Puligandla 1985, 31), objective truth turns out to be a certain rigor, a certain discipline of self-suspension, practiced by those who share a common paradigm. And shared commitment to a relative outlook is not Absolute Truth. In response to the query, "What is the ground of Absolute Truth?," Fa-yen Wên-I replied, "If there should be a ground, it would not be Absolute Truth" (Chang 1971, 244). Absolute Truth is groundless, unconditioned. The *conception* of Absolute Truth has no conceptual content. "Truth doesn't make sense!" (Lispector 1988, 11). "The term 'absolute truth' is part of the descriptive order, not part of the factual order. Like all other expressions, it is empty, but it has a peculiar relation within the system of designations. It symbolizes non-system, within the system of constructs" (Streng 1967, 84). Absolute Truth—not the conception, but the realization—is emptiness.

Chapter 2

Light upon Light

The Great Way (*magga*) of the Buddha is marked by the dialectical aston-ishment of finding ourselves abruptly delivered to our very starting point. The marvel of the Other Shore is that it is not "other," that the alterity of the *alter* is its seamless identity with the same. Having navigated the turbulent waters, having at last achieved solid footing, and having finally released the raft (*yāna*), we look about only to discover the familiar. *Here* we are, and *here* we return. Nothing has changed—but *everything* has! The very famil-iarity of the familiar has, in the course of our perilous journey, itself become unfamiliar. The prosaic has become poetic. *Nirvāṇa* is "continual freshness" (Corless 1989, 281). Corless here crosses out both words, "continual" and "freshness," installs in their place a *chi*, a chiasm of reciprocal encroachment, detaching these words from their usual play within the economy of bipolar contrast. "Continual" does not contest "interrupted"; "freshness" does not oppose "stale." "There is an Unborn, Unbecome, Unmade, Uncom-pounded," the Buddha teaches, which is the ground, or rather *Abgrund*, of the continuous and the discontinuous alike, that which is "born, become, made and compounded" (Conze 1994, 76). Right *there*, there in the very arising and subsiding of temporal phenomena, gleams the eternal. And there, also, in the very interplay of the exuberant, the spirited, and the inert, there is an enlivening, a quickening, a freshness. What Nāgārjuna achieves dialectically, we must pursue in our own phenomenological/ontological way: there is not the difference of hair's breadth between *nirvāṇa* and *saṁsāra*. Ch'ing-yüan Wei-hsin expresses this defamiliarized familiarity, the culmination of the "Zen dialectic," in his declaration:

Thirty years ago, before I began the study of Zen, I said, "Mountains are mountains, waters are waters."

After I got an insight into the truth of Zen through the instruction of a good master, I said, "Mountains are not mountains, waters are not waters."

But now, having attained the abode of final rest, I say, "Mountains are really mountains, waters are really waters." (cf. Abe 1985, 4)

Wei-hsin's "really"—mountains are *really* mountains, waters are *really* waters—is an expression of wonder, the child-mind's questioning openness in the face of the sheer suchness of things. "Thirty years ago" Wei-hsin would have hailed the wisdom of Sartre's quasi-dualism: mountains are mountains; waters are waters; all things imbibe the stolid self-identity of the in-itself. Wei-hsin later discerned, as must we, that, like the lotus, mountains and waters are themselves ecstatic, beside themselves. The ten thousand things of this world have taken on the idiosyncrasy of the Sartrean for-itself: they *are not* what they are. Wei-hsin bears witness to the interminable deferral of existence: the existence of each thing resides in its conditions; and the existence of those conditions is, in turn, deferred to their conditions. The chain has no final link. And there is, finally, *nothing*—no/thing—which exists. This is not the nothingness of the Sthaviras which "is like a termite hole—termites bore a hole into a piece of wood (absence of self in persons), but all around they leave thin outer walls standing . . ." (Conze 1994, 198). Nor is it the ontological vacuity of the Sartrean for-itself depicted as a bubble rising in the medium of being. Wei-hsin's intermediate vision is that of universal nothingness. There is no[thing]—no object, nothing objective, nothing remotely objectival, nothing in any way thematizable—*at all*. And we find here a certain concord with Levinas' reading of the *il y a* of phenomena as the "silence of infinite spaces . . ." (cf. Burke 1990, 94). Boundless vacuity is portrayed by an empty circle, the "all-meaning circle" of Shoichi (Stryk and Takash 1963, 3), in the eighth painting in the famous Oxhearding sequence: "No Ox, No Man." The eighth, however, is not the last. And Wei-hsin was not to rest at this intermediate stage. Subsequently, all things reappear in their wondrous suchness, and the ten Oxhearding paintings culminate "In Town with Helping Hands." Like Wei-hsin, we must take the final step. Boundless emptiness is itself empty. It is like a mirror which sharply remits illumination to its source. We cannot approach emptiness without being abruptly repelled, thrown headlong back to the world of discriminate form. And this deep negativity is elicited in the teaching of Shen-hui:

A bright mirror is set up on a high stand; its illumination reaches the ten-thousand things, and they are all reflected in it. The masters are wont to consider this phenomenon most wonderful. But as far as my school is concerned it is not to be considered wonderful. Why? As to this bright mirror, its illumination reaches the ten-thousand things, and these ten-thousand things are not reflected in it. This is what I would declare to be most wonderful. (Suzuki 1981, 51)

Our journey is not complete until, after the regressive movement—the intermediate work of a hyper-reflective phenomenology which interrogates the chiasmatic structure of phenomenal manifestation—we return, with Wei-hsin, to listen in admiration—"the innocent heart constantly awakening to the shock of wonder, like a child on Christmas morning" (Corless 1989, 281)—to the echo of the abyss.

The Buddhist dialectic is rooted in *naïveté*—mountains are mountains, waters are waters—the credulity of an unsuspecting registration of manifest reality, a childlike acceptance of the manifest with no awareness of the "as," which leaves the work of construal completely off stage. In an Hegelian supplement: "The concept makes the free, delivered *sense* (the "as," the being of what is) appear. As long as consciousness is 'consciousness,' it 'does not accept the 'as' " (Heidegger 1970, 104). And this resonates powerfully with the illuminationism of Husserl's view that we see—see both things *and* their *Sinne—with, in the light of*, the *eidos*. Like the sun of Plato's allegory, the *eidos* makes visible while cloaking "itself" in blinding radiance. Bedazzlement is testimony to the sun's relinquishment of self—or rather, its displacement of itself in the manifold *visibilia* of our experience. Buddhism repudiates the two-tiered construction which sequesters the existence from the sense of the perceptual object (*rūpa*). Hui-neng counsels us to rise "above existence and non-existence" (Price and Wong 1969, 27), to survey the domain of phenomena without ontic imposition. And the phenomenal terrain thus surveyed "is equally beyond negation as beyond affirmation" (Sartre 1971, 27). Guenther reminds us that "the Buddhists revolutionized the whole of Indian thought in that they did not speak of 'things' in terms of substance, whether physical or mental, but of 'meanings' " (1989 40). And if "meaning" signifies, not an abstraction lifted from the textured surface of concrete experience, but rather, that very experience itself prior to the intrusion of existential judgment, then we welcome the word, and concur also with Brand that "what *is* is being in its meaning" ([1955] 1967, 203). Meaning, the "as" of experience, gives voice to the mute impassivities of *naïveté*. Indeed, in the expansive sense which awakening has acquired within the Mahāyāna, we can even say that "the Buddha . . . *is* meaning . . ." (Guenther 1989, 282, n. 11).

But again, consciousness insensitive to its own hermeneutic contribution to experience is woefully naive. In Wagner's portrayal, "[n]aivete has no suspicions concerning what takes place within the unfathomable; it speaks without suspicion of the world, of man, and of his consciousness; it lives without suspicion in the world. . . . This naivete would come to an end if it should be asked: what does it mean to say that *there is* (a world, that we are within it, that we have our familiar capabilities)?" (1970 217–8). The "suspicion" induced by our awakening to the problematicity of the "there is" is not a wariness regarding some potential evil couched behind the veil of *phaínomena*. It may be that "[o]nly great pain is the ultimate liberator of the spirit, being the teacher of *the great suspicion* . . ." (Merleau-Ponty 1988, 10). But the manifestation of reality conceals nothing sinister or menacing. Nor do we suspect reality of subterfuge. Reality is not a fraud. Though we discover that nothing is "what" it is, nothing impassively coincides with its regulated modes of self-giving, the primal impetus of "suspicion" is not the misgiving that reality might be other than it appears to be. Indeed, "[t]rue radicalism will not be just this distrust, but also a 'distrust of distrust' " (15). Rather, the cessation of *naïveté* arises with the first inkling of alternative possibility: though in fact the world appears this way, it *could* appear otherwise, and its appearing as it does—in *this* guise instead of *that*—is a matter of contingency. Thus is awakened the "suspicion" that the way in which it presents itself is, not duplicitous, but simply conditioned. And with vigilance regarding the conditioned nature—thus "emptiness" (*śūnyatā*)—of all manifest phenomena, a vigilance which, at each successive iteration of conditionality releases ipseity into "the unfathomable," is born an authentic Buddhist phenomenology. "Philosophy," Solomon claims, "is not a particular body of knowledge; it is the vigilance which does not let us forget the source of all knowledge" (1972, 4). To be sure, philosophy is vigilance, attentiveness. And the "alertness" which this entails is, not an expectation of peril, but an openness to the vicissitudes of conditioned experience. But a distinctively Buddhist philosophy reminds us, on the contrary, that knowledge has no "source," no *fundamentum inconcussum*, that every purported fundament is, in principle, "concussable," that there are no cognitive "atoms," nothing intelligible or evident *in se*, that evidence (*Evidenz*), however compelling, is not *self*-evidence.

Buddhist phenomenology begins, then, with the contingent, not with the absurd. The absurd is the "contingent" without contingency, the disintegration of the world into independent fragments, each on its own, each existing by its own power, a mad anarchy of ontological sovereignty. The final word, the word which silences all other words, the word of harsh and irresistible authority, is that each *just is*. The absurd is the ontologically capricious. And arbitrariness, as Adorno discerns, is "the complement of compulsion . . ." (1983, 23). The being of the absurd is in no way elucidated by context or horizon. It is detached from its horizon, aloof, invulnerable, a pure inexplicable, unintelligible givenness. Its alienated implosion upon our intelligence gives no hint of functional dependence upon its perceptual environment. Its efficacy is *ab intra*. If it changes, the mainspring of its transformation is "within." If it pleases or happifies or satisfies, if it presents itself as a value, it does so out of its own presumed inner resources. If it exhibits itself, its manifestation is an eidol emanating from a certain interior pressure. It is kenotic. The absurd has, then, an "inside," an interiority entirely secluded from other fragments of reality, an "inside" on the verge of turning itself inside-out, discharging, exploding, overflowing, emptying itself. In Caputo's eloquent description, the absurd—exemplar of "heteromorphic difference"—"gathers itself into uncontainable fullness, becomes overrich and brimming over, and then erupts. . . . The forces break apart, break open, multiplying themselves in kind of joyful self-destruction and dissipation, in a work of profligacy and dissemination" (56). The volcanism of heteromorphic difference "prevents closure and occlusion" (56). Its "uncontainable plenitude" (56) discloses "the incapacity for totalization" (57). The wondering, child-like gaze of ontology occupies itself with the volcano; phenomenology concerns itself with the eruption. Ontology invests itself in the pregnancy and fullness of the absurd; phenomenology, in its irrepressible issue. Ontology discloses the heteromorphically different; phenomenology, the dispersal of heteromorphic difference. Ontology takes up the absurd—but not in its naive registration. The child already beholds the first faint intimations of dawn. It is the absurd *as such—as absurd*—which consumes ontology. That which is compacted and pressurized within the absurd, its uncontainable content, is the improvident profusion of conditions which the absurd conceals and which demand release. The self-existence of the absurd is no more than a way delusion has of totalizing, interiorizing, and cloaking the conditions to which the phenomenon defers its being. Dehiscence is a making-manifest of interior content, a making-evident of the utter absence of interior content, a transformation of the absurd into the contingent. Were they separable operations, ontology would see the bomb and phenomenology would see the fragments. But neither alone could see the explosion: an event the significance of which is to reveal the plenary as a locus of empty reference. Ontology is the "re/collection" that phenomenology requires in order to "watch the forms of transcendence fly up like sparks from a fire . . ." (Merleau-Ponty 1962, xiii). Without ontology, there would be no fire. Without phenomenology, there would be no sparks. And without their concert, there would be no "flying upward."

Interiority, the assumption of a dimension of inwardness, the lightless cave of the unmanifest, is convertible with absurdity. The naive registration that the mountain *is* a mountain by no means imports the thematization or problematization the "is." Danto points out that "[f]or us, our world is: *the world*" (1973, 257). From the standpoint of a naive privacy uninformed by the self- displacement engendered by the sense of one's own view as *a* view, "the distance between ourselves and the world which the concept of truth requires is automatically closed . . . because we do not think of the representation of the world, to which truth properly applies, but to *what* is represented, namely the world" (258). For naive consciousness, the mountain is absurd, discriminated from its horizonal environment, endowed with ipseity. It is "there"—without question, needing no explanation, having no relevance to the imposition of "why?" Buddhism, a contextualism without holism, joins with Caputo in abjuring an ultimate "Meta-event" that "organizes all other events, that puts them to rest, that arrests their play, that sweeps over them all and gathers them to itself in a final 'because' and gives them all a rest" (1993 222). But the ontological contextualism of Buddhist thought will not, without qualification, follow Caputo's inference that, therefore, "[t]he 'because' sinks into events, sinks off in what happens, faces away like an echo in space, leaving only the events" (223). The strident voice of absurdity does not pronounce the last word. We can agree that "the 'because' sinks into events." But this is because events are nothing over and beyond the wake of conditions to which they owe their being—not because the world is pulverized into inexplicable granules. There is inexplicability. Yes. But it pertains to the successive pulses of world's ongoing life; to open-ended wholes, not closed totalities, of conditions; to wakes of conditions which trail diachronically into the beginningless past; not to the isolated points of their convergence. This does not entail "a totalizing illusion induced by the idea of an ideal observer, an outsider taking the view from nowhere" (94). Each world-whole exceeds without boundary the com/prehension of any situated gaze. For each "view from somewhere" finds itself engulfed in a context of conditions which, because it has no outside, we can only call boundless or in/finite.

Merleau-Ponty notes that "the absolute positing of a single object is the death of consciousness, since it congeals the whole of existence, as a crystal placed in a solution suddenly crystallizes it" (1962, 71). Or with Adorno's somewhat different emphasis: "[p]hilosophical thinking crystallizes in the particular . . ." (1973, 138). *Naïveté*, or in a word more familiar to Buddhism, beginningless *avidyā* (ignorance, blindness), is not a lapse from a prior apprehension of theme-in-horizon, but the muddy bottom from which the lotus grows, and into which, by tracing out the roots, phenomenology must descend. And without this reflective, interrogative pursuit to the depths, "life would probably dissipate itself in ignorance of itself or in chaos" (Merleau-Ponty 1964b, 19). Horizonal blindness is the "ground" of awakening. And while the darkness of night is "absorption into the outside" (Bataille 1988, 17), we must recognize in the soil's turbidity, not the privation, but the interiorization of light. Every particle of absurdity wraps the resplendence of limitless horizonal illumination within a veneer of thematizability. "The horizon no longer emits light of itself" (Heidegger 1977, 107). That which is boundlessly environmental becomes a discriminated object of our apprehension. Extracting Sartre's description from a very different context, it is "as if interiority closed upon itself and proffered us only its outside; as if one had to 'circle about' it in order to understand it . . ." (1972, 84). Every absurdity is thematized, objectified, emptiness. The task of a Buddhist phenomenology is, then, to liberate this interior illumination by a certain dethematization, to pop the bubble, releasing its inner resplendence. This, in a sense approximating Bergson's, is an exercise of the spirit: "that faculty of seeing which is immanent in the faculty of acting and which springs up, *some*how, by the *twisting* [*torsion*] of *the will on itself*, when action is turned into knowledge, like heat, so to say, into light" (1944, 273). If "[i]ndistinctness . . . is interiority seen from the outside," if it is "the degraded projection of interiority" (Sartre 1972, 85), then in its infinite successive displacement of interiority—equivalent to the exteriorization of the interior—the obscurity and opacity of the "outside" is ruptured, and all turns to light. Foucault speaks relevantly of the "majestic violence of light [which] brings to an end the bounded, dark kingdom of privileged knowledge" (1973 39). Knowledge, in this sense, is clarity robed in obscurity. Buddhist insight (*prajñā*) penetrates the nebulous patina of experience, not with the violence of rapture, not to violate the modesty of a particular truth immured behind the murky appearance, but precisely to demonstrate that nothing—no thing, no being, no reality—huddles behind the veil. It is true, as Merleau-Ponty affirms, that "there is no *Schein* without an *Erscheinung* . . ." (1969, 41). But in this converse case, there is *Erscheinung* without *Schein*. In the intuitive demonstration (showing, *Erscheinung*) which strips away the phenomenal veneer, there is no[thing] to "shine," no[thing] with a "look" or appearance. There is appearing without the appearance *of something*. And this is the truth of Loy's deposition that "given the nature of the eyes, all we can ever see is light" (1988, 75). Indeed, "the *Erscheinen* of the *Erscheinende*, the 'birth' of truth is not the movement to another *Seinde*" (Merleau-Ponty 1988, 309,).

But the pronouncement of absurdity upon disengaged fragments of reality already exceeds the capacity of *avidyā*, and involves a decisive efflorescence, a rooted, but upwardly dynamic, transcendence of the ground. For a consciousness immersed in ignorance, mountains may simply *be* mountains. But the countenance of the world does not require our voice. Blindness is at the same time muteness. For to give voice to the absurd, to herald the absurdity of an unfathomable interior enshrouded in limiting and finitary indistinctness, of the *sva-bhāva*, is already, in some measure, to extricate oneself from sheer imperception. It may be true, as Bresson comments, that "[t]he phenomenological description is at the limit unrealizable and interior experience ineffable" (Bresson 1958, 156; cf. Merleau-Ponty 1969, 252). But as Caputo comments, " 'Ineffability' is a high-powered discursive resource, the product of a language that has been refined and defined until it is sharp enough and nuanced enough to announce all this ineffability. 'Unsayability' is a modification of what is sayable. . . . By the time one has said that something is ineffable, or that one cannot say a thing, one has already been speaking for some time and one has already said too much" (75). To encounter the absurd in silence is blindness. To entertain the absurd *as* absurd is the beginning of vision. The philosophical articulation whereby the mountain is brought to light *as* mountain, in its facticity and "thereness," its obscurity and its resistance to ex/planation, is what we might call "deictic" (de/monstrative) phenomenology. What are thus exhibited to deictic phenomenology, what are displayed in their absurdity, are the rattling seeds within a desiccated gourd, seemingly sovereign discriminata detached from the living vine. The field of investigation served by a deictic phenomenology is contoured by our capacity to discriminate *this* from *that*. Deictic phenomenology thus addresses the absurd *as such*. The absurd is then seen *as absurd* only to the extent that it submits to certain formal exigencies. *Qua* absurd, it is *contingent* upon its concealment of an explosive inner plenitude. Thus, the absurd is decisively surpassed with the first movement of phenomenology. There is, ultimately, no phenomenology of the absurd. To see the absurd *as absurd*, authentically to *see* what presents itself to us in our *naïveté* as self-existent, is thereby to see that "the absurd" is a vacuous category instantiated by no[thing], no *this* and no *that*, at all. The absurd is the unbegotten sightlessness from which Buddhism calls us to awaken. It is no accident that the in/sight (*prajñā*) which liberates is outwardly directed. "*Bodhi* . . . does not consist in the knowledge of, or union with, an Absolute, but in an understanding of, and a penetration into, the real nature of phenomena" (Sangharakshita 1987, 108). What primordially enthralls the benighted mind is the delusory presentation of permanence, unqualified value and ipseity. Conversely, the mark of a distinctively *Buddhist* phenomenology is its elucidation of the impermanence (*anityā*), unsatisfactoriness (*dukha*) and insubstantiality or selflessness (*anātman*) of all *dharmas*—a word which can be cast as broadly as "thing," but refers, more specifically to the thing *as an object of discrimination*, thus a thing *for us*—a phenomenon—*"mental components as I perceive them and physical components as I perceive them"* (Corless 1989, 123).

Buddhist phenomenology is instituted with the inaugural step beyond absurdity toward contingency, and thus involves the externalization of the interior—call it "ex/pression," if you will—which reenvironmentalizes the delimited theme. The meditative practice of concentration, as enacted in the cultivation (*bhavanā*) of inner peace (*samatha*), has precisely this effect. As concentration deepens, the theme "expands," absorbs ever more of the field of consciousness, pervades more broadly the spaciousness of mind. The ultimate effect is to deprive *it* of its "it." The boundary separating figure from its background, the earth from the heavens, lapses in the full depth of concentration. The object, previously falling to the clarity of another sky now dissolves into a heaven of its own, an open, immeasurable diaphaneity indistinguishable from the illumination which traverses it. In a similar way, and with the same experiential import, the realization of emptiness, the abyss into which an endless regressive analysis of conditionality plummets, serves, first, to dilate the thematic locus to encompass the theme-in-horizon, and this, again, to encompass the theme-in-horizon *in horizon*, and endlessly thus forward. With the dawning awareness of the "so forth," the sense that the dissolution of phenomena into their conditions is indefinitely continuable, there arises the intuition of the abyss, the intuition of emptiness, and *deictic* phenomenology gives place, finally, to *meontic* phenomenology. While deictic phenomenology investigates the discriminata of our experience, the "thises" and "thats" which populate the domain of conventional reality (*saṁvṛti*), with an eye to their evanescence, their deficiency of value and their insubstantiality (*anityā, dukha, anātman*), meontic phenomenology orders its exploration with reference to the privation of own-being (*sva-bhāva*) which affects all phenomena. The privation of permanence, intrinsic value and self all assume a privation of ipseity. There can be no phenomenology of the absurd. And neither can there be a phenomenology of emptiness. For in emptiness there is nothing—no[thing]—to see, nothing to investigate, no structure to articulate, no murky depths to elucidate. Emptiness is not an object, certainly not an object of investigation. But if the phenomenology of presence bears witness to the sparks flying upward, the phenomenology of absolute absence observes the endlessly progressive diminution of their inner fire into the limpid atmosphere of emptiness, and culminates in a clarity galvanized with the incendiary energy of presence.

Naïveté is voiceless. It stands helplessly before experience without comment, without construal, without *as* or *as such*. But the introjection of voice is not inevitably a source of illumination. Conceptuality can darken as well as brighten. Dōgen knew that delusion attends our advance toward the manifold objects of experience, that the imposition of concept eclipses reality, while the advance of the myriad things toward us brings light. The advance of things towards us requires our openness, our sensitivity, to their own appeal to our language. To be sure, *"[w]hat Zen objects to is not intellection or conceptual knowledge as such, but clinging to intellection, or to conceptualization within the clinging pattern"* (Chang 1971, 159). And this applies reflexively to delusion "itself." To the complaint, "I find myself utterly deluded," Hui-hai rejoins: "Having never been Illumined, how can you say that you are now deluded?" (Blofeld 1972, 90). Having been illumined, we are not deluded; and devoid of illumination, we have no experiential contrast on which to base the claim of delusion. The object before us cries out for expression. We give it voice. In Merleau-Ponty's description, we "make it say . . . what in its silence it *means to say* . . ." (1969, 39). Thus, "language realizes, by breaking the silence, what the silence wished and did not obtain" (176). It is "the expression of what is before expression . . ." (167). Indeed,

> The philosopher speaks, but this is a weakness in him, and an inexplicable weakness: he should keep silent, coincide in silence, and rejoin in Being a philosophy that is there ready-made. But yet everything comes to pass as though he wished to put into words a certain silence he hearkens to within himself. His entire "work" is this absurd effort. He wrote in order to state his contact with Being; he did not state it, and could not state it, since it is silence. Then he recommences. . . . (125)

"Thought is the suspension of the voice in language" (Agamben 1991, 107). And in this sense, language becomes "the very voice of the things, the waves, and the forests" (Merleau-Ponty 1969, 155). This is not to say that "there is some word that is the word of just this thing, that just melts away in favor of the thing itself, the word this thing would speak if it could, the thing that would just rise up into presence and be its own word" (Caputo 1993, 77–8). For the doctrine of the proper name, the proper word, of one-word-one-thing, induces the nominalism which a Buddhist contextualism must eschew. In the originary response of *logos*, "the a-venue of manifestation" (Fóti 1992, 8), to *phaínomena*—the neuter present participle of *phaínesthai* (to appear) and passive of *phaínein* (to show)—there is illumination. "Since the word, *logos*, brings something into the radiant appearance of its phenomenal "color" (*iro*) by carrying it unto the vast emptiness of *kū*, logos is the saying-together of *iro* and *kū* . . ." (Fóti 1992, 10). Concepts are not *applied* to reality. Rather, things are seen in their light. And to this extent, our concepts have a provisional, not a fixed, employment. Our role as

phenomenologists is to grope in the obscurity, on behalf of the object, for the conceptual switch which will dispel the darkness—a trope which disintegrates in the dialectic ingenuity of Nāgārjuna:

> There is no darkness in light or in its abode. What does light illumine when, indeed, it destroys darkness? [VI, 9] How could darkness be destroyed by a presently shining light? For, indeed, the presently shining light has not as yet extended over to darkness. [VI, 10]
>
> If darkness is destroyed by light which is not extended, then light, in such a state, will destroy the whole world of darkness. [VII, 11]
>
> If light illuminates both itself and other entities, then undoubtedly, darkness will also darken itself and other entities as well. [VI, 12] (Inada 1970, 66)

It is when our [pro]visional engagement with concepts becomes [pre]visional, when our concepts have congealed into system, when our conceptual scheme is laid against reality as a template, that the clouds gather over the face of experience. A template, of course, is not an unqualified figuration of obscurity. Certain colors and patterns of reality are permitted to the fore, and certain others are cloaked. The subject/object schema is, in this sense, a template that effaces the subject in the face of objective display. The figure/ground schema is likewise a template that obscures context and horizon in favor of a central saliency. "We continuously seek closure in our meanings and identities, yet we cannot tolerate the constrictions they lay upon us . . ." (Parsons 1976, 3). The impositional use of concepts permits only a half-light, a dim gloaming in which the contours of reality melt into indistinctness. Impositional conceptuality speaks before it listens. Open conceptuality listens in silence, in empathetic resonance, selflessly, without imposing its own inclinations upon experience. For it knows that "[t]he absence of language is pregnant with the pure possibility of all language" (Coward 1990, 101). Impositional conceptuality determines in advance what is to be seen, and then assumes that the way reality thus appears is the way reality stands in itself. Open conceptuality remains vitally alive to experience, sacrificing, in its gift of voice, both the rigid deductive ordering of concepts characteristic of system and the clarity of definition which informs the rationalist's clear and distinct ideas. The open concept is receptive, indeterminate. It is not inevitably clear whether a given determination or its complement belongs to an open concept. Nor is it inevitably clear whether a particular reality conforms to it. And this is not because the indeterminacy of the concept fails to select the relevant determination on the part of reality.

Reality is rather intrinsically open. Its silent appeal for expression is not a plea for con/formity, isomorphism. The open concept cannot mirror the purported determinacy of reality. The unfinished determinacy of reality is a coagulation *in progress* out of an environing soup of emptiness. The appeal to an inflexible ordering of well-defined concepts would either betray the soft viscosity of reality or represent, on the part of reality, a movement of self-determination. In either case, there would be no question of adequate [mens]uration.

Again, it is not that reality presents itself without determination. Nor are we required to suspend all *Vorhabe*. Philosophy, after all, is "the study of the *Vorhabe* of Being . . ." (Merleau-Ponty 1969, 204). Radical presuppositionlessness would leave us with nothing to see—unless, of course, "radical" is understood as *racinated*, "rooted in a dense and inextricable system of roots, of factical pregivenness, which antedates me and my attempts to disentangle it . . ." (Caputo 1993 254,). A phenomenology purged entirely of presupposition could only speak a language of proper names. Without a certain precomprehension, without a certain fund of assumptions, no matter how nebulous, we would be "utterly and totally unfamiliar" with the object, "completely unprepared for it, wholly unable to anticipate it" (Caputo 1993, 78). Thus, "we would not know it is a name, we would not use it or understand its use, and it would not get known because it could never be repeated" (78). And if, as a consequence, "[a] proper name . . . must have . . . im-proper features," if "[a] pure proper name would be an absolute secret . . ." (78), phenomenology, though it may aspire to a freedom from presupposition, can never attain it. We must not, then, presuppose the phenomenological possibility of radical presuppositionlessness. And in our empathetic attentiveness to experience we also must not neglect the positive constitutive role of presupposition. Thus Lyotard's description of phenomenology as "a combat of language with itself in its effort to attain the originary" (Dews 1988, 43). That which advances toward us entreating our voice is inseparable from the prearticulate fabric of meaning in which it is implicated. The phenomenon is a wave in a sea of meaning. And our attunement to its silence is an appeal for the expression of this concertion. *"Silence,"* as we hear from Agamben, *"comprehends the Abyss as incomprehensible"* (1991, 63). And we learn from Merleau-Ponty that "philosophy is the reconversion of silence and speech into one another . . ." (1969, 129). Phenomena are no more reclusive bundles of significance than cloistered and irrelative atoms of presence. Open conceptuality does not impose structure upon the reality which it serves. But it is attentive to the intricate tissue of meaning which supports and composes the phenomenon. It is, then, this textured context as concertedly expressed in the phenomenal text that is thus given voice. A Buddhist phenomenology does not rip out shreds of tissue, does not, in the originary sense, ab/stract, holding up the useless morsels before its gaze. It rather heals the rift, mends the lacerations, binds up the wounded corpus of significance, and, in the spirit of Nāgārjuna, demonstrates the inseparability of meanings from the living body of meaning which moves the phenomenologist to speak. Presuppositionlessness is possible, for a Buddhist phenomenology, not as the annulment of prior contexts of meaning, and not as the deoperationalization of significance, but only as a lucid awareness of the dialectic determination of a meaning by the context in which it is embedded. Thus, as Merleau-Ponty recognizes, "if it is to remain dialectical, speech can no longer be statement, *Satz*, it must be thinking speech, without reference to a *Sachverhalt* . . ." (1969, 175). At the very root of phenomena, in the functioning which allows their presentation, there works the empty[ing] (*śūnyatā*) of conceptuality which Nāgārjuna labored to express.

While Buddhist philosophy—"the conceptual formulation of the non-conceptual content of Wisdom or Enlightenment" (Sangharakshita 1987, 26)—does not pretend to presupposition-free discernment, its review of reality is empowered by its own distinctive *epochē*. The Buddhist repudiation of substantiality, like its other avowals and disavowals concerning the nature of manifest particularity, the "thises" and "thats" of our experience, must not be understood as a "position," certainly not a position which we "occupy," and certainly, also, not one which we "defend." The *dharma*—"*trans*formation manifesting as *in*formation" (Corless 1989, 124)—is not a citadel to be fortified and protected against the enemies of light. Light has no enemy, cannot be attacked and needs no protection. The rejection of *ātman*—an ambivalent term designating both that invariant "self" rumored to underlie the vicissitudes of our mental life, the residuum which, it is claimed, remains upon the pacification of mental fluctuations, and the continuous "itself" which underlies the accidental and variable idiosyncrasies of the object—is, if you like, a "gentle" affirmation, not a willful assertion. The ultimately real is the ground of all distinction, and subtends, thus, even the distinction between the substantial and the insubstantial. Reality (*paramārtha*) is neither. But the negation of *ātman* pertains to *realitas* as the domain of *res*. Insubstantiality is not, then, an absolute posit. It is not that ultimate reality is substantial by contradistinction. "The purpose of Nāgārjuna's negations is not to describe *via negativa* an absolute which cannot be expressed, but to deny the illusion that such a self-existent reality exists" (Streng 1967, 146). And Bhattacharyya perceives that the varieties of negation "indicate certain distinctive temperaments or attitudes towards truth, certain familiar modes of handling a given content" (1958, 210). The proclivity expressed in Nāgārjunian negation is an unqualified openness, absolute receptivity, pure affirmation which "does not affirm anything in-itself" (Caputo 1993, 45). The affirmation intrinsic to Nāgārjuna's negation "is not fed by the fire of opposition" (47). Negation is not exclusion. In its application to ultimate reality, the denial of substantiality can only be understood as the rejection of the categorial bipolarity which locks together appearance and reality. In its application to *saṃsāra*, however, to the realm of *res*, the deposition concerns all discriminata.

The Husserlian *epochē* is not, as often supposed, the confinement of philosophical attention to the apparent in contradistinction to the real. Nor is it the exclusive suspension of our belief in the real. A duality is a unity of two. And it is impossible to bracket one half of the oppositional duality of appearance and reality. The questionability of reality draws appearance into itself. And what is, then, bracketed is not the noumenal as distinct from the phenomenal, but the very distinction/connection between them. In Foucault's phrase, what is bracketed is human reality as "a strange empirico-transcendental doublet" (cf. Hiley 1988, 102–3). Or rather, what is bracketed is the naive unquestionability of our variegated experience which features within itself both the real and the apparent. Buddhist insight rejoins the Husserlian at exactly this juncture. In Hui-hai's words, "the 'right' dharma is neither wrong nor right" (Blofeld 1972, 118). Right view (*sammā diṭṭhi*)—singular, not plural—involves a refraining from "views," and has much in common with the method of withholding assent brought from India by Pyrrho of Elis at the time of Alexander the Great. Not unlike the Buddhist aspiration, though differently nuanced, "the Sceptic's end is quietude in respect of matters of opinion and moderate feeling in respect of things unavoidable" (Sextus 1933, 19). And somewhat like the *catuṣkoṭi*, the four-cornered negation, practiced by Nāgārjuna—though, again, not without divergence—"[a] Pyrrhonist's researches do not end in discovery; nor yet do they conclude that discovery is impossible. For they do not terminate at all: the researches continue and the researcher finds himself in a condition of [*epochē*]" (Barnes 1983, 5). Nāgārjuna refutes each of the four "corners," or forms of predication—that a thing *is*, *is not*, *both* is *and* is not, and *neither* is *nor* is not . . ." (where the ellipse is filled by one's favorite adjective). Sextus found himself "involved in contradictions of equal weight, and being unable to decide between them suspended judgement . . ." (19). If, as Merleau-Ponty proposes, philosophy is ineluctably autocritical, then "it is also essential to it to forget this as soon as it becomes what we call *a philosophy*" (1969, 92). Position-taking, the sponsorship, not of philosophy, but of *a* philosophy, is a relapse, an instability, revocation of epochē. Thus, "[a]t bottom, Pyrrhonism shares the illusions of the naïve man" (6). These "illusions" are simply held in a state of suspension. And inasmuch as the commitment to quiescence is itself a position, pyrrhonism becomes "the naïveté that rends itself asunder in the night" (6). Nāgārjuna actively *produced* such contradictions. But his suspension of conceptuality was not an admission of failure—as if the disequilibrium of decisiveness would otherwise ensue. Nor would he purchase *ataraxia* at the price of forfeiting the utility and value of forming ordinary, common-sense judgments. The Buddha was referred to as the Great Physician. And Nāgārjuna, regarded by some as a second Buddha, offered, not a theory, but a therapy, a healing procedure which involved the reduction of a proponent's position to absurdity (*prasanga*) by employing the assumptions and modalities of inference intrinsic to the conceptual scheme being refuted. In a sense, Nāgārjuna had no "opponents," since he was not on the attack, nor did he populate his world with theoretical "enemies." "The value of accepting the logical criterion of the opponent [or proponent, if you will] is that he can be refuted in terms of *his* principles of meaning or he must be judged inconsistent with *his* own principles" (Streng 1967, 97). Unlike the skeptic, for whom "*ataraxia* is hardly to be attained if he is not in some sense satisfied—so far—that no answers are forthcoming, that contrary claims are indeed equal" (Burnyeat 1984, 52), Nāgārjuna sweeps away even second-order judgments. The salutary cauterization of conceptuality leads, ultimately, not to the opposite position, and not to a blithe suspension between equivalently weighted absurdities, but to the breakdown of the partisan's expectation that, beyond its utility, beyond its halo of noncognitive value, *any* conceptual scheme could secure absolute truth. And with the invalidation of mediating conceptuality as the vestibule to truth, we find ourselves in im/mediate touch with the real.

The imposition of the appearance/reality schema upon living tissue of our experience is, within the context of Husserlian methodology, an open question. To bracket is to insist upon this openness. Husserl does not disclaim our natural "faith" in the reality of the world. He suspends our preepochetic world-positing: suspends it, that is, between the alternatives of veracity and untruth. One might say that what, for Husserl, is an open question, is, for Buddhism, firmly and irrevocably closed, that there is no question, certainly not a methodological or procedural question, of the applicability this ancient dichotomy to ultimate reality (*paramārtha*). It is inapplicable. And that, it seems, is that. It "is not a question of the suspension of judgment but of judgments of suspension . . ." (Caputo 1993, 107).

One *might* say this, and at a preliminary stage, this insistence would not be misplaced. But to do so with more than a provisional emphasis would be to miss the subtlety of the Buddhist dialectic. The Buddhist *epochē* bears witness our "judgments suspended over an abyss" (Caputo 1993, 107). Without wishing to hypostatize, we may speak of "the Ultimate" as the ground of any possible discrimination. "It" cannot take on as its "own" any determination which belongs to a one-sided discriminatum. It is free of "the onus of Ownness . . ." (93). It is not apparent as opposed to real, or real as opposed to apparent. And this is the provisional truth which oversees the closure of the Husserlian question. Like a mirror, the Ultimate welcomes and makes possible any figuration which dances upon it. But as a mirror does not "itself" turn blue in the presence of the blue sky, the Ultimate repudiates, as intrinsic character, any determination which it might "reflect"— and this includes, as a vital instance, the bivalence of truth and untruth. The Ultimate does not, then, arrogate to itself the nobility of truth as distinct from the debased status of falsehood. It is not (ultimately) *true* that the Ultimate is beyond truth and falsehood. Indeed, absolute "[t]ruth does not begin or end in declarative statements . . ." (Streng 1967, 163). Such doctrinal expressions are fingers pointing to the moon. The finger is not a form which could possibly con/form to the contours of lunar reality, for the Ultimate has no contours. No bond of adequation spans finger and moon. Nor does such a formulation express the dis/closure, the re[veil]ation, the a/letheia of the Ultimate. For the Ultimate is neither open nor closed, neither patent nor concealed, neither veiled nor unveiled. Murdoch is assuredly correct in his recognition that "Our minds are continually active, fabricating an anxious, usually self-preoccupied *veil* which partially conceals the world" (1970, 84). In the Husserlian epochē, world-faith is neither true nor false. It is suspended between the two. And the question in which this issue is methodologically suspended is *which*. This is not a question for Buddhism, because the Ultimate is demonstrably neither. But this does not import a repudiation of the Husserlian view. The Buddhist "neither" draws both Buddhist and Husserlian posits into itself. Which is *true*: the Buddhist or Husserlian position? *Neither*. The ultimate "truth" of the Buddhist "neither" is that it lies beyond (relative) truth.

A meontic phenomenology discloses exactly this "truth," the truth beyond truth. A deictic phenomenology, the investigation of conditioned *res*, and of the integrity of their synthetic unity, *realitas*, reveals the insubstantiality of phenomena, the absence of a dimension of ontological depth. There is nothing standing under or behind the manifestation. Manifestation is not, then, the ex/pression of something deeper than the apparent. But the attribution of in/substantiality to phenomena subtly assumes the disjunction of the apparent from the subtending real. The distinction holds, but one side is vacuous. There is a conceptual niche for substance, but this niche remains vacant. In its application to the domain of "conventional" reality (*samvrti*) the denial of sub/stance is angular—sharply opting for *this* position in contrast to *that*—and unbalanced—the native equipoise of the impartial scale of truth being disrupted by the evacuation of a presumed ontological depth. There is a relative truth: namely, that, although the alternative position is fully and equally conceivable, nothing, in fact, subtends the apparent. The two positions are indifferently conceivable. The one, and not the other, is preferentially *true*. The "truth" of meontic phenomenology, on the other hand, is like a slippery bar of soap: ungraspable with the wet hands of discriminate conceptuality—even with the "hand" of truth. The truth of deictic phenomenology is preferential, slanted, unbalanced, tipped outside itself. Its ec/stacy, its overflowing of "itself" beyond itself, the auto-constitution of "itself" as a being beyond "itself," is the vectorial directed-ness of the finger. And directedness is asymmetrical.

Husserl distances himself from the Cartesian posturing of incertitude in his contention that Descartes' "attempt to doubt universally is properly an attempt to negate universally" (1982, 59). Or as Merleau-Ponty ex-presses it, "doubt as a destruction of certitudes is not doubt" (1969, 106). Descartes is concerned to contrive conceivable narratives which, if true, would render certain of our ordinary commitments false. While the dy-namic of Cartesian doubt is an urgency in the direction of possible false-hood, the doubt of Husserl's Cartesian path to the reduction is rather an authentic vacillation before the alternatives of truth and falsehood. Transcendental subjectivity, the residuum which survives the Cartesian "*hy-pothesis of the Nichtigkeit of the world . . .*" (172), also outlives the presump-tion of existence. But as Merleau-Ponty points out, to think of subjectivity as a "residuum" at all is "to define it not by what it gives us, but by what in it *withstands* the hypothesis of *non-existence*; it is to identify from the first the positive with a negation of negation; it is to require of the innocent the proof of his non-culpability, and to reduce in advance our contact with Being to the discursive operations with which we defend ourselves against illusion, to reduce the true to the credible, the real to the probable" (39). As Wagner affirms, "I perform the *epoche* in order to distinguish between world and 'world' . . ." (1970, 221). But "world"—world *in quotes*—is a world which, when disquoted, will fall to one side or the other of the alethic di-vide. Quine tells us that "[t]he truth predicate serves the function of . . . dis-quotation" (1970, 97). Bracketing merely relieves the pressure of de/cision which would otherwise erupt in "the violence of unleashed quantification" (Adorno 1973, 43). If Cartesian doubt is the suspicion of possible false-hood, Husserlian doubt is irresolution before the "which?" Bracketing qui-ets the insistence upon resolution. The resolution of doubt is always a clarity with regard to the "which?" And this lends content to Merleau-Ponty's observation that "doubt is a clandestine positivism" (1969, 120). In the Hegelian vision, which Merleau-Ponty treats with evident approbation, doubt is "the whole history of consciousness." It "inserts itself into truth ([since] the object and work of consciousness reflect each other exactly)" (1988, 20).

But there is, as one of Husserl's closest students attests, a very different sense of our registration of the bracketed world. Fink reminds us that "[w]hat is of decisive importance is the awakening of an immeasurable astonishment over the mysteriousness of this state of affairs [i.e., the reality of the world]. To accept it as a self-evident fact is to remain blind to the greatest mystery of all, the mystery of the being of the world itself . . ." (1970, 109–10). This is Husserl's own "interrogative word of adoration in the ear of . . . the Abyss." Far from an indecisiveness in the face of live options, an inability to commit, this "immeasurable astonishment" is a decisive cessation of doubt. We find ourselves frozen, breathless, stilled and overwhelmed by the overpowering and indubitable enigma of the "there is." And "the explanation of an enigma is the mere repetition of the enigma" (Lispector 1988, 127). The mystery of world-presence repels our usual tendency to take the world for granted. And as Fóti (1992) advances, "*poiēsis* remains mindful of the 'mystery' or the lack of any inherent, positable reality in the happening of manifestation . . ." (13). While the world may be the deepest-set invariance accessible to our intuition, the givenness of the world itself remains altogether baffling from the vantage point of naive, prereflective, pretranscendental consciousness. Husserl (1982) assumes that reflection broaches the intentional act at right angles, that the linearity, the vectoriality of the act is taken up into reflective consciousness, and thus that, *behind* the naive display there are complex flows of constitutive activity. But as Merleau-Ponty insists, "reflection cannot feign to unravel the same thread that the mind would first have woven, to be the mind returning to itself within me, when by definition it is I who reflect" (1969, 34). For a reflective investigation which peers behind the immediacy of the given, there is, then, no enigma. Mystery resolves into lucidity. Self-evidence is reestablished. Mystery, for Husserl, merely motivates the pursuit of clarity. And this pursuit achieves its end in transcendental reflection. But in the achievement of transcendental self-evidence, there is a trade-off. For to quote Fink back at himself, this consciousness remains "blind to the greatest mystery of all, the mystery of the being of the world itself." There is loss: loss of mystery. The quality of immediate apprehension which strikes us with such consummate impetus, the atmosphere of the enigmatic in which it is unwrapped, vanishes with a shift of posture. Mystery is apprehensible only for a consciousness suitably placed to apprehend it. There is no absolute, irresolvable mystery. But whether the Husserlian epochē is conceived as vacillation, hesitation, the implosion of an ontological *mysterium* upon our wide-eyed receptivity, or "the first authentic *discovery of the belief in the world* . . ." (Fink 1970, 221), it seems to bear at least one similarity with the hyperbolic drive to possible falsehood which informs Descartes' thinking. As Sokolowski writes of the Cartesian stratagem:

The attempt to doubt is naturally performed in order to change the modality of our belief in a certain object or to reconfirm with new reasons, what we already believe. . . .

The disconnection from a convinced life effected in the attempt to doubt is carried out in order to return to the same life with better conviction. . . . (1974, 173–4)

Cartesian doubt is a means to an end: the end of securing a rational foundation for our beliefs which is impervious to doubt. Doubt seeks its own extinction. And Husserlian mystery likewise seeks its own annulment in the transcendental reclamation of certitude. Granted that Husserlian suspension can never be deployed self-consciously as a practice or technique, since "[t]he reduction becomes knowable in its 'transcendental motivation' only with the transcending of the world" (Fink, 105), still the effect is the same: cognitive security. In this respect, the *epochē*, the "switching off" of the world, bears an unmistakable resemblance to *nirvāṇa*:

Literally, the word [*epochē*] means 'switching off,' as when we switch off an electric lamp. The lamp is still there, but now as one of the objects in the room, not as that which illuminates everything else. This is what the phenomenologist does when he 'switches off the world' or, more precisely, the common-sense assumption that the world explains experience. The world, like the lamp, is still there, but no longer as that which makes experience 'visible' (here, intelligible). (Kohák 1978, 36–7)

Writes Sangharakshita: "The 'world' being a positive datum of experience, and mankind having on the whole no knowledge of anything beyond the world, Nirvana had necessarily to be described to them in terms of the cessation of the world . . ." (1987, 145). Fink's wonderful portrayal of the *epochē* as "the most extreme striving for a theoretical self-surmounting of man" (126) simply marks a shift to another "self"—the grim transcendental ego that surveys the constitutive dimension of experience, and for whom there can, in principle, be no mystery. Buddhist nonsubstantialism repudiates the artifice of a transcendental, right-angled intuition of the presumed linear directedness of consciousness. Self-surmounting is free-fall through the abyss, through the fathomless emptiness which permits the reception of experience in ever widening horizons of constitutive conditions. With each successive dilation, each event of releasement of phenomena into their radiance of conditions, there is light. But the bottomlessness of this descent is consonant with "the awakening of an immeasurable astonishment." For Baudrillard, "fundamental thought is bottomless. It is, if you wish, an abyss" (183, 21). And emptiness does not induce an insensitivity to the ir-reducible mysteriousness of things. There is no "self-evidence," because there is no "self" to be evident. Emptiness witnesses the perpetual dissolu-tion of "self" and "itself" into nonself. And though this very dissolution elu-cidates and brightens, there remains deep mystery in the interminable expansibility of illumination.

Natanson claims that, in Sartre's ontology, "the Husserlian method is put aside as inadequate," that "no *epochē* or reduction has been performed," and thus that "whatever its merits or insights," Sartre's ontology "is not a phenomenological analysis" (1951, 70). And Solomon concurs that Sartre "explicitly reject[s] the reduction in all its forms" (1972, 20). Sartre was, of course, very deeply influenced by Husserlian phenomenology. He writes that "Husserl had gripped me, I saw everything through the perspectives of his philosophy . . ." (1984, 183). His early novel, *La Nausée*, "traces the ex-perience of living through the reduction" (Busch 1980, 21). *L'Imaginaire* was written "under his [Husserl's] inspiration" (Sartre 184). And *La tran-scendence de l'ego* was written "against" Husserl, "but just insofar as a disciple can write against his master" (184). Certainly, by the composition of *L'Etre et le néant*, Sartre had begun to wrench himself away from the authority of his "master." In a letter to Beauvoir, he confides that "I no longer think with an eye to certain strictures (the Left, Husserl), etc. . . . " (1993, 14). And it is not surprising, then, that certain of Husserl's methodological strategies receive comparatively little attention in *Being and Nothingness*, or that they have been deeply transformed in the process of appropriation. The *epochē*, for example, "is no longer . . . an intellectual method, an erudite procedure: it is an anxiety . . ." (1972, 103). And "the significance of Sartre's appropri-ation of the phenomenological reduction emerges as the possibility to 'disconnect' our reflective life from its natural impulse," namely "the psy-chological impulse toward absolute being" (Silverman and Elliston 1980, 3). The Sartrean "reduction" institutes a profound hemorrhage in the "ab-solute being" of consciousness. The "reduction" is rupture, rent, cleavage. It is the nothingness whereby consciousness is torn from itself, the occasion of our freedom from our "natural impulses," from ourselves.

Findlay affirms—and cogently—that, to the question of how mind can be ecstatic or self- transcendent "it does not seem a sufficient answer at a suf-ficiently deep level of reflection to say that such ecstasy, such self-transcen-dence, is the very mark of the mental" (1970, 244). And neither is "the mystery of consciousness"—the paradox, in Sokolowski's words, that "real-ity, something which is transcendent to consciousness, is accessible to con-sciousness in its very transcendence" (Sokolowski 1964, 135)—dissipated in the least by appealing to intentionality. There is, perhaps, an unintended dimension to Bernasconi's priceless quip that "intentionality can be traced back to insomnia . . ." (1988, 242). And a second, rather tired, but more pertinent joke is at Aristotle's expense: that their soporific quality does not *explain* the fact that our lectures put freshmen to sleep. Ecstasy, self-transcendence, intentionality can be no more than a means of vocalizing a vital enigma. Though clarifying the concepts deployed in phenomenological description, Husserl's eidetic reduction in no way *explains* the comportment of consciousness or resolves the deeply problematic issues of how consciousness lives in its object by dying to itself. At best, eidetic intuition displays (and splays) the determinations analytically derived from a host concept. But deduction is impoverishment. The filaments of significance spun from a given conceptual skein can be no richer in content than the original. And, of course, "[t]o deduce is not to elucidate" (Levin 1970, 11). It may be useful to observe, with Gurwitsch, that in the eidetic reduction

> . . . the real existent is divested of its actuality, of its existential character. . . . Every real existent can be regarded as an actualized possibility. Under the eidetic reduction, the fact of its actualization is considered as immaterial, and hence, is disregarded. What is en-countered as a matter of fact, is "irrealized"; i.e., considered as to its imaginable ness and not as to its actuality, it is transformed into a "pure possibility" among other possibilities. From the status of a real existent, it is transferred to that of an example or exemplar . . . (1966, 383)

Still, if what we seek is the essence *of consciousness*, irrealization is out of the question. To the precise extent that consciousness achieves self-transcendence its purported presence evaporates before the object. "[C]onsciousness has a *'punctum caecum'* . . ." (Merleau-Ponty 1969, 247). The eye cannot see itself. The mirror cannot reflect itself. Or rather, the "self" of self-reflection is displaced outward. "Consciousness," Sartre tells us, "cannot escape its imma-nence, cannot be an object of its own will, unless it projects its passivized image to the other side of the world" (1984, 40).

In the only phenomenologically available sense, the "self" which is seen *is* other. "[T]he self is a non-self . . ." (Silverman 1980, 87). The othering of self, the equivalent diaphaneity of consciousness, ensures that there is no "real existent" which could be modulated into the register of "pure possibil-ity." Thus, the application of eidetic reduction is, *pace* Husserl, baldly impracticable. And if consciousness offers to reflection no discernible artic-ulation of presence, no "fact," its ecstatic dynamism becomes, not merely problematic or puzzling, but straightforwardly inconceivable. For "[t]he idea is in the strict sense the possibility of the fact" (de Muralt 1973, 320), and without the fact we cannot postulate its possibility. Or in Merleau-

Ponty's concomitant ruling, "[t]he possibilities by essence can indeed envelop and dominate *the facts*" (1969, 110). Possibility "animates and organizes *their facticity*" (110).

Derrida is magnificently insightful in his contention that "[i]deality is the preservation or mastery of presence in repetition" (1973, 9–10), and thus, "the very form in which the presence of an object in general may be repeated as the *same*" (9). No *eidos* reigns over unrepeatable presence. One may, indeed, question whether Husserlian presence is conceivable in default of eidetic repeatability. Manifest quality must be diachronically re/cognizable as *the same*. Otherwise, there is nothing to nourish eidetic intuition. And for the Husserlian, who envisions the intentional object as a continuity woven through the discontinuous strands of givenness, "[o]bjectivity is identifiableness" (Gurwitsch 1940, 136). Merleau-Ponty refers to the invariants of eidetic variation as "*hinges* of Being" which are "accessible through quality as well as through quantity—" (1969, 236): the same quality given through a quantitative diversity of intuitions. And indeed, "the solidity, the essentiality of the essence is exactly measured by the power we have to vary the thing" (111). Buddhist insight is thus incompatible with a phenomenological essentialism, and sponsors that "awareness of the essencelessness of things, which is another way of expressing *nirvana* itself" (Misra 1971, 174–5). Thus, as Conze puts it, "Nirvana is 'unthinkable', or 'inconceivable', if only because there is nothing general about it . . ." (Conze 1962, 57). And in Streng's statement, "[s]tatements about *nirvāna* or metaphysical statements were not meant to be unassailable semantic pillars on which to construct a system of necessary propositions . . . " (1967, 157). The realization of impermanence permits, at best, only the similarity, not the identity of diachronic exhibitions of quality. Given the momentariness of our experience, possibility provides no way in which successively presented determinations could be immediately compared. For similarity assumes a dimension of comparison, a respect or prospect in which *two* determinations can be said to be *one*. And either this is available to us in the moment, in which case, as moments succeed one another, we have a multiplicity of such "respects" incapable of being brought under the purview of a single intuition, or else there is a single transtemporal vantage point from which the vanishing moments of presence can be surveyed and their qualitative identity registered. It is, however, of no use to assume an immovable reviewing stand opening out upon the animated parade of phenomena, a *nunc stans*, aloof from the world, from which the temporal proflux can be safely and impassively regarded. For if consciousness *is* the revelation of its object, if its *being* is wholly bound up with the *appearing* of our evanescent world, then either the dynamism of our experience would upset the atemporal equilibrium of the frozen standpoint or the timelessness of the standing now would effect a radical cryogenesis of our outlook. "*Nirvāna* is realizing the true, *empty* structure of becoming, which then becomes religiously 'more,' but metaphysically 'less' than 'being' or 'becoming' " (Streng 1967, 81).

What Barthes proclaims with respect to the arrested image of oneself in a photograph, the "specter" of the self othered and immobilized, we conscript for the spectator. The solidified outlook encases "a micro-version of death." The spectator has become "[d]eath in person." And much as "[d]eath is the *eidos* of that Photograph" (1981, 14–5), the unliberated fixation of an essentialized self can be visioned only in the black light of the lifeless. For to live is to be released from stability, to die to the immutable self and to find one's life in dynamic profluence toward the other. And this is no insignificant deliverance of Buddhist wisdom for which "[i]lluminating and acknowledging life and death is the ultimate concern . . ." (Kotoh 1987, 202). Sartre is right that "[t]he existent does not *possess* its essence as a present quality. It is even the negation of essence." Thus "the green *never is* green" (1971, 267). It escapes fixed determination by cascading into the possible. Its essence "comes from the ground of the future"—we would say the possible—"as a meaning which is never given and which forever haunts it" (267). But there is *self*-transcendence only in the sense of an illuminating transposition of our sense of self. It is not that the authentic life blood of the phenomenon is rendered up to the greedy fangs of its carnivorous conditions, but rather that what, in our originary delusion, we once regarded as a self-existent entity harboring its own fund of intrinsic and monadic predicates turns out, on closer inspection, to have no intrinsic self or self-existence, and that the only "self" which it rightfully possesses is its other. And if, as Adorno teaches, "[t]he concept of entity pure and simple is the mere shadow of the false concept of Being" (1973, 138), we must foreswear both the shade and the tree. Or in Caputo's brusque "theory of *Seinsvergessenheit*: Forget Being!" (1993, 69). Moreover, emptiness imports that the being of a phenomenon dissolves into its temporal wake, and that this "wake" is extended—and thus differs—with each passing moment. Nothing, then, remains the same. And there can thus be no acts of repetition. In Baudrillard's analysis of the famous Warhol painting, "the multiple replicas of Marilyn's face are there to show at the same time the death of the original and the end of representation" (1983, 136). Repetition requires a "first," either in the order of exemplifications or in the order of the ideal. And Buddhism will countenance neither. Even the Buddha could see no beginning of *samsāra*. Or in Bourdieu's sonorous proclamation, "[i]n the beginning is the *illusio* . . ." (1983, 1). And we can find no warrant for regarding ideality as an exemplar. In Nietzsche's startling pronouncement, "All ideals are dangerous: because they debase and brand the actual; all are poisons, but indispensable as temporary cures" (1967, 130). Buddhism does not deny infinity. Emptiness itself is the possibility of infinite disintegration. But we cannot accept Derrida's proposal that "absolute ideality is the correlate of a possibility of indefinite repitition" (1973, 52). For in the strict sense, there is, and can be, no ideality, no essence, no *eidos*. Nothing ensures that "the possibility of . . . repetition may be open, *ideally* to infinity . . ." (6)—a decided relief, if, as Corless tells us, "[s]amsara is repetition" (1989, 281). Emptiness, on the other hand, ensures the indefinite proliferation of the different.

There may, however, be another way of thinking about this. As Llewelyn suggests, "[t]he presentation of the *eidos* is a depresentation. For the eidos is intrinsically extrinsic . . ." (1988, 198). Buddhism has no objection to idealities which, like all other phenomena, loose themselves in their conditions. The *eidos* is that in light of which phenomena are seen, and vanishes with direct inspection in a surfeit of illumination. Like the sun which relinquishes its brilliance to the potentially visible, the *eidos* both brightens and conceals itself (its "self") in bedazzlement. Its *self* is "othered" in the visible. And it has no being beyond that which is multiplied among the manifold associated visibilia. The *eidos* is thus the inverse of evanescent subjectivity. Consciousness annuls itself in the presence of its object. The *eidos* annuls itself in its frontal presence to the subject. Or rather, both are seen *as they are*—thus, *are not seen*—in immediate presence. The visibility of phenomena is conditioned by the obliqueness of our glance. We see. But we cannot see that whereby we see. There is light. And there is ineluctable mystery.

While the *eidos*, as "intrinsically extrinsic," denies its own immediate presence in a blinding superfluity of presence, and thus offers nothing (or nothing but *nothing*) to the curious, investigatory gaze of phenomenology, the "sense" (French: *sens*), its direction or grain, its bearing or proclivity, is present within experience as its visible *Gestalt*. Merleau-Ponty likens the ideational lattice-work of experience, the figuration which exhibits its vectorial dynamic, to the veins which form and support the material tissue of the leaf: "As the nervure bears the leaf from within, from the depths of its flesh, the ideas are the texture of experience, its style, first mute, then uttered. Like every style, they are elaborated within the thickness of being and . . . could not be detached from it, to be spread out on display under the gaze" (1969, 119). Thus, "the philosopher could not possibly have access to the universal by reflection alone . . ." (Merleau-Ponty 1974, 104). "The ideas," Adorno tells us, "live in the cavities between what things claim to be and what they are" (1973, 150). Things do not *have* an essence as one might have a dog on a leash. Essence is not a detachable possession. And we must not, in this way, abjure the "the essencelessness of things"—which Misra ap-

)

propriately conflates with emptiness (cf. Misra 1971, 174–5). But the *Gestalt* rendering of "essence" permits a clear sense in which "Buddhism is the study of mind—its essence, nature, and functioning . . ." (Hayward 1989, ix). Puligandla elucidates:

> . . . mind is no more and no less than mental activities; for this reason, mind is best construed as a field of energy; it is sheer dynamism, a nexus of activities and potential for activities—mental activities. To be aware of mind is to be aware of one's thoughts and the activity of thinking. Mind is not a container of thoughts; rather, thought and thinking *are* mind; mind is an energy field, the fluctuations in which are phenomenologically cognized as thinking and thoughts. (1985, 75)

"Mind" can only betoken the pervasive flow pattern, the "style," which informs the fluid phenomena of our mental life. Subject to the same influence, Sartre exhibits throughout his philosophical writings, and right from the very beginning, the formative pressure of a *Gestalt* analysis of the structuration of experience. In the *Transcendence of the Ego*, for example, he represents the empirical self as a *Gestalt* of elements in contrast to the position which he imagines Husserl to hold, namely that the ego is an ideal pole "indifferent to its states" (1972, 74). In Sartre's reading, Husserl's theory of the ego is informed by a certain reading of Aristotle: "What is logically first are unilateral relations by which each quality belongs (directly or indirectly) to this X like a predicate to a subject" (73). Aristotelian substantialism was in significant respects formative for Husserl's outlook. But curiously, the example—that of the unitary melody—which Sartre offers in refutation of the presumed "Husserlian" position is lifted directly from Husserl's musings on our experience of lived temporality:

> If we take a melody . . . it is useless to presuppose an X which would serve as a support for the different notes. The unity here comes from the absolute indissolubility of the elements which cannot be conceived as separated, save by abstraction. The subject of the predicate here will be the concrete totality, and the predicate will be a quality abstractly separated from the totality, a quality which has its full meaning only if one connects it again to the totality. (1972, 73–4)

The Sartrean ego is, then, a "melody," an "interpenetrative multiplicity" (1972, 86), of states, acts and qualities. It is "the infinite totality of states and actions which is never reducible to *an* action or to *a* state" (74). And far from being indifferent to its elements, is rather "compromised" (74) by them. We actually do *see*—and not merely interpret or construct—the rows of chairs in a classroom. And in fact, it is typically the *row*, and not its elements, the chairs, which comes first to our notice. The contribution of the elements comes to our attention when they are reconfigured, when, for example, the same chairs are arranged in a circle instead of a row or when chairs are added to or deleted from the composition. Though it remains "[a] whole that does *not* reduce itself to the sum of the parts . . ." (1969, 204), the *Gestalt*, as "a diacritical, oppositional, relative system whose pivot is the *Etwas*, the thing, the world, and not the idea—" (206) is helplessly dependent upon its constituents. A "square" of chairs becomes a "triangle" by the simple removal of an element, and a "pentagon" by the addition of one. The "square," the "row," the "circle," are, in exactly the Buddhist sense, *empty*: fully and vividly present, yet having no being detachable from their elements. The "triangle" exists *in* the three chairs. There is no question here of a "fallacy of simple location" (*à la* Whitehead). For the configuration exists only among the configured elements. As Merleau-Ponty makes plain: "In so far as the content can be readily subsumed under the form and can appear as the content *of* that form, it is because the form is accessible only through the content" (1962, 102).

Sartre marvels at the advances of "modern" (we might prefer the anachronism "postmodern") thought (1971, 3). If, as Lyotard suggests, postmodernism represents an "incredulity toward metanarratives" (1996, 482), phenomenology is at least willing to bracket our credulous confidence in the "metanarrative" (general thesis) of the world's existence until a counterpart is installed in the domain of phenomenological *Evidenz*. This aside, however, Sartre sees in phenomenology the hope for a resolution of a number of classical dualisms, including as a poignant instance, the disjunction of *being* from *appearance*, and then, as another, of *appearance* from *essence* (cf. 1971, 3–5). The inference is inescapable: being and essence cannot be disjoined. Thus, in Sartre's delineation, the inseparability of *Gestalt* and elements is potentiated to the point of interfusion: "the concrete 'flesh and blood' existence must *be* the essence, and the essence must itself be produced as a total concretion; that is, it must have the full richness of the concrete without however allowing us to discover in it anything other than itself in its total purity. Or, if you prefer, the form must be to itself—and totally—its own matter. And conversely the matter must be produced as absolute form" (1971, 267–8). And we find here a significant resonance with the Buddhist deployment of the Pāli and Sanskrit "*rūpa*" (form) which can denote the material "this." A "form," then, is not, as the substance was for Aristotle, a morsel of formed matter, a designated quantity of corporeal (for later science, corpuscular) "stuff" *with* a form. Nor is it simply that [m]atter is 'pregnant' with its form . . ." (Merleau-Ponty 1964b, 12), as if (in the Aristotelian scheme) form were potential within matter. The material object *is* its form. For Dōgen, the object exhausts its potentiality, without reserve, in being exactly "what" it is. It does not conceal within its metaphysical depths a fund of potentiality in virtue of which it could "become" something else. There is no continuity underlying the supplantation of one form by another. Neither Sartre nor Merleau-Ponty would wish to abandon the canonical notion of "form." Nor, of course, would Buddhism. But form becomes concrete in the *Gestalt* and materialized in Sartrean interfusion.

Merleau-Ponty pointedly claims that the phenomenon, the very subject matter of phenomenological investigation, "is a 'figure' (*Gestalt*)," and follows this with the arresting claim that, far from an impassive formal object, the *Gestalt* is itself " 'figurative' knowledge" (1988, 18). And in a similar vein, Lyotard can say that the *Gestalt* "is not *in itself*—that is, it does not exist independently of the subject who fits his relation to the world inside it . . ." (Lyotard 1991b, 85). For Lyotard, as for Merleau-Ponty, the primal formation, that within which all others occur, is that whereby the scissiparity of subject and object presents itself as a unity. In Kwant's representation, this *Gestalt* is "the most fundamental and primordial compenetration of subject and world" (1963, 65). This "mutual implication" is "the primordial interconnection, within which all other connections exist . . ." (68). Sartre would append that this totality is "detotalized," that there is no vantage point from which it can be intuitively recovered. As he says, "[n]o consciousness, not even God's, can 'see the underside'—that is, apprehend the totality as such. . . . no point of view on the totality is conceivable; the totality has no 'outside' . . ." (1971, 400). And in this light, the claim that consciousness and its world form a "totality" at all is an extraordinary admission. For Sartre posits, as an unequivocal ontic certitude, the existence of totalities which, in principle, can enjoy no phenomenological warrant. Though speaking with the latitude of a general metaphysical concern, Severino could be prompted to concur: "Appearing is not the infinite appearing of Being, the epiphany in which the completed totality is disclosed and in which, therefore, no further revelation can occur. As finite Appearing, eternal truth is contradiction" (1988, 182). The existence of an infinite "completed totality" is unquestioned. Only the possibility of its "finite appearing" is disclaimed. And it is difficult to see what advantage might be offered by an authoritarian leap of metaphysical speculation which, in principle, cannot be warranted by our experience. Totality appears, not as detotalized, but as impossible. But consistency would then expect a concomitant declaration that the subject/object totality is consequently "impossible." Instead, it is exalted to global proportions: the form of all forms, the first and most encompassing *Gestalt* within which all other formations are inscribed.

Aligning himself with Levinas, Bernasconi assumes that "[p]hilosophy . . .
is always 'to one side,' independent and critical. It is to be understood as 'a
rupture of our participation in totality' " (1988, 235). For Merleau-Ponty,
such a "rupture" would forfeit our "natal bond with the world" (1969, 32).
"Philosophy is not a rupture with the world, nor a coinciding with it, but it
is not the alternation of rupture and coincidence either" (99). For a philosophy of reflection, a product of "the reflective cramp . . ." (57). Thus, "[t]o
reflect is not to coincide with the flux . . . it is to disengage from the things,
perceptions, world, and perception of the world. . . ." (45–6). The "philosophy of reflection" which Levinas exemplifies "is not wrong in considering
the false as a mutilated or partial truth: its error is rather to act as if the partial were only a de facto absence of the totality, which does not need to be
accounted for" (42). But our reflective probes into the dim undercurrent of
experience do need to "account" for, or at least warily (with awareness) suspect, the disturbance which they themselves occasion. We must not only
see—as if that were enough—to the extent possible, we must also see clearly
the transformation of the *seen* wrought by the *seeing*. We must, in Merleau-
Ponty's coinage, enact not a detached and impartial reflective observation,
but a "hyper-reflection" which descends into the tissue of experience with a
lucid appreciation of its own work of disruption. And this entails the commitment "not [to] allow ourselves to introduce into our description concepts issued from reflection, whether psychological or transcendental: they
are more often than not only correlatives or counterparts of the *objective*
world" (157). Or in an Hegelian response to Kant: "the instrument modi-
fies the thing. The milieu alters its image. The means runs counter to the
end" (Heidegger 1970, 8). Among the impositions to be dropped at the
portal of phenomenology, as a condition for its work to begin, are the notions of *matter* and *form* (cf. 158). We cannot assume, from the outset, that
experience *has* a form, or *is* a form. We must disclose the formalities of experience within hyperreflective circumspection.

Of course, the reflective palpation of experience could deform what it
manipulates only if the *subject* of reflection and the "object" (act) on which
operates are systemically integral, only, that is, if the "two" are *one* in an environing conformation: the vectorial *Gestalt* of intentionality. If reflection
"ruptures" our participation in the totality, it then represents an extrasystemic intrusion. Hyperreflection is intrasystemic. Though we cannot
simply *agree* with the "environmentalism" of Sartre, Merleau-Ponty and
Lyotard, or in larger profile, of Severino, Bernasconi or Levinas, neither can
these views be summarily dismissed. On the one hand, declamations which,
in principle, cannot be authenticated by "one's" experience, by the experience of any/one, can only be promulgated ex cathedra. And philosophy in-
stinctively recoils at the authoritarianism of this privileged modality of

assertion. Merely to reject this authoritarianism, however, remands us, on the other hand, to a new "authority," that of a certain privileged presence, an experiential *Evidenz* which enforces assent. And this is incompatible in spirit with a hyperreflection which lightly descends into experience by means of a cobweb ladder incapable of supporting the weight of such ponderous authority. Rather than scattering the elements of primal configuration in a gale of assertion, hyper-reflection whispers, almost inaudibly, the suspicion that its presence may distort presence. And yes, even this whisper, which approaches silence as nearly as possible with voice cannot fail to send tremors throughout the lacework of experience. Bataille reminds us that *"the word silence is still a sound . . ."* (1988, 13). And our own vocal ruminations are far from the silence *about* silence of which Heidegger speaks (1993, 424). The secret of silence is undecidability. But this is not a vacillation or oscillation between competing disjuncta. There is no wavering. There is "the noiseless ringing of stillness" (420), a serene awareness that, for all our experience certifies, it is *exactly as if* a situated subjectivity were hopelessly enmeshed within fabric of the observed and, at the same time, *exactly as if* the scene were to shift spontaneously in correlation with certain appreciable indices normally, if also naively, associated with the "position" of the subject. Environmentalism and transcendentalism are equally adept at "saving" the appearances. If, in the Buddhist deposition, "[t]he effect is nothing over and above the presence of the totality of its causes" (cf. Conze, 1962, 148–9), it is also the case that the cause is nothing over and above the totality of its effects. *"The door to the invisible must be visible"* (Daumal 1974, 42). The invisible current of electrons which we call electricity simply *is* the incandescence of the filament, the whirring of the electric motor, the heating of the coil, the movement of the dial. And if electricity empties itself into its manifestations, so, presumably, must subjectivity. If subjectivity in no way affects the structuration of our experience, if it makes no difference, it is either non-existent or transcendental. Hui-neng declares that "[i]ntrinsically our transcendental nature is void and not a single dharma (thing) can be attained" (Price and Wong 1969, 26). And much like Vedanta with its divarication of *manas* (mind), the phenomenal "object" of reflection, from *vijñāna*, pure consciousness, Buddhism discriminates a benighted *vijñāna* (phenomenal consciousness, the locus of delusion) from *sati*: pure awareness. Consciousness disturbs its object. Awareness does not. If thought, or in Severino's phrase, "finite Appearing," prohibits the silent registration of totality, we must, at the same time, posit a larger unity in which the "totalized" totality available to awareness is distinguished from the domain of "detotalized" totalities accessible in their partiality to limited subjectivities, a totality of totality and partiality. (1988, 182) And with the assumption of an environing subject/object formation, *this* totality could be seen *in its to-*

tality only by positing, in turn, a totality of yet a higher order. As Adorno writes, we spare ourselves the regress only by ceasing "to enter into collusion with the compulsion of totality" (cf. Dews 1988, 232). Either experience is not de/fined, de/termined, has no boundary or outline, no "outside" in virtue of which it could offer itself up to our gaze as a delimited whole, or awareness of experience does not assume a subject/object totality. Distinguishing totality from wholeness, we must concur with Levin that "[n]ormal perception, the ontical perception of anyone-and-everyone, is inveterately grasping, as the very word itself should remind us. It is an anxiety-driven, restless intentionality: a grasping *of* light and a grasping *in* the light. But such perception cannot see the whole of things, because wholeness, unlike totality, is not something that can be grasped" (1970, 234). As a contextualism without holism (or rather, totalism), Buddhism will recognize neither an "outside" of experience nor an external observer. Its "transcendentalism" is not an egology writ large. *Sati* is environmental, not as a distinguishable element of a global *Gestalt*, but as a boundless "space" which pervades all phenomena. In Burke's eloquent delineation, "the imagination, in search of totality, finds itself flooded by something wild and unseen, by the simultaneity and eternity of everything, by an abyssal presence, both visible and invisible, out of which it (the imagination) arises but which it cannot frame" (1990, 93). *Sati* is not the detotalized term of an intentional flow, but the very condition for the arising of any such term. *Sati* is silent. It is not an "authority." So our worries over a privileged pontification ex cathedra are unfounded. Buddhism knows that "[l]ogical and discursive thought as a process of meaning is a selective process, and this selectivity prevents it from being able to express the totality of existence, or the total human experience of existence" (Streng 1967, 97). And *sati* sponsors no angular "position," no slanted theoretical posture. It is the voice of no/one—certainly not of an anonymous, but denominable, subject. If proper names harbor "a core of impropriety, of *différance* . . ." (Caputo 1993, 226), the [no]one is the very impropriety of the proper. Nor is *sati* an impersonal standpoint which, in deference to democracy, permits any/one, or every/one simultaneously, to occupy it. For this would be no more than a special instance of that "ludicrous immodesty of decreeing . . . that there can only be a legitimate perspective from our nook" (Nietzsche 1964, 340). And the "evidence" which it provides is not "compelling." It does not impel selection between competing options. Its "presence" is that of ineluctable ambiguity. It offers radical undecidability, the *koan*, the openness of the question which cannot be foreclosed by any degree of confirmation.

Chapter 3

Questioning Sartrean Questions

Sartre's explication of the nature of nothingness commences, not with consciousness, not with nihilation, not with decompression, but with the question. The present chapter seeks to uncover the source of Sartre's theory of nothingness in ontological interrogation. Much as *Dasein* is the key to Heidegger's understanding of Being, consciousness, in Sartre's emphatic formulation, "*is a being such that in its being, its being is in question in so far as this being implies a being other than itself*" (1971, 24). The being of consciousness *is* the apprehension of the being of its object—and not, we would add (*contra* Sartre), the apprehension of "itself" as the apprehension of objectual being. The interrogation of the being of consciousness unfailingly discloses the being of the world. This is the engine of Sartre's "ontological proof," the passage from "the *pre-reflective* being of the *percipiens*" (21) to the transphenomenal being of the object, from the for-itself to the in-itself, a movement intended to commute the solitary confinement to which an Husserlian constriction of attention to the "phenomenon of being" (distinguished, by Sartre, from the "being of the phenomenon") would remand us. By seizing upon the very *being* of the world, indeed, by *being* that very act of seizure, consciousness shatters the confining walls of solipsism. In the Anselmian proof, the divine essence, formulated as unsurpassable greatness, entails God's existence; in the Sartrean, though consciousness is "a being whose existence posits its essence," the in-itself, inversely, is "a being, whose essence implies its existence" (24). Thus in its intentional reference to worldly being, its penetration "beyond" appearance, "beyond" the essential structuration of appearance, to a final absorption in the very being of the world, the for-itself "must produce itself as a revealed-revelation of a being which is not it and which gives itself as already existing when consciousness reveals it" (24). It is self-identity in the rich sense of self-fusion, the utter abolition of any internal differentiation, which "implies," or rather, assumes, the existence of the in-itself. Being-in-itself is the condition for intentional objectivity. If "[t]he appearance refers to the total series of appearances . . ." (4), then the appearance of an object is differentiated upon the ground of the "indifferent" unity of the in-itself. And "[t]he essence . . . is radically severed from the individual appearance which manifests it, since . . . it is that which must be able to be manifested by an infinite series of individual manifestations" (6). Were "essence," in this sense, a coherent notion at all, we could legitimately posit "the cube itself, with six equal faces" as being "only for an unsituated gaze, for an *operation* or inspection of the mind seating itself at the center of the cube, for a field of *Being* . . ." (Merleau-Ponty 1969, 202). Consciousness is a being *in question*, thus *questionable*. And its own being is subject to question to the exact extent that it reveals the in-itself. "Being is" (1971, 29) is a fundamental postulation, an "axiom," perhaps a definition, of Sartre's systematic ontology—a distant echo of Anselm's derivation of deific being. And the in-itself is defined in terms of identity. Being-in-itself is not the abstract infinity of the sequence of appearances which present the object, it is the unity of this inexhaustible manifold. The distinctness and multiplicity of this extravagance of profiles dissolves into the primal oneness of objectual being. And transposing Husserl's distinction, being-in-itself becomes "immanent" and being-for-itself becomes "transcendent." Or almost. To be sure, the coincidence of *presence-to* and *self-presence*, Husserl's "principle of principles," is displaced in Sartre's ontology (though not overcome). The in-itself is "glued to itself"; it inheres "in itself without the least distance," and is thus "an immanence which can not realize itself" (27). But "the transcendence of the for-itself" (1984, 180) is ill-at-ease beside the "absolute law of consciousness" for which the being of consciousness and its appearing to itself are flawlessly fused. This, the identity of being and appearing, is precisely what Husserl means by "immanence." Self-identity, self-coincidence informs Husserlian immanence. It here informs Sartre's rescripting of Husserlian transcendence (Sartre's "immanence").

For Husserl, it is subjectivity which is apodictic. For Sartre, it is subjectivity which is "in question." The question into which the for-itself has plunged, the source of its questionable character, is not, of course, an expression of casual coffee-party curiosity. It is not an interrogative appeal either to one's colleagues or to the gods. Nor is it the ponderous *Seinsfrage*: Heidegger's weighty question, "What is the meaning of Being?" Expressed without the usual technical regimen, this is Sartre's question: "Is there any conduct which can reveal to me the relation of man with the world?" (1971, 35). Transcribing into his more usual idiom: Is there any activity of consciousness whereby the for-itself reveals to itself its own relationship with the in-itself? The question is unanswerable, since the "conduct" of the for-it-self is unavailable in its enactment. And its retrieval in reflection provides, assuming the notion is at all coherent, only the "outside" of consciousness, not consciousness *as lived*. For Sartre, the in-itself could fail to exist *only if* we were capable of conceiving the nonexistence of absolute plenitude. We will witness the dissolution of fullness into emptiness—the most effective demonstration of its conceivability—showing that the "in-itself" is not only contingent, but entirely dubitable. But for Sartre, the in-itself exists of (systemic) necessity. Its existence is *beyond question*. The for-itself is questionable in so far as it implies a being which is unquestionable. This is surprising, since nothingness arises in the world through the interrogation of being. It is vital to discriminate the insipid, featureless plane of being-in-itself from the ravaged, cratered, craggy terrain of *nihilated* being, being which has begun to "decompress," to display its jagged detail, the irregular determinateness of its quality, its structure, its relatedness, to our notice, being, that is, which has become *salient*. If prenihilated being is, indeed, beyond question—as also beyond conception—it cannot be the subject of the for-itself's interrogation. It is "implied" by the questioning activity of the for-itself, not as object, but as ground. Sartre seems often to conflate the two.

But we must pause to question the questionability of the for-itself as a questioning of being. The dyad of seemings, transparentism and translucentism—each an answer to the question of whether manifest quality (presence, including "self-presence") is transcendent or immanent—is informed by reciprocal exclusion and radical undecidability. Undecidability is not skepticism—though like Hellenistic skepticism, undecidability, far from a "bleak expedient," may be seen as "a highly desirable intellectual achievement" (Sedley 1984, 10) and as an "*activity* for perpetuating mental health" (Hiley 1988, 11). It is not that we cannot *know* which construal is valid. Rather, there is simply nothing to know. There is no *answer* to the question, "Which is true?" Both *seem* to be true. Neither has any more purchase upon consciousness than the other. And the two are incompatible. Consciousness cannot resolve the issue. For both are wholly compatible with consciousness. Yet consciousness could subject "itself" to question, its being could be "in question," only if, with Sartre, we assume translucentism. If, as we have seen, consciousness is hopelessly and irresolvably ambiguous, then its very questionability is hopelessly and irresolvably questionable. Sartre is not "wrong" in regarding consciousness as self-questioning. For the transparentism with which his position conflicts is not contrastingly "right." He is rather "wrong" in assuming that the questionability of the for-itself is unquestionable. Of course, had he recognized the questionability of questionability, he would not have posited, as unquestionable, the self-questioning of consciousness. And conversely, his willingness to put forward this deposition assumes an overlooking of second-order questionability. For the *assertion* of self-questioning is possible only in virtue of an implicit rejection of the deep ambiguity of consciousness. Assuming ambiguity, then although translucentism is not "wrong" (and also not "right"), the *assertion* of it *is* wrong. And admitting from the outset that transparentism is not "right" (and also not "wrong"), we must, for parallel reasons, recognize that the *assertion* of it is wrong. Consciousness, then, is that for which it is never proper to posit the transcendence or the immanence of the presence which it reveals; that for which there can be no *answer* to the question of whether transparentism or translucentism is the more fitting construal; and therefore, that for which this issue is always "beyond question." Paradoxically, perhaps, the undecidable ambiguity of consciousness, which ensures that it is always improper to *answer* the question of the questionability of consciousness leads to an affirmation of its unquestionability. Consciousness cannot *be* as it appears. For the incompatibility of its seemings would then sunder it in two. It *is not* as it appears—*however* it appears. Thus, it "itself" does not appear. It is, finally, transparent. Not translucent. We cannot confess the impropriety of the two seemings without being immediately restored to the seeming of transparentism. Transparentism is like a boomerang. We relinquish it, and its negate, only to find it coming back to us. It would betray experience not to relinquish it. But paradoxically, we "have" exactly what we discard.

Emptiness, as we know, is ruthless and thorough. It sweeps away every last crumb of ipseity, demanding the exhaustive relinquishment of the "*se*" to the manifold of sustaining conditions. And consciousness is not spared. "[C]onsciousness is born *supported by* a being which is not itself" (Sartre 1971, 23). Being empty, it is sheer, unimpeded openness to the world, pure manifestation, and conceals nothing of "itself" in this manifestation which could be reclaimed by reflection or by an environmental, nonpositional, awareness of the act of consciousness in its enactment. There is, then, nothing of "itself" to question. It can have no questions for "itself," since *for itself*, it has no self. It is not simply that the appearing of an object presumes its objectual being. There would be genuine passage in this case from appearing to being, and thus, an authentic ontological proof. It is rather that, as a circuit, an ontological arc—the flux of borrowed being and the reflux of being returned to the lender—consciousness has no being beyond the being of the objects which sustain it. Not "itself" subject to question, all interrogation must therefore concern itself with the world. It is the in-itself which is questionable.

By returning a negative response to our questioning, ontological interrogation exposes the veins of negation in the granite of being. But this runs afoul of Sartre's description of the being subjected to interrogation. The infinitary unity (or unitary infinity) of prenihilated being precludes conception. Being-in-itself, prenihilated being, cannot respond with negation or with affirmation to our queries, since it is devoid of articulate determination. It is wanting in the "salt" of saliency, prosaic, without ecstasy. Nothing "stands out," so nothing casts a shadow. If the postulate, "being in-itself *is*" (1971, 29), provides a systemic pillar of Sartre's ontology, a framing conception comparable to an axiom, then despite his contention that "being can neither be derived from the possible nor reduced to the necessary" (29), the being of being-in-itself exhibits the sort of necessity which is imposed by the system. Its truth is practically definitional. And the systemic tautology of this claim is destabilized in the presence of Sartre's insistence that being-in-itself is contingent. The *assertion* that being is cannot be false. Or rather, the presumption of its truth is so central to Sartre's thinking that its denial would ring holistic changes in his systematic ontology. The non-necessity *of being* hardly accords with the necessity that *being is*. And the complaint that we have failed to distinguish *de re* from *de dictu* necessity is of no avail. It may, of course, be necessary (*de dictu*) that being be without it being at the same time a necessity (*de re*) of any particular being that it *be*. But necessity *de re* is wholly inapplicable to prenihilated being. It is only subsequent to nihilation that our world is populated with *res*. Lingis asks of the intentionality thesis—the contention that "[a]ll consciousness . . . is consciousness *of* something" (1991, 11)—"[i]s this 'apodictic insight,' like the laws of natural science, undecidably a law or a definition?" (91). As a central postulate, the "being thesis" may be afflicted with a similar undecidability. If it is a law—a "cognitive monster," in Lyotard's phrase (cf. Caputo 1993, 13, n. 43), "something that makes a monstrous show (monstrare) of itself against the regular succession of the phenomenal world" (Caputo 1993, 13)—its repudiation explodes the system. And if it is a definition, then the nonbeing of being is tautologically impossible. In either case, the being of prenihilated being is unquestionable—and is especially so, since being, for Sartre, is inconceivable. But assuming, now, that it is nihilated being with its discriminated world of "thises" and "thats" that is subjected to interrogation, questioning can at best disclose a determinate landscape *already* pocketed with nothings; the "no" returned for our ontological questioning can play no part in the nihilation of being. And this is deeply puzzling, since *both* nihilation *and* baffled interrogative expectation are said to account for the fissures of nothingness which open rhizomorphically in the plenary ground of being. In any case, despite the inconceivability of being, despite its (systemic) exigency, despite its unquestionability, we stand "before being in an attitude of interrogation" (Sartre 1971, 35).

The question is not, however, merely the expression of an impotent wish to know. It is posed (with the ambiguity of the French *demander*) as a demand. "[T]he question is a kind of expectation; I expect a reply from the being questioned" (Sartre 1971, 35). The question assumes a certain effectuality, if not the brute power to extort a reply, at least the ability to gain the ear of being, and is thus prepared to take the echo of silence not as an index of deafness, but as a positive reply. "I expect from this being a revelation of its being or of its way of being. The reply will be a 'yes' or a 'no.' It is the existence of these two equally objective and contradictory possibilities which on principle distinguishes the question from affirmation or negation" (35). Sartre's fundamental question does have its possible "no." But not every question can be answered with a simple "no." Every question can, however, be answered in the negative. For questions of degree ("How much?" "How many?"), there is "none." For "Where?" there is "nowhere." For "When?" there is "never." Sartre is here concerned not with the "no," but with the possible negativity of the response.

The Sartrean question thus has much in common with the "Belnap question" discussed by Annette Baier:

> Belnap questions are disjunctions, of possibly indefinite length (one proposition and its negation being a limit case, yielding questions with *yes-no* answers), accompanied by a request for a selection of a correct alternative, all the correct alternatives, or a "complete list" in which all given alternatives are explicitly accepted or rejected. Belnap questions are multiple choice tasks. However little the one who asks himself such a question knows, he knows that the answer lies on the list before him, unless the question is a trick question, a disjunction which is false. (Baier 1985, 24; cf. Belnap 1963)

While questioning is conditioned by "the non-being of knowing in man" (1971, 36), Sartre must admit that the questioner "knows that the answer lies on the list before him." Sartre concedes as much in affirming that the question is posed "on the basis of a preinterrogative familiarity with being" (35). Only in this case, we know significantly more than the subject of Belnap's multiple-choice exam. Belnap's subject might be surprised to discover that *these* are the response-options. In hurling our questions into the ear of being, *we*, however, can never be surprised in this way. And perhaps this is why "philosophical questioning habitually knows more than its audience" (Rancière 1991, 246). The for-itself is not the passive recipient of a preformulated list, but is rather the author of those options with which it confronts being. And, of course, this assumption of privilege bespeaks a certain audacity: these are *my* alternatives, and being *must* respond in *my* terms. Baudrillard complains of this sort of usurpation, speaking of "the impossibility of obtaining for a *directed* question any answer other than *simulated . . ."* (1983, 129–30). Indeed, "yes"/"no" questions are disingenuous exactly to the extent that we control the options. Far from expectation or demand, remote even from gentle request, Bataille finds the spirit of interrogation in earnest entreaty: "Philosophy is never supplication; but without supplication, there is no conceivable reply" (1988, 36). For Bataille, it is supplication that gains the ear of being. And it is supplication that grounds philosophy. Sartrean audacity, the *demand* for an answer, must be tempered by a twinge of humility. While wonder, the primordial question, shares little of the abjection of supplication, it vibrates not at all with the arrogance of "expectation."

But in another sense, Belnap's subject might not be surprised. The Belnap question seems more closely allied to the true/false than to the multiple-choice exam. The question is visible at the stem of the multiple-choice item and ramifies into response-alternatives, each of which is explicitly intended as a possible answer *to the question*. Questions cannot, then, be analyzed into anything like a multiple-choice task on pain of circularity. On the other hand, the items of a true/false exam are not severally taken as possible answers to *a single* question. Rather, each is taken, individually, as the content of the implicit question, "Is this statement *true?*" Baudrillard sees in the true/false examination the prototype of digitalization, "infinitely divisible question/answers, all magnetized by a few great models in the luminous field of the code" (1983, 139). And we, like tireless robots, assign our "Ts" and our "Fs" to the bits and the bytes of information conveyed past our sensors. Supplied *only* with a list of statements, and asked to identify the true ones, we might wonder why we are being subjected to this useless experiment, how the fiendish experimenter came up with just these statements, and how our assignments of truth are to be used and evaluated, but we would *not* be perplexed at the unexpected restriction or expansiveness of the list as a set of possible responses *to a question*. There is more to a question than a disjunction of responses and a request. And there is *less*. Possible *answers* are not analytic constituents *of the question*. Merleau-Ponty perceives that "the interrogative is not a mode derived by inversion or by reversal of the indicative . . ." (1969, 129). The question is not a proposition fronted by an interrogative, rather than an assertoric, operator. Every question first opens upon what *might* be true, only then settling upon what *is*. The "more" is the sense of interrogativity, the sense that this list did not materialize magically out of thin air, that the items on the list are not arbitrary statements selected, perhaps, at random, but that each item is a possible *answer*, and thus a possible answer *to a question*. The authentic interrogativity of the question is felt as a vacuum, a lack, an absence of security, and the response is not merely a disembodied assertion, but an avowal experienced as succumbing to the negative pressure of this void. Belnap displays no sensitivity to this requirement. And Sartre seems little more enlightened. Both construe the question as a request (for Sartre, a demand) for selection from a number of "multiple-choice" alternatives. And both, in consequence, offer themselves to the charge of circularity—defining "question" in terms of the *question*—and then depriving the question of its proper function of invoking possible, not merely settled, responses.

Suppose, now, to take up Baier's suggestion, that the question *is* a trick question, "a disjunction which is false" (1985). Or suppose (a further specification) that the question is loaded, thus implying a false disjunction. We know the Buddha's response to Mālukyāputta's litany of freighted inquiries. "That every view is ultimately false is," Streng tells us, "a corollary to the recognition that ultimate reality is not a thing to be 'possessed'" (1967, 87). But in plumbing the response of being to our false disjunctions, how would we discriminate an analogous noble silence from a negative reply? Indeed, how would we discriminate a negative reply from uncomprehending deafness, the "no" from a nonresponse? In Llewelyn's involuted confession, "I am made deaf (*sourd*) to what takes place there, supposing there is something that takes place there, supposing there is a place there, supposing there is a there supposed . . ." (1988, 197–8). Perhaps we, like Lispector, are rather afflicted with deafness: "I had the ability to question but not the ability to hear the answer" (1988, 127). Though Sartre is clear that "if I *expect* a disclosure of being, I am prepared at the same time for the eventuality of a disclosure of non-being" (1971, 39), he seems singularly *un*prepared for a nonresponse. Despite the "the non-being of knowing," the for-itself seems to know even more than we had thought. For now it seems to know—or at least to find unquestionable—that being *will respond* either affirmatively or negatively. But again, suppose that being has withdrawn in sullen silence, or cannot hear our question, or issues a negative response intended not to repudiate one, but rather, *both* of the available options, intended, that is, to repudiate the question itself. Is the celebrated *absence* of Pièrre (the "no") a simple alternative to Pièrre's *presence* (the "yes")? Only if Pièrre *could* have been here instead. The spot where Pièrre *would* have been is now saturated with the subtle fluid presence of non-being. But if Pièrre *could not* have been here instead, then the "no" of Pièrre's absence is not optional, and cannot be disjoined from Pièrre's presence. The "no" declines the question. The interrogation of being regarding the presence of Pièrre is, of course, simply the distinctive modality of openness/closedness exhibited in our *looking for* him. If Pièrre *could not* have been here, the "no" signals, not a contingent failure of the search, but the impossibility of the search.

Could Pièrre have been here instead? Speaking in London, and evidently in the presence of the appropriate artifact, Saul Kripke rhetorically queried, "Now could *this table* have been made from a completely *different* block of wood, or even of water cleverly hardened into ice—water taken from the Thames River?" His response, concordant in spirit with that of Buddhism, is instructive:

> We could conceivably discover that, contrary to what we now think, this table is indeed made of ice from the river. But let us suppose that it is not. Then, though we can imagine making a table . . . from ice, identical in appearance with this one, and though we could have put it in this very position in the room, it seems to me that this is *not* to imagine *this* table as made of . . . ice, but to imagine another table, *resembling* this one in all external details, made of . . . ice. (1972, 113–4)

Contingency has not herewith been expunged from the world. Kripke's point is simply this: *Given* that this table is made of wood, then *this very table* in the specificity of its detail—the table which is, in fact, made of wood—could not have been a product of the ice carver's craft. It is the "giving" which is contingent, gratuitous, *de trop*. Once given, its woodenness cannot coherently be taken back. And similarly for Pièrre. It is, of course, a purely contingent fact that Pièrre is not at the party. But *given* that he is not at the evening's affair, it follows that *he* could not have been there instead. *Another* person, resembling Pièrre in every other respect, perhaps with the same name as well, might be there. But of course, given that this "other Pièrre" is there, *he*, then, could not have been absent. Only the indeterminate, the ontologically lacunary, could enjoy genuine alternativity. If Pièrre were *neither* here *nor* there, it would still be possible for him to be *either* here *or* there. But the determinate closure of that gap spells the foreclosure of alternativity. Pièrre could be here *instead of* there only prior to being assigned a determinate location. Like Merleau-Ponty, I regard the fallacy of determinate being as a want of philosophical vigilance. *Nirvāṇa* is entirely indeterminate. And we have no reason to suppose that a humble dust mop is entirely determinate. But to the extent that our questions are addressed to the determinately absent, the "yes" is not a possibility. Granted that "[t]here exists then for the questioner the permanent objective possibility of a negative reply" (Sartre 1971, 36), we must adjoin that there exists *only* the possibility of a negative reply. And if the existence of a negative *and* an affirmative possible reply "distinguishes the question from affirmation or negation" and does so *in principle*, as Sartre insists, then we cannot genuinely *question* the determinately absent. The absent is beyond question, unquestionable. And absent the absent, we are confronted, not with the in-itself, porous with nothingness, but with prenihilated being which is, by definition, beyond question. "Matter asks no questions, expects no answers of us. It ignores us" (Lyotard 1991a, 11). The consciousness which ingenuously interrogates the absent determinate is thus bewitched by a "trick question." To *look for* Pièrre would be harmless were Pièrre presently *nowhere*. Given that Pièrre is not here, to look for him here is to be deceived, to be under the spell of *avidyā*.

A declamation propounded *prior to* inquiry is not, properly speaking, an answer. The question enjoys both a logical and a temporal precedence over its response. Granting that reversal of this order is possible, and often effective, in rhetoric, we must also remember that to the extent that the answer is assumed beforehand, the rhetorical "question" is not a genuine *question* at all. In Bataille's more histrionic scripting, "[N]o answer ever preceded the question: and what does the question without anguish, without torment mean?" (1988, 36). In this sense, the question comes first. The interrogative void is not, then, a contoured hollow awaiting a predetermined shape, like the gap in a puzzle into which, sooner or later, the missing piece will be inserted. Thus, as Merleau-Ponty imparts, "the 'object' of philosophy will never come to fill in the philosophical question, since this obturation would take from it the depth and the distance that are essential to it" (1969, 101). But think, once again, of the "yes" and the "no" of being. The *presence* of Pièrre is, for Sartre, being's affirmation; the *absence*, being's negative response. Does Pièrre's presence come invariably as a result of our seeking? There are times when, quite without looking for him, we simply encounter Pièrre as we might trip over a misplaced rake. As the stray sentence is not felt as the satisfaction of inquiry, the accidental encounter is not taken as an affirmative response to a question.

In a deeper sense, the question assumes not only logical and temporal priority, but a certain doxastic priority as well. To issue the question with the answer up our sleeve is, of course, a rhetorical posture. But even to gravitate, even to be ever so slightly inclined, toward one alternative response to the exclusion of the other is, to the extent of the attraction, no longer genuinely to *question*. Questioning is always a state of absolute equilibrium. "Thought," writes Gillan, "is suspended in the daze of the question" (1980, 142). To be tilted one way or the other is *already* to have ceased questioning and to have fixed upon the answer. We question *in order to* upset our complacent equipoise, *in order to* be tumbled off our feet by the abrupt extraction of the carpet which conditions our pseudo-security. For Sartre, "consciousness is a slippery slope on which one can not take one's stand without immediately finding oneself tipped outside onto being-in-itself" (1971, 786). Response to an authentic, heartfelt query always takes one by surprise. But as philosophers, we must " 'surprise the surprise,' be at home in the marvel and in the division" (Agamben 1991, 94). We may expect that *either* Pièrre will be present *or* he will not. But to expect that he *will* be present is no longer to question. If, as Sartre claims, "non-being always appears within the limits of a human expectation" (1971, 38), Pièrre's absence, though emerging on the basis of thwarted anticipation, is not the negative response *to a question*. Sartre is not entitled to hold that thematic nothingness (*négatité*) is *both* interrogative response *and* the product of baffled expectation.

Our "preinterrogative familiarity with being" cannot, then, assume any commitments which would slant us one way or another toward a possible answer. Thus, the question cannot "answer itself." The radical interrogation of Merleau-Pontyan hyper reflection, the movement of questioning which finds nothing whatever *beyond* question "provides a reflective and intuitive access to Being which philosophers of intuition and reflection quickly sought to close up by trying to prove that the answer was already contained in the question; for them the 'meaning'of Being was prior to the question, for it was contained a priori in the mind . . ." (Burke 1990, 88). The answer must be adventitious, coming from beyond the question. It cannot be folded into the question's stock of presuppositions. With Burke, we must acknowledge that "[t]his does not mean that the ontological question has no answer. On the contrary, it means that we do not know a priori what answers are forthcoming. It means that if answers come, it will be only as a result of our having recognized the interrogative space, the abyss, within which alone Being can freely and continually manifest itself" (89). In Heideggerian terms, the question "awaits" response, it does not *wait for* any particular response. Still, "preinterrogative familiarity" (Heidegger's "pre-ontological apprehension" of Being: *Vorhabe, Vorbegriff*) must have more content than the vacuous truism (if not truth) that any object exemplifies either a given property or its complement. *Mind as Mirror* repudiates the principle of bivalence (cf. Laycock, 1994, 54–57), and there is no need to resuscitate that discussion here. But inasmuch as Sartre regards neg-entities as responses to a question, and is thus unwittingly committed to the indeterminacy of being, he thereby assumes the invalidity of bivalence. We cannot, then, expect "preinterrogative familiarity" to consist in this principle. To know, for example, of the neighbor's cat that she is either green or not, and then, *solely* on this basis, to seek to determine which, is not to pursue the satisfaction of a genuine question. Valid or not, the clean, dry, mechanical functioning of logical principles, a sort of immaterial *perpetuum mobile*, is insufficient to motivate questioning. No excluded middle or the principle of contradiction. Logic cannot inspire interrogation. And if Sartre's "yes" and "no" are not only "contradictory possibilities," but also exhaustive, they do not, for the same reason, determine a question.

Specific questions (e.g., "What color is the neighbor's cat?") are motivated as much by what we know as by what we do not. Chloe darts through the tall grass in pursuit of a squirrel, and we cannot be sure whether that streak was grey or light tan. We *know* it wasn't green. It *could* have been somewhat orangish, and might have been a bit more brown than we recall. Our perception is indeterminate, and the delineation between what we clearly *know* and what *might* be is blurred into mist. It is the mind's incessant struggle against the fog which motivates questioning, not the attempt to settle accounts between clear, exclusive and exhaustive options. We *know* what we saw—an indeterminate flash of grayish, tanish felinity—and when Chloe pauses from her pursuit or lapses into stalking mode, we will also have the answer to our question. It is our clear cognition of unclarity, which, in Burke's fine image, "anchors" our inquiry: "The perceptual faith is a prepossession of Being, it is what gives our questions their relevance and their anchorage. It is the confidence that there is an answer *there* at the same time that it prompts the question 'What is there?' and even 'What is the *there is*?'" (1990, 83). Like Merleau-Ponty, Sartre was concerned to secure perception to the existence of things, not to their detached appearances (thus, the "ontological proof"). This mooring, kindred to Merleau-Ponty's "perceptual faith," is not the naive assumption that perception inevitably gets it right, but "the confidence that there is an answer *there*." "What color is Chloe?" assumes its own answerability: Chloe *has* a determinate color, and we can discern what it is. The question, while leaving open the possibility of Chloe's *not* being grey or tan, is nonetheless closed to the pertinent species of Sartrean negativity. "How much?" has its "None." "When?" has its "Never." But "What color?" does not have its "Colorless." And this is surely a deliverance of "preinterrogative familiarity." Some questions are simply not open to negative reply. In fact, "Chloe is devoid of color" ruins the answerability of "What color is Chloe?" It is a repudiation of the question, not an answer to it. In this case, answerability is incompatible with negative response. Thus, to ground perception in existence, and thereby to assume answerability, is to abandon the conflicting Sartrean thesis of negative possibility.

If, as Michel Meyer propounds, meaning is not the monadic possession of a given proposition, but is rather constituted in the "relationship between the answer and the question it solves" (cf. Golden and Jamison 1990, 345), and if, in Burke's concordant deposition, "there is no positive statement that does not have an interrogative halo" (p. 88), we may have to rethink even the fund of propositional securities which our questions take for granted. We will later explore the reductive descent by which the existence of an object is distributed among its conditions, leaving the object "empty" (*śūnya*) or devoid of self-existence (*svabhāva*). The significance of the assertion, affirmative or negative, is likewise to be factored out among its conditions, and the conditions for its significance lie in its capacity to saturate interrogativity. Independent of the questions to which it responds, a statement is drained of meaning. Independent of its correlative questions, it is, then, no *statement* at all. Alter the stock of questions to which it might respond, and the statement is thereby transformed in significance. Abolish that stock entirely, and the statement evaporates, leaving behind only an assemblage of indecipherable marks. The indisputable, the undeniable, the *hors-question*, that which withdraws from question in order to secure its own apodicticity, is, then, the insignificant. And the Cartesian proclivity to erect the edifice of philosophy upon unshakable foundations would result, were it possible, only in meaningless scaffolding. The very *being* of the statement is displaced, deferred, residing not within itself, but within each of its associated questions. It is, then, nothing over and beyond its questions. Preinterrogative familiarity is thus drained of its indicative pretense. We do not have a store of "background knowledge," but a fund of background questions.

For Sartre, as we have said, it is unquestionable that being *will respond* to our inquiries. And Sartre thus shares Merleau-Ponty's preinterrogative "confidence that there is an answer *there*." But such affirmations would lapse into nonsense were they not, at least implicitly, expressions of responsiveness to their associated questions: "*Will* being respond?," "*Is* there an answer?" Everything meaningful is also questionable. The disjunctive question which we pose in the face of being is not the logically first. Assuming response, and assuming, more generally, answerability, Sartre's question is derivative. "*Will* being respond?" and "*Is* there an answer?" are prior questions. But is there a "first" question, a question which does not presume? Certainly, it is not Sartre's original query, "Is there any conduct which can reveal to me the relation of man with the world?"—a question staggering under the weight of a thousand assumptions, a thoroughly "loaded" question. A first question would be analogous to the first principle of Fa-yen Wên-I's account:

> Question: "What is the first principle?"
> Master: "If I should tell you, it would become the second principle." (Chang 1971, 246)

A question becomes derivative in its formulation. The primordial question is not the linguistic form, but the existential modality of openness which we have called "wonder." It is not a grammatically formed expression of inquiry, but that which is expressed thereby. Wonder is "a question consonant with the porous being which it questions and from which it obtains not an *answer*, but a confirmation of its astonishment" (Merleau-Ponty 1969, 102). Nāgārjuna would agree that "'final answers' were not to be found because there were no essential self-determined questions" (Streng 1967, 87).

Final answers are, in Meyer's useful epithet, *apocritical*, beyond question. They present themselves as the termini of inquiry, impeding the dynamic of ongoing interrogation, withdrawing into timeless conclusiveness. But as Heidegger said of the question, "What is called thinking?" "To answer . . . is itself always to keep asking, so as to remain underway" (1968, 169). And though, correspondingly, we cannot properly identify the *real* questions, the essential questions, the questions without issue in further interrogation, we can find, palpating at the living center of any question (self-determined or not) the reverent openness of wonder. Wonder is the preinterrogative question which floats like a feather, with a wisp of a wish, into the lap of being: "[w]onder . . . is the originary question that the look addresses to the world, but, unlike the questions of cognition, does so without expectation or demand, without only a 'wish' that this open world remain open to its savage witness" (Burke 1990, 93). The earth child marveling at the ad/vent of being's auroral blush is not the unsophisticate which we had supposed. For being does not deposit itself into an account ready to receive and to contain. Being dawns, not for the mind which returns its gift in affirmation, but for a mind which is pure question. It is the spirit of unadulterated wonder, pure interrogativity, unmixed with the arrogance of presumption, which grounds and nourishes the advanced investigations of phenomenology. Being will not speak upon the anvil under the hammer blow of demand. We must learn to be as little children.

We have spoken of the question as a certain vacuum, the lived absence of the answer which is experienced, though quite differently, in casual curiosity as much as in the passionate quest for truth. To the query, "what is my treasure?" the Zen tradition records the response: "It is he who has just asked the question. It contains everything and lacks nothing. There is no need to seek it outside yourself" (cf. Chang 1971, xi.). Merleau-Ponty concurs: "we ourselves are one sole continued question" (1969, 103). Thus, as Sylviane Agacinski affirms, "the status of the subject is inseparable from the status of the question" (1991, 9). Indeed, "consciousness 'questions' even 'before' it can be 'questioned' " (11). There is deep wisdom in Sartre's subjection of being to question; and there is deeper wisdom still in his assimilation of questioning to the being of the for-itself. But we must plunge to the sea bed. For Brentano, the philosophical psychologist seeking to demarcate the region of his concern, intentionality was seen as a criterion of the mental. Husserl modulated this foundational notion into the *essence* of consciousness. Sartre, in turn, radicalized the Husserlian conception of intentionality, transforming it into the very *being* of consciousness. Consciousness is not, for Sartre, essentially world-revealing. It *is* the very revelation of the world. We must, then, achieve the same degree of radical penetration. Questioning is not merely essential to consciousness. Nor is it merely an *existentiale*, an ineluctable structure of the being of consciousness. It *is* that very being.

When Merleau-Ponty declares that "the existing world exists in the interrogative mode" (1969, 103), he is clearly not claiming that the world is composed of questions, even less that it is comprised of certain typical units of language. He is here calling attention to the indeterminacy of the world. With Dummett, Merleau-Ponty agrees that the important issue is "not whether the reality that rendered our statements true or false was *external*, but whether it was *fully determinate* . . ." (Dummett 1978, xxix). Being is pervious, spongy with absence. We have seen that the enlightened gaze is not obtrusive. "Buddha contemplates the flower without picking it" (Irigaray 1991, 171). And one thus content to let the flowers of this world be, and "to witness their continued being," one "who therefore limits himself to giving them the hollow, the free space they ask for in return, the resonance they require, who follows their own movement" (1969, 101) is regarded, by Merleau-Ponty, as "a question consonant with the porous being which it questions and from which it obtains not an *answer*, but a confirmation of its astonishment" (102). To be enlightened is not to question, but to *be* a question—a question, "consonant" with (we might say, "indistinguishable from") the absolute nothingness which peers forth in the countless pools of absence which imbue the indeterminate being.

The Zen koan, distilled from living interaction and used as a subject of meditation, is a question which, in principle, cannot be rationally resolved. The experience of sudden illumination (*satori, kensho*) is sometimes thought to blossom on the grave of rationality, conditioned by insupportable friction of vigorous interrogation against the rationally irresolvable. But it cannot be the simple breakdown of rational functioning which gives rise to enlightenment. This would open the door to pathologies of all sorts. We would then have to count among the enlightened those who simply need our compassionate treatment. It is not the abrogation of reason which nourishes the seeds of enlightenment. The discourses of the Buddha are masterpieces of conceptual clarity and precision. The work of Nāgārjuna, regarded by some as a "second Buddha," exhibits extraordinary dialectical acumen. There is not the least hint of irrationality here. But logic, in Nāgārjuna's hands, "becomes a tool to break open the semantic fetters with which the logicians have bound themselves" (Streng 1967, 150). Rather, the irresolubility of the enigmatic koan is the prop which holds the question permanently open, allowing the mind to take up residence within this vacancy, and indeed, to *become*, not merely to prosecute, the question itself. The koan thus represents a specific modality of openness. The insight (*pra-*

jñā) which thus arises is not an adventitious propositional accretion, nor even a certain message released from the depths of the mind. As Margaret Gibson confirms, in the Zen experience,

> . . . I enter the complete
> absence of any indicative event,   (1991, 88)

Merleau-Ponty remarks that "we ourselves are one sole continued question . . ." (1969, 103). Insight is *being-question*. Decidedly not a species of knowing-that, it is much more closely allied to a certain know-how. To gain insight is to learn *how* to remain open, *how* to preserve one's equipoise without succumbing to the gravity of resolution.

Surface questions, questions of a purely pragmatic or instrumental nature, are unstable. "Did I leave my lights on?" is instantly resolved—and abolished—by a quick glance out the window. The question has vanished, and, like a population of rodents distracted for an instant by an unfamiliar sound, we scuttle back into our ordinary affairs untroubled by the possibility of a dead battery. Zaner observes that

> Any 'problem' (or: disturbance, crisis, dilemma, in life) stands out from a background of what is unproblematic; in fact it is only by reference to the latter that anything can stand out as 'problematic', 'unfamiliar', 'unexpected', and the like. Moreover not only does the unexpected, unfamiliar or unusual call attention to itself, but what has hitherto been accepted as familiar, expected and usual is brought into question. . . . To the extent the person takes his situation—ultimately, his life—seriously, the problematic situation is critical for him; and to the extent that he seriously *seeks to know* 'what and how things actually are', he is himself called on to be critical: to question, seek, find out, assess, justify. That is, he must cease taking for granted what has been up to now accepted as unquestionable. (1975, 134)

Our quotidian transactions, the affairs of "everydayness" pursued within the secure and unproblematized womb of our "natural" concerns, afford little occasion for question. At best we vault briefly into query like salmon jumping into the air—but then only to return immediately to the comforting milieu of the familiar. Philosophy is born, however, with the attempt to live more consistently in the liberating atmosphere of interrogation and to widen the boundaries of the questionable.

Despite the original pretensions of the *soi-disant* "analytic" philosophy—which, in any case has "turned upon itself and committed slow suicide" (Rorty 1882, 227)—the domain of the deeply and lastingly questionable cannot be parceled out to teams of specialists so that, acre by acre, inch by inch, the blight of questions which has infested the land will have been brought to extinction. Indeed, "[t]he history of analytic philosophy may be read as a history of failed forms" (Danto 1980, 615–6). Thus, "what remains of analytic philosophy is only a style: a sort of generalized legalistic expertise, a skill with cases, claims and arguments" (Rajchman 1985b, xi). Short of suicide, lobotomy is the only means of dispelling the furies of philosophical interrogation. Only by transforming itself into positivist science could philosophy be rid of its questions. Philosophy seeks not, however, to abandon its questions, but to *live* in them. Philosophical questions are not transient shimmers of practical concern. Nor are they eternal. Though philosophy advances by the nativity of new questions, and though it sometimes succeeds in scraping away the ossified remains of questions outlived, it is nonetheless true that philosophical questions are experienced as perennial. "Philosophy does not raise questions and does not provide answers that would little by little fill in the blanks" (Merleau-Ponty1969, 105). And "philosophical interrogation is . . . not the simple expectation of a signification that would come to fill it" (Merleau-Ponty 119). The value of addressing the irresoluble can, if questionably, be compared to the value of doing isometric exercise. Though "movement" on basic issues may be inachievable, we gain, nonetheless, a certain intellectual vigor, a certain strengthening of sinew and ligament, a certain growth in grit and mettle in the attempt. Of course, if all that is wanted is intellectual exertion, the same effects might accrue to a game of chess. Philosophy is not, for us, merely a means of intellectual muscle building. It is, perennially, if also hopelessly, the appropriation of a certain loose inventory of questions. It is the *questions* which we find of intrinsic interest, not their abolition through resolution, and not, again, the epiphenomenal effects garnered from our efforts to respond. The distinctiveness of philosophical questioning lies, for Merleau-Ponty, in a certain double vision:

> "What is the world?" or, better, "what is Being?"—these questions become philosophical only if, by a sort of diplopia, at the same time that they aim at a state of things, they aim at themselves as questions—at the same time that they aim at the signification "being," they aim at the being of signification and the place of signification within Being. It is characteristic of the philosophical questioning that it return upon itself, that it ask itself also what to question is and what to respond is. (1969, 119–20)

The reflexive questioning of questioning is thus an inalienable feature of philosophy. Philosophy interrogates interrogation; it asks what it *means* to ask; it wishes to know what it *means* to wish to know. In this vortex of questioning and self-questioning, nothing is sacred, nothing is *hors-question*, nothing is apocritical, nothing is allowed to withdraw into the pseudo-authority of conclusiveness, nothing is granted the last word. The self-effacement of perception in the face of being does not deliver it from interrogation. And the self-effacement of reflection in its disclosure of perception is likewise not spared. We shelter from interrogation what we take ourselves to be. But the vortex of interrogation washes us out of our unilluminated rat-holes of self-identification—not to perish in the sun like so many bloated jellyfish on the shore, but, without the artificial buttresses of delusion, to stand forth serenely in an infinitely expanded sense of who we are. Brown suggests that "[p]erhaps, in view of *the form* in which *we* presently *take* ourselves *to exist*, the mystery *arises from* our insistence on *framing* a question where there is, in reality, *nothing* to question" (1973, 105). The mystery of boundless identity is not unquestionable. But "[t]he reason we talk about it at all is because questions are raised concerning it. If no questions are raised about it, there would be no discourse" (Suzuki 1981, 30). Or as Bataille observes, "[i]t is not beyond expression—one doesn't betray it if one speaks of it—but it steals from the mind the answers it still had to the questions of knowledge. Experience reveals nothing and cannot found belief nor set out from it" (1988, 3-4). We are on the verge of emptiness.

Chapter 4

Nothingness

Standing aside from direct engagement with the object, at right angles to our live perceptual proflux, Sartre offers the guileless, but vitally ramifying observation—indeed, the fundamental conception of his ontology—that consciousness *is not* its object. The "is not" does not, however, mark the Cartesian divide segregating "thinking thing" from "extended thing." Indeed, "Descartes' conclusion that he was a thinking thing was the product of his question, and that question was a product of specific practices—those of disembodied, unmindful reflection" (Varela, Thompson, and Rosch, 1992, 28). We do not have in Sartre a dualism of substance: "Consciousness has nothing substantial" (1971, 17). It is a "nonsubstantial absolute" (17). (Buddhism regards consciousness as a nonsubstantial *relative*.) And if consciousness is, as Sartre inculcates, precisely *nothing*, the very absence of all conceivable thingliness, we do not have a dualism which divides two varieties of "thing" at all. Consciousness is not "something" which then stands in a relationship of *difference* to its object. "It" (a problematic reference) does not *differ* from the in-itself. It is rather the very event of *differing* describable as the dis/integration of the in-itself. To say that the for-itself *is not* the in-itself is exactly to say that the in-itself undergoes the event of relaxation, disintegration, decompression.

This refusal of identity—or rather, the internal breakdown of self-identity—is no mere abstraction, however, no impassive state-of-affairs: the impalpable dis-identity of subject and object. Once again, it is an occurrence: the event of *nihilation*. Consciousness is the event of *differentiation* whereby the lifeless, formless and stolidly integral domain of being-in-itself begins to crumble. The in-itself is an absolute plenum without the least hint of porosity. The for-itself, on the other hand, "corresponds . . . to an expanding de-structuring of the in-itself, and the in-itself is nihilated and absorbed in its attempt to found itself" (Sartre 1971, 133). The in-itself is informed by absolute identity. This is not, however, the paltry truism that each thing is formally identical with itself, but the rich, if also paradoxical, notion that in the object of consciousness, all attributes, all relations, all dispositions, all structures, fuse; all are melted indiscernibly into a pool of identity. It is not that a profusion of qualities are fitted into a complex matrix of relations, but rather what, in the disintegration of the in-itself, articulate into multiplicity are, in its primordial fullness, not merely subsumed under the form of unity, but perfectly and seamlessly *identical*.

Being-in-itself is a deeply troubled notion, afflicted by massive incoherence. It represents the liquefaction of all discriminable qualities, thus melding within this "vast swill" (Sartre 1984, 132) qualities which contend with one another. And we would then expect the in-itself to be the site of the most brutal strife. As Adorno remarks, "[t]otal contradiction is nothing but the manifested untruth of total identification" (1973, 6). Merleau-Ponty palliates: "the accusation of contradiction is not decisive, *if the acknowledged contradiction appears as the very condition of consciousness*" (Conze 1962, 19). For Sartre, of course, the in-itself does give itself as the foundation of consciousness. And from the Buddhist quarter, "[z]en knows no contradictions; it is the logician who encounters them, forgetting that they are of his own making" (Suzuki; cf. Conze 1994). Extracting discriminate qualities from the soup of being cannot fail to generate conflict. In their primordial state of deliquescence, however, there is no multiplicity, and thus no binary opposition.

Still, in Merleau-Ponty's confession, "I cannot even for an instant imagine an object in itself" (1962, 16). The in-itself is a phenomenological, not an ontological or a conceptual, category, and stands as the reference point of an explosion of detail and structure which, over time, comes progressively to salience. Sartre's contention is not the stale logical truism the each thing is identical to itself. As Wittgenstein discerns, "to say of *two* things that they are identical is nonsense, and to say of *one* thing that it is identical with itself is to say nothing at all" (1974, 52). Merleau-Ponty, somewhat closer to Sartre's view, saw that the duality of identicals already interpolates between them a nothingness: "Nothingness is . . . the difference between the identicals" (1969, 263). And whether the identicals are two or one, if identity preserves its customary sense, an in-itself defined in terms of self-identity lapses, as Hegel would promote, into unintelligibility: "no mind thinks or forms conceptions or speaks, in accordance with the law of identity, A is A, and . . . no existence of any kind whatever conforms to it" (Lowenberg 1929, 136–7). To speak of oneness, instead, is unhelpful both because of its suggestion of a unification of diversity (and thus, a tacit institution of non-being) and because, even to count to one, we must stand outside the one counted (*one* implies *two*), and at this point, prior to nihilation, the in-itself has no second. These perplexities aside, the in-itself

> . . . is the noema in the noesis; that is, the inherence in itself without the least distance. From this point of view, we should not call it "immanence," for immanence in spite of all *connection* with self is still that very slight withdrawal which can be realized—away from the self. But being is not a connection with itself. It is *itself*. It is an immanence which can not realize itself, an affirmation which can not affirm itself, an activity which can not act, because it is glued to itself. (Sartre 1971, 27)

Nihilation thus amounts to a liberation of the distinctiveness of the object's detail, a relaxation, or decompression, of the taut internal intimacy of the in-itself. A gossamer suggestion of metaphysical myth is evident in Sartre's proposal that "[e]verything happens as if, in order to free the affirmation *of* self from the heart of being, there is necessary a decompression of being" (1971, 27–8). The circuit whereby nothingness arises upon the ground of the in-itself, and the in-itself, now inflected with the selectivity of liberated detail, becomes, to this extent, meaningful, describes the rudimentary "self," the prereflective *cogito*. The in-itself "is this self. It is itself so completely that the perpetual reflection which constitutes the self is dissolved in an identity. . . . In fact being is opaque to itself precisely because it is filled with itself. This can be better expressed by saying that *being is what it is*" (28). Decompression is the emptying of the in-itself *of itself* and the consequent ontological permission for the emergence of *self*. There is no self so long as the in-itself is full of itself. In decompression, the "self" of the *itself* is drained; the self of the for-itself emerges. The depletion of the one and the repletion of the other are inverted images of each other.

The cherry tree in the garden is never simply *seen*. At first sight, much of its detail is compacted, compressed. It is given impressionistically, its detail submerged, indistinct, flowing together. With time and exposure, this general shape, this vaguely greenish, brownish haze, begins to articulate itself into a more definite form. A green cloud becomes a profusion of distinct leaves. Leaves regiment themselves into vein-patterns and distinctive edges. Detail "comes out," emerges from a sea of indistinctness, like the shower of scintillae from the explosion of fireworks. And this emergence, this coming-to-notice, is decompression. It is as if the variegated qualities and relations of the cherry tree were held in by a sort of effort, and as if, in relaxing into detail, the tree exhaled its relief, scattering detail everywhere. Merleau-

Ponty reminds us that "[t]here really is inspiration and expiration of Being . . ." (1964a, 167). The for-itself is not the spectator of progressively atomized detail, but is rather the very exhalation of the in-itself. It is not the witness of decompression, but decompression itself.

The for-itself is, then, the activity of emptying—an activity which, in its progressive explication of qualitative determination mirrors the classical "spatio-analytic" de/monstration of *śūnyatā* (cf. Sangharakshita 1987, 120) so remarkably that we are impelled, here, to credit Sartre with an unwitting refinement of the Buddhist deposition. From its inception, Buddhism regarded the phenomena of our experience as composite, thus decomposable, "as a lump of dried clay is crumbled between the fingers into millions of fragments" (121). A contemporary Thai meditation teacher reminds himself whenever a glass breaks that "it is broken already" (Levine 1982, 98). "[W]hen . . . it falls to the ground and shatters, I say, 'Of course.' But when I understand that this glass is already broken, every moment with it is precious. Every moment is just as it is and nothing need be otherwise" (99). It is only the bonding of component elements which forestalls utter disintegration. Breakage is the release of select bonds. What we see as the unbroken glass is a cloud of shards held together through various modalities of attraction. It is not that the glass is "breakable," *potentially* broken. It is *already* in pieces. At the limit, it is not infinitely divisible, but infinitely divided, continuity vanishing utterly into discontinuity. Its apparent intactness is, though "real" enough for practical purposes, nonetheless illusory.

Sartre's decompression is closely allied to the *écart* which, for Merleau-Ponty, simply *is* consciousness. Decompression is the event whereby particular figural elements come to stand out against their perceptual ground. "Each element of the setting, a person, a table, a chair, attempts to isolate itself, to lift itself upon the ground constituted by the totality of the other objects, only to fall back once more into the undifferentiation of this ground; it melts into the ground" (1971, 41). The ground is both alpha and omega, beginning and end, for its phenomena. Phenomena describe a great solar arc, blazing plasma flaring from the surface of the sun only to merge, once again, into the sun's fiery substance. Or if the ground appeals to us more as a mysterious mood than an eruptive declaration of presence, we might borrow the Hindu image of the drop of water arising from and rejoining its source. The beginning and the end are indiscernible. The abyss which devours articulated detail is not distinct from the ground. Emptiness, which is the destiny of infinite decompression, is there from the beginning as primordially nihilated being, being opalescent with the "shimmer of nothingness" (294). But consciousness "refuses to have a destiny, that middle ground between opacity and transparence" (Haar 1980, 187). Articulation, explicitation of detail, occurs upon the ground. Inasmuch as decompression *is* this grounded emergence into saliency, it is the "rejection," thus the Merleau-Pontyan *écart*, intimated in Sartre's proposition that "in perception we constitute a particular object as a *figure* by rejecting another so as to make of it a *ground*, and conversely" (1971, 54). The ek/stasy of the figure is, then, a dual negation: figure is cloven from ground as much as ground from figure. And Sartre compatibly affirms that "what is offered to intuition is a flickering of nothingness; it is the nothing of the ground, the nihilation of which summons and demands the appearance of the figure, and it is the figure—the nothingness which slips as a *nothing* to the surface of the ground" (42). The primal nihilation of being would afford only the undifferentiated consciousness of the ground. Or rather, if we can speak of a moment "before" the fissure of figure from ground, prior even to "name-and-form" (*nāma-rūpa*) which, in Buddhist phenomenology, "wraps itself about the subject of consciousness in the form it assumes prior to division of subject and object" (Takeuchi 1983, 80), there would be experience without objectual differentiation. If conscious at all, we would be conscious *of nothing*, no *thing*. If Merleau-Ponty is correct, "the knowing of nothingness is a nothingness of knowing . . ." (1969, 85). And knowing lapses "because there is nothing hidden" (Varela, Thompson, and Rosch 1992, 225). Positional consciousness, consciousness *of* . . . demands the eruption of saliency. Figural detail—itself a nothingness—emerges from "the nothing of the ground." To perceive a figure on a ground is to see a nothingness upon a nothingness, the two sequestered by a nothingness.

Sartre diverges from Buddhist insight, however, in assigning destruction to our subjective originary powers: "man is the only being by whom a destruction can be accomplished. A geological plication, a storm do not destroy—or at least they do not destroy *directly*; they merely modify the distribution of masses of beings. There is no *less* after the storm than before. There is *something else*" (1971, 39). Of course, were we incapable of expecting those "masses of beings" to remain "distributed" as before, and were we incapable of recognizing that they are not, we would be blind to destruction. To this extent Sartre's wisdom runs deep. Buddhism would question, not the *conditions* for our perception of destruction, but our purported *production* of thematic nonbeing. Sartre's contention is disjunctive: either nothingness originates in the in-itself or in the for-itself. Since "it is inconceivable that a Being which is full positivity should maintain and create outside itself a Nothingness . . . for there would be nothing in Being by which Being could surpass itself toward Non-Being" (57), the option remaining is that human existence is the demiurge of nothingness. But we must query the assumption that nothingness is *produced* at all. Distinguishing, with Sartre, the thematic absences (*négatités*) which are the correlates of our thwarted anticipations—"non-being always appears within the limits of a human expectation" (38)—from the disintegration of being which is the for-itself, we can render unto Sartre what properly pertains. We are, to be sure, responsible for the emergence—*for us*—of neg-entities. "[T]his intra-mundane Nothingness can not be produced by Being-in-itself" (56). Were we incapable of leaning doxastically into the future, the evening's soirée would not be haunted by the absence of Pièrre. The agency which introduces noematic absence into the world "can not be passive in relation to Nothingness, can not receive it; Nothingness could not *come* to this being except through another Being—which would be an infinite regress" (57). The agent of thematic nothingness must *be* nothingness in order to bestow nothingness. Should it emerge, however, that the "in-itself" is *always already* porous, lacunary, encysted with nothingness, that there is, in effect, no "time," no occasion, at which an originary event of nihilation could have taken place, then we must reconsider. And we will shortly find reason to repudiate Sartre's curiously theological conception of creation whereby human consciousness, through a radically institutive event shrouded in impenetrable mystery, comes to be. While it is harmless to acknowledge that the *négatités* which pocket our world cannot be produced by a being of "absolute plenitude and entire positivity" (48), neither can they be produced by the for-itself in so far as the latter is conceived as arising, once for all, through an originary occurrence of nihilation. It is not that we would presume authorship of our own being. Our being, the being of the for-itself, is assuredly an endowment, a gift, a gracious bestowal. We are neither its foundation nor its architect. But if our being has its source in the momentous event of nihilation, and if "only *Being* can nihilate [make nothing of] itself . . ." (57), we may have come to the rather embarrassing strait of having to confess our nonexistence.

Are destruction and fragility engraved, then, upon the smooth face of being entirely through human imposition? Sartre tells us that "[f]ragility has been impressed upon the very being of this vase, and its destruction would be an irreversible absolute event which I could only verify" (1971, 40). In its deconstruction of egocentric, and more largely, anthropocentric, points of vantage, Buddhism would agree that we can "only verify" the destruction of the vase. This "irreversible absolute event" is imbued with a certain objectivity. Buddhism would not, however, acknowledge that fragility is merely "impressed." The splintered fragments of the vase now lie separated on the floor, at a certain distance from each other, the shattered "vase" (if we can still speak of a *vase* at all) now clutching the only ontological dignity it can in existing *partes extra partes*. But is this a degradation? Or did the destruction of the vase do no more than make manifest the prior externality of its *already* fragmentary elements, the shock of terrestrial encounter simply dispelling the allure which preserved its illusory integrity? Sartre observes that "[t]wo points are distant when they are *separated* by a certain length. The length, a positive attribute of a segment of a straight line, intervenes here by virtue of the negation of an absolute, undifferentiated proximity" (54). It seems frankly counter-intuitive to suppose that it is *we* who interrupt the coincidence of the termini by interpolating a nothingness between them; that without *our* generation of *négatités*, all the points now distanced by our interposition of negativity would once again collapse into a single point. Separation must, of course, be negatively defined. Indeed, "any definition is negative" (47). And Buddhism is quite content to recognize, with Sartre, that negativity is not primarily the province of propositions and definitions. But fragmentation introduces a novel, and for our purpose, pivotal species of nothingness: nothingness as the medium of disintegration, spatio-analytic emptiness. *This* nothingness is absolute. It is neither produced nor does it come to be. It is there from the beginning. And destruction is simply its disclosure.

If, then, the seemingly integral vase is "broken already," if it is a nimbus of *already* disintegral constituents, then what we see is a blur, or what, after Watts, we can consider as "fuzziness":

> For when we examine anything we see first of all the pattern, the shape, and then we ask the question, "What is the shape composed of?" So we get out our microscope to look very carefully at what we thought was the substance of, say, a finger. We find that the so-called substance of the finger is a minute and beautiful design of cells. We see a structure, but then when we see these little patterns called individual cells, we ask again, "What are they made of?" and that needs a sharper microscope, a more minute analysis. Turning up the level of magnification again, we find that the cells are molecules but we keep asking, "What is the stuff of the molecule?" What we are in fact discovering through all of this is that what we are calling "stuff" is simply patterns seen out of focus. It's fuzzy, and simply fuzziness is stuff. Whenever we get fuzziness into focus, it becomes patterns. So there isn't any stuff, there is only pattern. This world is dancing energy. (1970, 13–4)

What at one level seems solid, continuous, real, becomes at the next, a simple index to the poverty of our vision. Everything—all the objects of our blurred perception—crumble into fragments; and these fragments, in turn, into dust. It is only our practical limitations, our failure of acuity, the deficiency of our instruments, which—for us—prevents the bottomless plunge of atomization in the direction of sheer nothingness. The *telos* of this descent is nothingness, the infinite decomposition of presence. And the Abyss which swallows up this endless plummeting is also a nothingness, nothingness as the space of free fall. "Abyssal Being," Burke reminds us, "envelops the conditioned/condition schema and thus cannot be subject to it" (1990, 89). There is nothingness as a destination; and there is nothingness as a path. The "two" are absolute and are *one*. Or perhaps better: the two are dimensions—that of vertical abandon and that of horizontal dissolution—of the one Abyss. "This absolute lack of ground constitutes the abysmal darkness of human existence. At the bottom of our existence is total nothingness which repels any kind of reasoning from the human perspective" (Kotoh 1987, 201). We are in endless free-fall. There is no *fundamentum inconcussum* to conclude the plunge.

In the West, spiritual realization is depicted as homecoming. The soul, now embraced by its creator, returns to its primordial habitation. The world is a wilderness, a trial, the vale of alienation and unfamiliarity. We long for rest, for peace, for the familiarity of childhood. The spiritual quest is motivated by a species of nostalgia, homesickness. The procession, though marked by reversals and diversions, is essentially linear, a progress which traverses the demarcation between categories: *from* the alien *to* the familiar. The questions of Mālukyāputta—whether the world is eternal, whether it is also infinite, whether the *jīva* (the Indian equivalent of *psuche* or vital principle) is to be identified with the physical body, and whether the *tathāgata*—that within us which transcends and, in Takeuchi's fine coinage, "transdescends" (cf. 1983, 56)—continues to exist after death—are intended to plumb the nature of this traversal. Does our journey take us *from* the temporal *to* the eternal; *from* the finite *to* the infinite; *from* identification with the body *to* somatic detachment; *from* mundane *to* otherworldly existence? The Buddha, as we know, maintained a "noble silence." And to borrow Watson's words from another context, "[t]his silence is rather the silence of another order, another frame of reference, of a 'view' which cannot be retrieved or subsumed, of a phantasm which cannot simply be structured like a language, i.e. 'substituted' or represented (either 'from above' or 'from below')" (1988, 179). For the assumption which braced this battery of questions was entirely misplaced. Buddhism does not represent the inversion of this serial order, but its convolution. Renunciation begins, of course, by "going forth" (*prabājja*) from home into homelessness. But *nirvāna* is not our final dwelling. It is the unfamiliarity of the familiar, the uncanniness (*Unheimlichkeit*) of the pedestrian, the extraordinary wondrousness of the everyday, the knelling significance of the utterly trivial, the astonishing shock of the unsurprising. To be homeless is to be at home everywhere. The Buddhist path does not take us from the profane to the sacred. It finds the holy, the wholly other, in a gem of dew languishing on a leaf, a bead of water casually abandoned by the faucet. The destination *is* the path. In Takeuchi's splendid trope, "The needle on our terrestrial compass that points the way to the goal of salvation turns around: one might say that Buddhism seeks the beyond of the beyond (the *epekeina* of *epekeina*) and finds it in the here-and-now immediacy of daily human existence" (9). Our authentic destination is reversion to the path with the wonder of a child.

But the infusion of the path by the destination, the means by the end, thus the bi-dimensionality of the Abyss, is not available to Sartre. Sartre never queries the "end" of decompression. He never asks what would appear were the cherry tree *completely* to relax, were *all* of its inexplicit presence to release itself into definition, were *all* of the tight cords of identity restraining its features suddenly to rupture, were all of its positivity to vaporize into negativity, were the microscope which delivers us, level after level, from impression to structure—a microscope of limitless powers of magnification—to find, after one final turn of the knob, nothing further to disclose. We are, for Sartre, perpetually in medias res. And we must be. For the final turn, the final volatilization of the in-itself, would spell the extinction of consciousness. Absolute relaxation is *nirvāna*. For Sartre, absolute decompression would be, not the experiential vacuum of deep sleep, not nothingness in any of its Sartrean senses, but simply death. There could be no experience of absolute decompression. The for-itself is intrinsically, ineluctably, the nihilation of the in-itself. The in-itself is its ground. Were the in-itself to evaporate in consummate decompression, the for-itself would thereby be abolished.

But on second thought, is it *death* that grins behind absolute decompression? "At my limit, at that infinitesimal instant of my death, I shall be no more than my past" (Sartre 1971, 169), and the past "exists *in-itself*" (1984, 335). "Death reunites us with ourselves. Eternity has changed us into ourselves" (1971, 169). But we could only *be* ourselves by crystallizing into the integrity of absolute plenitude. Ex hypothesi, this option is excluded. The in-itself has vaporized. Absolute decompression would leave us without ontological habitation, neither in-itself nor for-itself, neither living nor dead. Were the realization of *śūnyatā* understood as the asymptotic vacuity that orients this endless approximation, we would thus be lead either to acknowledge, with Sartre, the futility of the course on which consciousness inescapably finds itself or—the more reasonable option—to reject the assumption that ontological status is a privilege bestowed only upon entities that fall determinately to one side or the other of the Sartrean divide.

Elsewhere I have spoken of the Sartrean *apeiron* which functions invisibly in Sartre's thinking much as the Boundless functioned (though quite explicitly) in the philosophy of Anaximander (cf. 1991, 406–7). The *archē* which spawns the manifold phenomena of our world cannot, as Thales had supposed, be one of the four great elements. Thales had postulated *hydor* (the fluid, the wet) as the source of all. But his student, Anaximander, discerned that, since the elements are belligerent, waging war one with another, obliterating one another, we would have no way of accounting for the other elements were one selected as primordial. Water is wholly antithetical to fire. Its primordiality would—contrary to observation—ensure the latter's nonexistence. Crediting common experience, the source must, then, be without limits or determination (*a-peiron*). What is most deeply archaic is neither this or that element (*neti, neti*). The Boundless is indeterminate. The futility of our passion to be God is the systemic impossibility of being both the foundation of our own being (the in-itself) and yet conscious of this very foundation (the for-itself). "God is man's vain wish . . . to be as dense as a rock and as free as a thought" (Haar 1980, 185). The "self" of reflective self-consciousness is ejected from consciousness "like some noisy visitor" (Sartre 1984, 324). The assimilation of objectivity into subjectivity is inachievable. The project of cartesian self-reflection is a dream which can be realized, in pale simulation, only in nonpositional self-awareness, consciousness (of) consciousness. As the pillar, the support, the resting place of consciousness, the in-itself is always "outside," separated from the for-itself by the nothingness that consciousness is. And this is ineluctable. Sartre's atheism is the repudiation—constitutive of his systematic ontology—of the *en-soi-pour-soi*, conscious self-existence. "Everything happens as if the world, man, and man-in-the-world succeeded in realizing only a missing God. Everything happens therefore as if the in-itself and the for-itself were presented in a state of disintegration in relation to an ideal synthesis. Not that the integration has ever *taken place* but on the contrary precisely because it is always indicated and always impossible" (1971, 792). God, the "ideal synthesis," is missing. And the *apeiron* is, then, the *ni-en-soi-ni-pour-soi*, the very absence of God. Sartre maintains a covert "theology" of creation presented under the guise of nihilation. "I didn't renounce the absolute," Sartre reminisces, "but by a very natural slippage it came to cloak man's works" (1984, 87). He reports that he was "an atheist out of pride. . . . my very existence was pride: I *was* pride. There was no place for God beside me: I was so perpetually the source of myself that I didn't see what part an Almighty could play in it all" (325). But despite Sartre's candid confession of ontological hubris, we sense, in his thinking, the subtle intrusion of a deific, not a supremely human (*übermenschlich*), presence. For the *absence* of God, the futility of the hope that the being of consciousness might be transcategoreal or bicategoreal, suspended between the in-itself and the for-itself, is exactly the ontological imprint of God, the negative contour which *would* be replete with God's presence *were* God possible. Silverman reminds us that "negative theology is the view that God *is* only in terms of his absence" (1988 297, n. 2), and this negative God partakes of the deep paradox which afflicts the for-itself: "God is what He is not, and He is not what He is" (298, n. 2). It is not clear that Sartre's missing God centers a "negative theology." But Deity does seem unmistakably present through its ineluctable absence. And it would be a splendid irony, comparable to the agony of Sisyphus, if, at the end of its quest, the for-itself could *be* God only by relapsing immediately into its own distinctive, all-too-human, modality of being. The "neither" (*ni-en-soi-ni-pour-soi*)—the *apeiron*—is the empty space where the "both" (*en-soi-pour-soi*) would be. And as *space*, the neither gives clandestine permission to the both. The great imprint, emblazoned deep in Sartre's ontology, which bears the form of an absent God assumes the possibility of deific presence. Thus, what is systemically repudiated is, at the same time, systemically affirmed: God is both possible and impossible. Bataille remarks that in inner experience, "all possibilities are exhausted; the 'possible' slips away and the impossible prevails. To face the impossible—exorbitant, indubitable—when nothing is possible any longer is in my eyes to have an experience of the divine . . ." (1988, 33). We must say the same, then, with respect to the vital and the extinct. Nothing, for Sartre, is *both* in-itself and for-itself, dead and alive. But systemic binary exclusiveness of any sort culminates in *aporia*. The absence of the *both* is the presence of the *neither*. And the *neither* assumes exactly what is forbidden by the *both*.

For Sartre, consciousness is nothing—no/thing at all—because it *is not* any of its thematic objects, actual or potential. It is the nihilation of all possible *things*—the paramount, and flagrantly paradoxical, case being, of course, the "thing" which it gives itself to be in self-objectuating reflection. It is thus that "the being of *for-itself* is defined . . . as being what it is not and not being what it is" (1971, 28). Even the exceptionless abnegation constitutive of the for-itself remains, however, from the Buddhist point of view, a merely *relative* nothingness. It is a "hole of being at the heart of Being" (786), but not the utter absence of the whole of being. In Conze's words, "The relative nothing ("this is absent in that") cannot be hypostatized into an absolute nothing, into the non-existence of everything, or the denial of all reality and of all being" (1962, 61). Sartre is, of course, correct in finding us in medias res. The authentic experience of absolute emptiness is available only in advanced states of *samādhi*, the "absolute samādhi" of which Sekida speaks, in which "[p]rofound silence envelops you. It is as if you were going down into the depths of the sea . . ." (1992, 76). But not only does decompression remain, for us, an endless journey, it is a journey which begins only from where we presently stand, and where we *are* is always where we have *arrived*. If our journey has no end, it also has no beginning. If, to advert to Watts' serviceable example, we begin with the finger only to discover beneath the macrolevel a well-defined colony of distinct cells, we must also see that the finger in turn plays "cell" to a possible higher-level impression. Our macrolevel is "micro" from a more elevated vantage point. Elevation is simply a way of speaking of the liquidation of detail. As there is no maximum magnification, there is also no maximum altitude. Decompression cannot, then, begin with maximally compressed being. If there is no highest point of vantage, there is no radical inception of decompression. And there is, for the for-itself, no solid and irrevocable ground of nihilation. Nihilation must always operate upon the already nihilated. It cannot, then, cogently be claimed that the in-itself "is full of itself, and no more total plenitude can be imagined, no more perfect equivalence of content to container. There is not the slightest emptiness in being, not the tiniest crack through which nothing might slip in" (Sartre 1971, 120–1). If we can imagine a more elevated panorama, we have *thereby* imagined a more total plenitude. Thus, the vivid contrast in Sartre's thinking between the absolute plenitude of being and the absolute vacuity of consciousness—a contrast constitutive of the for-itself—is fatefully compromised. The contrast is lost in thick fog. And the beginning and the end are never where we are. Absolute compaction is suchness (*tathatā*); and absolute dissolution is emptiness (*śūnyatā*). Both are asymptotes, approximable but never attainable, in successive increments.

As Merleau-Ponty observes, Sartre's view "begins by opposing being and nothingness absolutely, and it ends by showing that the nothingness is in a way within being, which is the unique universe." "When," he asks, "are we to believe it? At the beginning or at the end?" (1969, 66). We cannot, as we have seen, believe it at the beginning. Nothingness is incapable of mounting an absolute opposition to being. The "opponent" would simply give way. The battle of the Titans turns out to be a sally into mush. But neither can we believe it at the end. The for-itself, depicted as a hole in the Swiss cheese, a bubble in the waters of being, is conceived on analogy with the "local space" of the Abhidharma and Theravāda traditions:

> The Abhidharmakosa defines local space as a hole or cavity in which there are no material objects, but which, like the mouth or the aperture of a gate, is near them and can be perceived. The Therevadins concur by describing it as the gaps, interstices, vacua, holes, apertures, etc., which occur between visible, etc., objects, as for instance doors, windows, mouth or nose cavities. In them there is nothing to be seen or felt, but they delimitate forms, set bounds to them, environ them and make them manifest, and are the basis of such notions as "below", "above", "across", etc. Local space is just lack of matter, and is finite, visible and conditioned. (Conze 1962, 164)

Local space is not a privation, however, but a modality, of presence. There is no assumption here that space is a sort of negative fluid which seeps into the pores and interstices vacated by materiality. Yet Parmenides (and after him, Sartre) did seem to hold an analogous fluid conception of nonbeing. Being must be unbegotten, reasons Parmenides, otherwise, prior to Being, there would—*instead*—be non-being. And of course, nonbeing is not. Parmenides thus assumes that reality is unfailingly replete. *Were* Being to withdraw, there would be no genuine vacuum. For the void thus created would already be sated with the subtle presence of nonbeing. Only a closet Parmenidean could puzzle over why there is anything at all *instead of* nothing. But as Merleau-Ponty affirms, "there is not something *rather than nothing*, the nothing could not *take the place* of something or of being . . ." (1969, 64). Buddhism is not prepared to acknowledge the contest of being and non-being as ultimate. In Hui-hai's proclamation, "[t]hinking in terms of being and non-being is called wrong thinking, while not thinking in those terms is called right thinking" (Blofeld 1972, 49–50). As Nishitani remarks, "true nothingness means that there is no thing that is nothingness, and this is *absolute nothingness*" (1982, 70). Wonder is not contrastive. Ontological wonder is a questioning openness in the presence of being—not the *surprise* (perhaps closer to the Greek *thaumatzein*) which belies an expectation that being continue, as ever, not to "be." As Caputo advances, "[w]ere a surprise absolute, were we confronted with something absolutely novel, that would make it impossible to recognize the surprise *as* a surprise. We would not know that we were being surprised or indeed that anything was happening at all. A surprise means that something else happens relative to a horizon of expectations; conceding this 'horizonality' and 'relativity' means that the surprise is not absolute" (74). We do not, of course, expect being not to "be," and are never surprised that it "is"—though the indeterminacy of Being fosters no concrete anticipations which could be foiled by a countervailing reality. "Being does not have a proper name" (70). If we *did* expect being not to "be," our surprise at its not "being" would, then, be absolute. Wonder is also an event of being "caught-up" (sur/prised), transported, elevated; and in its deepest sense it is "absolute." No[thing] can thwart its projections. For it has none. It is openness, not imposition. But unlike the astonishment at there being anything at all, wonder discloses, not being, but the emptiness which grounds both being and non-being.

Heidegger, as we know, had worked with a Chinese scholar on a translation of the *Tao Te Ching*. And in a passage resonant with an epigram attributed to the legendary Lao-tzu, he reminds us that

> When we fill the jug with wine, do we pour the wine between the sides and the bottom? At most, we pour the wine between the sides

and over the bottom. Sides and bottom are, to be sure, what is impermeable in the vessel. But what is impermeable is not yet what does the holding. When we fill the jug, the pouring that fills it flows into the empty jug. The emptiness, the void [*die Leere*], is what does the vessel's holding. The emptiness, the void, this nothingness [*dieses Nichtes*] of the jug, is what the jug is as the holding vessel. (1971, 169)

The well-known Zen story of the audience which Nan-in held with a rather pompous and inflated university professor makes a similar point. Offering tea to his guest, Nan-in continued to pour until the cup overflowed. At the professor's consternation, he remarked: "Like this cup . . . you are full of your own opinions and speculations. How can I show you Zen unless you first empty your cup?" (Reps 1989, 5). A filled cup is a thoroughly solid and impermeable object. It is emptiness, not fullness, which holds the wine of life. Lao-tzu saw that the emptiness of the vessel is its usefulness, the impermeable sides and bottom being merely profitable. Were we planning to sell a golden goblet, we might wish for less emptiness and more materiality. But this would do us no good in quenching our thirst. Still, in order to slake our thirst, the vessel must be filled. The cup is thus *useful* only so long as it is not being *used*. And to *use* it is once again to render it *useless*. Local space is relative in just this way. It is bounded by its solid limits, and sacrifices itself in accommodating its nemesis. Since it is defined as the absence of solidity, the presence of solidity excludes it. Surely, however, Nan-in did not urge the professor to empty his cup so that *he* (Nan-in) could then fill it with a different brew, thus reducing it, once again, to uselessness. Nan-in had in mind an infinitely more expansive sense of evacuation. Not demarcated by plenary limits, universal space is immeasurable. Embracing the dense and the rarified, the compact and expansive, the solid and the locally spacious alike, it cannot be filled up. In the deepest sense, it is universal emptiness which "holds" both the vessel and its local emptiness—not the local nothingness of the jug.

Nothingness neither opposes nor replaces being. Boundless empty space is a common trope for emptiness. Far from opposing its plenary inhabitants, space rather welcomes them, offering not the least impedance. Nor is space itself excluded, expelled, displaced by their presence, but rather pervades them. Were it not for this intimate infusion, space would be inhabited by nonspatial residents. There is not the least antagonism, either on the part of space or on the part of its spatial occupants. Suchness neither excludes nor is it excluded by emptiness. Were the Parmenidean position correct—were reality comprised of a plenum of Being—space would not be displaced in the least. And were the more general Parmenidean assumption also correct—were nonbeing a modality of fullness, and thus, were reality, whether its repletion was constituted entirely by Being or by Being *and* nonbeing nonetheless plenary—space would still be unaffected. Space is not Parmenidean nonbeing. Were space legitimately to be conceived as a subtle ether, it would be a spirit of infinite subtlety, subtle to the ultimate degree of presenting absolutely no impedance to its inhabitants, a measureless, featureless and insubstantial specter haunting all things. And all things would be, for it, a community of mere ghosts, passing wraithlike through its vastness. The absolute nothingness of *śūnyatā* permeates the presence of all things without in any way displacing or affecting them. It is pure openness, permissiveness, giving place to solidity and vacuity alike. The firm, unquestionable deposits of our experience, the levers of our trust, the funds of our investment, are, though not depleted of the least quality of vividness and coherence, nonetheless mere apparitions, pure "show." The pageantry of depthless *Schein* exhibits the "heteromorphic difference" which "loves the theatre, the show, a plethora of masks, plays within plays, disguises, masquerades, pseudonyms, assumed forms, temporary roles. It makes a fantastic, carnivalesque display of differences, variety, and variegation" (Caputo 1993, 61). And while ontology marvels at the spectacle, the spectral, phenomenology peers around to witness the rootedness of these flowers in the void. And "From a certain point of view, phenomenology is the whole truth" (Merleau-Ponty 1988, 9).

We have spoken of the "occupants" of space. But space is not a *house*. It may more aptly be considered a *home*. We come closer to the mark with Blofeld's remark that "[t]his void is at once the container and the contained" (Blofeld 1972, 32), that, like the self-lucidity of nonpositional (self-) consciousness, space is self-containing, and is so without containing a "self." But we must eschew any intimation of space as a receptacle. Guenther reminds us that "[t]he Buddhist always knew space to be an opening-up and simultaneously a force that constrains. Only now, after the advent of non-Euclidean geometry, have we in the West come to understand space other than as a passive nothingness or an empty container" (1989, 79). Space "constrains" by its curvature. It is, for us, and for the wondering child of ontology, exactly as if space were a "passive nothingness." And it remains to phenomenology to investigate the "curvature," the formative dynamism, of space. *Mount Analogue*, Daumal's delightful and provocative, though regrettably unfinished, metaphorical adventure, queries: "may there not exist unknown substances—unknown for this very reason in fact—capable of creating around them a much stronger *curvature of space*? . . . Because of it, *everything takes place as if Mount Analogue did not exist*" (1974, 64–5). Setting aside the laws of gravitational physics, we can imagine a great peak wrapped so snugly in its blanket of space, and with just the right folds, that light otherwise obstructed by the mountain would be bent out of its linear course, would circumvent the mountain, and would be remitted directly at the point where an unobstructed beam would rejoin it. And in this way, space could "make nothing of" (nihilate) its enfolded object. And in similar, though perhaps more complex, ways, the modulations of space could, for us, institute fissures and rifts at the granite core of monolithic being. Breaches in the in-itself may not so much be "in" space as simply *be* space. Concomitantly, nihilation may not be in augurated by the in-itself. For Heidegger, nothing "noths" (*das Nichts nichtet*). Dasein is not the agency responsible for clearing the clearing (*Lichtung*), but rather *is* the clearing itself. The clearing could only have come about through the self-abnegation of the dark forest of nothingness. Being is the nonpresence of nonpresence. And *nirvāna*, in Hwa Yol Jung's assimilation, is "a clearing for the truth of Being in the depth of its beauty and goodness" (1987, 262). In Sartre's very different, but perhaps concordant, myth of origin, "everything happens as if" the in-itself initiated its own nihilation. In our own playful speculations, everything—the same things—happen as if the modulations of nothingness brought about the little nothingnesses which rend the in-itself. We need not regard this institution as an assault. For the mountain is wrapped peacefully, without harm, in the secure comforter of space. Nihilation is, then, only *quoad nos*. The in-itself is partially submerged in invisibility. Nothingness does it no violence. Absence is then interiorized presence, presence enfolded in nothingness.

The physicist David Boehm offers an intriguing analogue for this "implicate order." Drop a bead of ink into glass cylinder of glycerine, and rotate the cylinder one full turn. Seen from above, the ink, unsurprisingly, will have been drawn into a thin circle. With a few more turns, the circle will become thinner still, and will finally disappear. What is surprising, however, is that if we now rotate the cylinder backwards the same number of turns, the circle will reappear and when our subtraction reaches zero, the bead of ink will appear once again in its pristine globular status. The enfolded state *seems* entirely empty, diaphanous. But concealed within its very clarity is the nebulous darkness of ink: the opaque enfolded within the transparent. Thus, "[e]mptiness is not a vacancy—it holds in it infinite rays of light and swallows all the multiplicities there are in this world" (Suzuki 1957, 30). Sartre thinks that "[t]o introduce into the unity of a pre-reflective *cogito* a qualified element external to this *cogito* would be to shatter its unity, to destroy its translucency . . ." (1971, 125). Consciousness, darkened by a muddying opacity, would cease to exist. Sartre had not met Boehm. *Kenosis* is *pleroma*. And emptiness is brimming with unmanifest presence. Concurring, in this instance, with Heidegger, Buddhism, though not rejecting the dialectical *nihilum*, localizes it, frames it within a larger conception.

[N]othingness, as the not-ness of beings, is the sharpest opponent of pure nothing. Nothingness is never nothing; even less is it a something in the sense of an object. It is being itself, to the truth of , which man is converted when he has overcome himself as subject, and that means when he no longer posits beings as objects. [*Aber das Nichts ist als das Nichthafte des Seienden der schärfste Wiederpart des bloß Nichtigen. Das Nichts ist niemals nichts, es ist ebensowenig ein Etwas im Sinne eines Gegenstandes, est ist das Sein selbst, desen Wahrheit der Mensch dann übereignet wird, wenn er sicht als Subjekt überwunden hat und d. h., wenn er das Seiend nicht mehr als Objekt vorstellt.*] (1950, 104)

The whetted opposition of absolute and dialectical nothingness is a certain modality of liberation analogous to the parturition of specific differences from the Derridian *différance*: "the nature of this constituting act is that it denies itself to that which it affirms, it holds itself to itself and thus crosses out its own constituting act, releasing this relation from bondage" (Brogan 1988, 36). Absolute nothingness embraces all presence, enfolds all presence and is present in all presence. In Heidegger's words, once again, "It belongs to that which is present. Being and nothingness do not exist alongside each other. One uses the other in an affinity whose fullness of essence we have hardly begun to comprehend . . ." [*Es gehört zum Anwesen. Sein und Nichts gibt es nicht nebeneinander. Eines verwendet sich für das Andere in einer Verwandtschaft, deren Wesensfülle wir noch kaum bedacht haben . . .*] (Heidegger 1967, 247).

Nāgārjuna has taught us that *nirvāna* and *samsāra* are *not different*.

Samsara (i.e., the empirical life-death cycle) is nothing essentially different from *nirvana*. *Nirvana* is nothing essentially different from *samsara*. [XXV, 19]
The limits (i.e., realm) of *nirvana* are the limits of *samsara*. Between the two, also, there is not the slightest difference whatsoever. [XXV, 20] (Inada 1970, 158)

Buddhism does not to regard the ultimate and the mundane, the sacred and the profane, the transcendent and the immanent, as states, locations, ontological regions, or in a suitably expansive sense, as "things" at all, and certainly not as things to be identified. Their *nondifference* is not a positive identity uniting positive entities. Rather:

Nirvāna and *samsāra* have a "negative identity" whereby the nature of reality in *nirvana* consists in the lack of self-sufficient reality in

the factors that constitute *samsāra*. The emptiness of the phenomenal world is also the emptiness of any "non-phenomenal reality" that is conceived as self-existent. *Samsāra* is no more
"empty" than *nirvāna*; nor is *nirvāna* more "empty" than *samsāra*
from the highest point of view—though *nirvāna* is more "empty"
than *samsāra* from the conventional, practical perspective. (Streng
1967, pp. 75-6)

Tsung-mi's crystal ball exhibits two seemingly quarrelsome possibilities for
apprehension. It *seems* itself a murky medium pervaded by a vaguely diaphanous ghost of color. And it also *seems* an aperture open without reservation upon an external exhibition of color. The crystal is not *given* in these
two different ways. It is *taken* in one way or the other. The very being of the
crystal is januarial. It would not be what it is, were it not afflicted with ambiguity in just this way.

The apertural vacancy, the nothingness or emptiness, of the second
seeming is thus, in Sartre's sense, a dialectical pole of opposition, and the
environing saturated presence of the first seeming is its dialectical correlate.
Conceived as *local*, being and nothingness, suchness and emptiness, are assuredly antithetical. And "[t]o oppose being and nothingness as thesis and
antithesis, as Hegel does, is to suppose that they are logically contemporary" (Sartre 1971, 47). In Sartre's view, "non-being is not the opposite of
being; it is its contradiction." Thus, "nothingness is subsequent to being
since it is being, first posited, then denied" (47). This is voiced in response
to Heidegger's view that "[n]othingness does not form the concept antithetical to Being, but from the start, the essence of Being itself involves
Nothingness" (1955, 35). And Haar comments that "[w]hat shocks
Sartre's Cartesianism is that the world, or the in-itself, might be able to lose
its consistency and take on a coloring, so to speak, of unreality and of nothingness" (1980, 176). But shocking as it may seem, from a Buddhist perspective, the "in-itself" (suchness) is always already saturated with
emptiness, infinitely porous, insubstantial.

Do being and nothingness spring, like twins, from the same womb, or
is being the matrix of nothingness? While the latter represents Sartre's official posture, there is much between the lines to suggest a preference for the
former. There is *being* (in-itself) and there is *nihilated being*. The two must
not be confused. Nihilated being is being pocketed with cysts of vacuity,
being which has already begun to expire, to exhale the spirit of nothingness
rising vaporously from its internal disintegration. Consciousness is the
odor of rot. Prenihilated being is fresh, entirely integral. As a fresh-fallen
apple, first plump and full of itself, begins to decay, it offers initially the
form and blush of the new fruit. But little by imperceptible little, its form

collapses, its burnish fades, until at the end what remains is barely, and then wholly, indistinguishable from the earth. When has it ceased to be an apple and become the nourishing richness of the soil? Perhaps the matter is practical, and depends on our continued willingness to consume it. Or perhaps it is aesthetic, and depends on its continuing to *look* like an apple. Or perhaps it is chemical, and depends on the continued presence within it of certain complex reactions and interactions. But such replies are arbitrary, relative to purpose and motivation. There are, it seems only two nonarbitrary possibilities: the endpoints of this continuous process of degradation. Sartre does not, however, allow that the apple of being can rot away utterly into emptiness. For we are always *in medias res*. Thus, the only response available to him, though one he seems not to recognize, is that being is radically modified by the event of decompression. There is a discontinuity between the fresh and the decomposing fruit. The moldering "apple" is no more an *apple* than a dead horse is a horse.

The in-itself is not, without qualification, to be identified with prenihilated being, but is rather the ontological twin of the for-itself. Nihilated being is the dialectical correlate of the nothingness which arises from nihilation. There is no evacuation without vacuity, and no vacuity without evacuation. Ineluctably, the worm of nothingness lies coiled at the heart of the in-itself (Sartre 1971, 56). No less ineluctably, prenihilated being is entirely free from the gnawing of the worm. Nihilated being is, however, exactly being in decay. And Sartre displays an implicit awareness of this distinction in his claim that " 'Before' consciousness one can conceive only of a plenum of being of which no element can refer to an absent consciousness" (16). The worm-eaten in-itself arises, not after, but *with* the for-itself. Sartre's insistence on the logical subsequence of nothingness is confused. To be sure, the for-itself is subsequent to prenihilated being, but it is a strict contemporary of nihilated being. What Sartre says of "the most abstract of abstractions and the poorest" (45), the dialectically first thesis and antithesis of the Hegelian logic, we must return to his own conception. The in-itself and the for-itself are "two complementary components of the real-like darkness and light. . . . strictly contemporary notions which would somehow be united in the production of existents and which it would be useless to consider in isolation. Pure being and pure non-being would be two abstractions which could be reunited only on the basis of concrete realities" (44). Sartre's alternative to "the Megarian, antidialectic isolation of essences" (119) seems to be the very complementarity which he wishes to reject.

In Sartre's penetrating observation, "[s]pace is not the world, but it is the instability of the world apprehended as totality, inasmuch as the world can always disintegrate into external multiplicity. Space is neither the ground nor the figure but the ideality of the ground inasmuch as it can always disintegrate into figures; it is neither the continuous nor the discontinuous, but the permanent passage from continuous to discontinuous" (1971, 254). Sartre here speaks of space in intriguingly active terms. Space is "instability," "passage." It is ideal to the extent that it particularizes itself, looms forward into figural definition. It is as if the figural phenomena which absorb our attention were, as modern physics says of the electron, "condensations" of a universal field of force. This suggestion resonates unmistakably with Einstein's observation that "[s]pace has devoured ether and time; it seems to be on the point of swallowing up also the field and corpuscles, so that it alone remains as the vehicle of reality" (Thiel 1958, 345). We have no quarrel with Sartre's view that, the world, apprehended *as a totality*, is "unstable," that our apprehension of this totality is immediately repulsed and deflected back into the figural domain, and thus that the world remains, for us, always ground, never figure. But if "world" does service for "being," there is a certain discord in Sartre's remark that "[w]hat being *will be* must of necessity arise on the basis of *what it is not*. Whatever being [the world] is, it will allow this formulation: "Being is *that* and outside of that, *nothing*" (1971, 36). If being *were* thus defined in terms of nothingness, it could not, contrary to Sartre's postulation, enjoy the logical precedence and independence which he requires. Moreover, this formula could be verified, could ground itself in phenomenological evidence, only from a purported standpoint outside of being, and that would seem to compromise our existential status as being-in-the-world. Of course, Sartre is explicit that "[n]othingness can be conceived neither *outside of* being, nor as a complementary, abstract notion, nor as an infinite milieu where being is suspended" (56). But then, if nothingness is not extrinsic to being, being could not be defined as *that* and nothing besides. And indefinability is even more inimical to Sartre's ontology than complementarity. For it is not simply that being and nothingness—while remaining distinct—flow into one another, like the interchanging fluids released from two bottles, only to discover their perfect homogeneity. Even their *apparent* duality is unavailable. Sartre's third exclusion, nothing as "an infinite milieu where being is suspended," Boehm's "implicate order," our opacity-within-transparency, is then the only remaining option. The emptiness of Buddhism is not "the abstract concept of 'nothingness,' as the opposite to being or 'somethingness'-in-general" (Streng 1967, 162). As Heidegger maintains,

> Nothingness is neither an object nor a being at all. Nothingness neither comes forth by itself alone nor together with beings to which it clings, as it were. Nothingness is the making possible of the openness to beings as such for human Dasein. Nothingness does not first stand as a counter-concept to beings, but belongs

originally to their very essence. [*Das Nichts ist weder ein Gegen-
stand noch überhaupt ein Seiendes. Das Nichts kommt weder für sich
vor noch neben dem Seienden, dem es sich gleichsam anhängt. Das
Nicht ist die Ermöglichung der öffenbarkeit des Seienden als eines
solchen für das menschliche Dasein. Das Nichts gibt nicht erst den
Gegenbegriff zum Seienden her, sondern gehört ursprünglich zum
Wesen selbst.*] (1967, 12)

To be consistent, Sartre must hold that the world is unthematizable, and
that being is indefinable. He rather contends that "nothingness is given as
that by which the world receives its outlines as the world" (1971, 51). But
if—consistently, but contrary to Sartre's contention—being is indefinable,
there is nothing within being to distinguish it from nothingness. Sartre has
not, in any remarkable way, exceeded Hegel.

Nor, from the Buddhist standpoint, would the surpassing of Hegel
represent a significant accretion of wisdom. As Streng explains, "wisdom, in
the context of emptiness, negated any one-sided assertion which required
bipolar distinctions, e.g., production—destruction, or reality—nonreality"
(1967, 86). As Merleau-Ponty elucidates, dialectic self-mediation is "a
movement through which each term ceases to be itself in order to become
itself, breaks up, opens up, negates itself, in order to realize itself" (1969,
92). Nāgārjuna has demonstrated the ultimate untenability of conceptual
contrast. Were we to divide a field, say an unremarkable acreage of grass,
into a northern and a southern half, we could not, then, apply the epithet,
"northern" (or "southern") to the entire meadow. It is always illegitimate to
attribute to the whole what, by definition, pertains *only* to a portion of it.
Reality—the larger sense of Mālukyāputta's "world"—is *neither* eternal *nor*
temporal, *neither* finite *nor* infinite. These distinctions represent demarca-
tions of the grassland, and cannot, then, be invoked to characterize the terrain itself. Reality is the ground of distinction, the field of distinction, and
remains unfailingly hospitable to distinction. But reality is, of itself, undistinguished. But even our pedestrian, nonmetaphysical attributions, characterizing, not reality at large, but bicycles and puppy dogs in fine, fare no
better. At Nāgārjuna's impulsion, we may have come to shun grand-scale
declamations, avoiding even the thought of reality depicted in this hue or
another. But to say of my bicycle, a humble ontic particular, that it is red is
already to have committed myself to the nature of reality. It is to say, of reality, that it is host to a red bicycle. And this determinate species of hospitality
contrasts with its opposite, inhospitality. Reality is the field of *any possible*
distinction; and this includes the distinction between containing, and not
containing a red bicycle. Even our fine-grained attributions thus embroil us
in contradiction. Distinction would be impossible without subtention. And

for this reason, we cannot abandon the field. But we need not assume that our attributions plough a furrow across it. Distinction may no more etch the surface of reality than the International Date Line carves a groove into the surface of the earth. The delicacies of language express, from the Buddhist point of view, merely imaginary constructions (*vikalpa*) that play over the surface of the real without giving us access to it" (Nagao 1979, 32). Such artifices are *useful*—not *real*. If (*contra* Hegel) being and nothingness are abidingly distinct, if they are not to dissolve dialectically into one another, then we must affirm what we have already affirmed in the case of "northern" and "southern," "eternal" and "temporal," "finite" and "infinite." *Existence* no more applies to "ontic" particulars than to ultimate reality, since, as Nāgārjuna avers, "[t]here absolutely are no things" (Burtt 1955, 170). Or as Sprung reiterates, "[t]here are no things on the middle way; they disappear into the way itself" (1978, 136). And neither, for precisely parallel considerations, do *they* fail to exist. Like any other conceptual contrast, the distinction between existence and nonexistence is not so much a line as a crevasse through which all the "things" of our world disappear.

We must press Nāgārjuna's logic forward one final dialectical step. While distinction does assume the field, we cannot conclude from this that the field *exists*. Up this point, the ground of distinction may well have been mistaken for the indeterminate Absolute (*Brahman*) of Vedānta realized as infinite *sat* (existence or truth). And, as Merleau-Ponty discerns, "[p]hilosophy cannot conceive the absolute except as the other side of the 'appearance' or the phenomenon" (1988, 39). In Heidegger's iconography, Being "is" (*is* in quotes). And while the existence of beings belongs, for Vedanta, to the illusory ontic realm of *māyā*, Brahman, likewise, "is." Buddhism will not permit even this guarded, bracketed, positing of *nirvāṇa*. *Nirvāṇa* neither *is* nor *is not*, and indeed, neither "is" nor "is not." Being and nothingness are *seemings*. Tsung-mi's crystal can be *seen as* clouded or clear. Its experiential presence is compatible with both seemings, but compels neither. Magliola perceives that "a Nothing can only operate in dialectic with a non-Nothing . . . so that any theory of nothingness 'buys into' a theory of presence" (1986, 25). But emptiness is not, in this sense, "a Nothing." The *concept* of nothingness exhausts itself in its reference to *nothingness*, a finger pointing to the moon. In the remarkable dialogue with Fa-yen Wên-I (885–958 C.E.):

> A monk asked, "As for the finger, I will not ask you about it. But what is the moon?" The Master said, "Where is the finger that you do not ask about?" So the monk asked, "As for the moon, I will not ask you about it. But what is the finger?"
> The Master said, "The moon!"

The monk challenged him, "I asked about the finger; why should you answer me, 'the moon'?"

The Master replied, "Because you asked about the finger." (Chang 1971, 242)

Concepts are, one and all, taken up into configurations of binary opposition, the terms of which "are inevitably contaminated by each other, each inwardly disturbed by the other" (Caputo 1993, 63). But nothingness, while it enfolds presence, does not "buy into" a *theory* or a *concept* of presence.

Chapter 5

Emptiness

The aporias of Sartre's early theory of nothingness stand forth, for us, not as the levers of dismissal, not as so many excuses for turning our backs upon a vision of immeasurable depth and subtlety, but as the faults and quagmires, the unexpected sinkholes and pitfalls, of an ontological terrain of luxuriant richness and fruitfulness. From the outset, we must chart these dangerous turns in an effort to liberate thought for a more consistent vision, and offer here a brief budget of philosophical perils:

- A phenomenology which stands aside from perception in order to describe it discloses to itself only the dry husk of perception, perception-reflected-on, not the palpating act in the flush of its vivid, if also transient, existence.

- Being can be analyzed in terms of identity only by positing within it a subtle multiplicity; and it can be counted as unitary only if it posits beyond itself a prior nothingness.

- "Everything happens as if . . ." is an echo, in a quasi-mythological register, of a more candid metaphysical account. Sartre's posture is disingenuous, since he is not entirely prepared to "own" the straight-forward thesis that being decompresses "*in order to* [emphasis added] free the affirmation *of* self from the heart of being." This would assume purpose, motivation, agency, prior to their possibility.

- We have no reason to assume that, independently of consciousness, nothingness would fail to interpolate itself between the fragmentary remains of an object destroyed. Destruction is not, then, produced, but only disclosed, by the for-itself.

- Since consciousness is grounded in the in-itself, the exhaustive vaporization of the in-itself in absolute decompression could only spell the extinction of the for-itself. Yet death, for Sartre, is reintegration into the plenitude of an in-itself which—ex hypothesi—no longer "is." Sartre's recourse is to posit human existence as always "on the way." The Buddhist meditative experience of absolute nothingness is, however, the realization of the *end* of this way.

- Sartre seems merely to invert theology. The *absence* of God is constitutive of Sartre's systematic ontology. But this absence, the Sartrean *apeiron*, bearing the contour of God, assumes, against Sartre's explicit protest, the possibility of God. God is both possible and impossible.

- Nihilation cannot begin with absolute plenitude. For there is no highest "altitude" from which a maximum compression could be witnessed. Sartre's unequivocal professions notwithstanding, nihilation can operate only upon the prenihilated.

- Sartre harbors a certain Parmenidean conception of nothingness. As an "ontological fluid," nothingness seeps into, and utterly fills, the crevasses and fissures which open within the in-itself. It is displaced by being and displaces being, and in this sense, obeys the logic of a merely local nonbeing.

- Sartre confuses being (the *apeiron*) and being-in-itself. Consistency requires their discrimination. And since the in-itself (not the *apeiron*) and the for-itself are coimplicates, he lapses into the very dialectical conception of nothingness which he has taken pains to refute.

- The definability of being, inapplicable to the *apeiron*, serves only to confirm the dialectical complementarity of the in-itself and the for-itself.

- Thus, Sartre's ontology can offer no legitimate resistance to the Buddhist conception of nothingness as an implicate order, "an infinite milieu where being is suspended."

The Buddhist conception of emptiness does not succumb to these snares. We turn, then, to emptiness.

Sartre's theory of decompression is a mirror of what Sangharakshita calls the "spatio-analytic" (in contrast to the "dynamic-synthetical") demonstration of emptiness (cf. 1987, 120). In its quest for the "atom" (the Greek *atoma*: that which cannot be further cut or divided), contemporary physics has watched the purported floor of physical reality crumble into fragments, and when these fragments have consolidated into an accustomed level, it has watched the subfloor give way once again. Emptiness shatters every last pellicle of plenitude. Thus, "a thought no less than a thing, an idea equally with an empire, is resolved into a complex of infinitely extensive relations between infinitesimally small parts" (Sangharakshita, 123). "Events divide infinitely into other events. There are no irreducibly simple events to put an end to the analysis of events, to bring it to a satisfying rest" (Caputo 1993, 94). And though pragmatic considerations inhibit experimental verification, there seems to be no theoretical limitation on the depths of our insecurity. Though excusing the nihilation which is Sartre correctly reports the scientific wisdom of his day: "If . . . a single one of the atoms which constitute the universe were annihilated, there would result a catastrophe which would extend to the entire universe . . ." (786). Accordingly, to indulge a thought-experiment, the operation of instruments of such fantastic power as to enable us to witness the dissolution of even the smallest known particle into lucid nothingness may absorb all of the energy in the universe. Fantasy balks, however, at the fact that our imaginary instruments themselves will reserve a significant quantum of potential energy, and the point of "annihilation" will not have been reached until *all* of the energy in the universe has been deployed. The practical impossibility of the *empirical* verification of emptiness is thus evident. As Watson points out, "the extension *in indefinitum* of verification could find the requisite strictness and closure only in failure, in refutation, that is, in 'cancellation' " (1988, 174). But each time the foundations crumble, a direction is established, a vectorial indication of sheer emptiness is, level by level, confirmed. Our imaginary experiment could be concluded only if the potential energy languishing in the massiveness of our instrumentation were volatilized into kinetic energy. The event of annihilation, of dissolution into the limitless *nihilum*, would be, not an explosion, but an implosion, pulling all things—our instruments and ourselves included—into the enstatic maelstrom. And it bears notice that depictions of the experience of enlightenment are not infrequently painted with similar strokes. Descending into absolute *samādhi* is like falling into a black hole. Time, space, causality, all objects and events, are swirled down into the vortex.

Perhaps it is our need for security, our desire for solid groundwork, for sub/stance, which gives rise to invigorated attempts to discover the basic particle. And perhaps scientific claims, naive though they may be, to have done so express the anxious hope that now, at last, we may stand firm, ungripped by the deep terror of loosing our footing to the abyss. If it is true, as Demartino represents, that "[a]ll forms of anxiety come from the fact that there is somewhere in our consciousness the feeling of incomplete knowledge of the situation" and that "this lack of knowledge leads to the sense of insecurity and then to anxiety with all degrees of intensity" (1981, 108), then the cognizance which would allay our disquiet before the ch[i]asm is an ontological intuition of emptiness. We might expect, with the disintegration of foundations, that the great edifice erected upon them would teeter and reel, sinking in starts and tremors into the interstitial dust beneath. And the dread of this monumental collapse contributes to the horror. Successive demonstrations of insecurity have not, however, come as upheavals. The revolution is silent, without shock, leaving everything in place exactly as it was. The superstructure has not sunk, has not felt the propagation of the least vibration. We dine with our friends and family as we always have, disquieted, if at all, by the quiet recognition that our mashed potatoes, our fork and our hand have been discovered to be a little more porous than we had thought, that the peas, the dinner rolls, our own corporeality, and that of our dear ones, while altering not the least in appearance or practical significance, have been seen to be a little more spectral, apparitional, rarified, that quietly, unobtrusively, we have become more like ghosts, and all this without anything changing.

Children just learning to float are given two important instructions: Hang on to the side of the pool—and relax. We need to feel the stability of the solid edge. Without the security of the solid, the plenary, the impenetrable—the in-itself—we could not comfortably release ourselves to the buoyancy of our watery milieu. But once we have learned the exquisite art of floating, once we have learned to release our hold, to entrust ourselves to the uplifting water, the terror of separation from the solid is dissolved. And once we have learned not only to endure, but positively to enjoy the state of bobbing aimlessly like a cork, relaxed and fully supported, we can no longer imagine why we once clutched so desperately to the side of the pool. There are, then, two ways of achieving security: one for beginners, and one for the advanced. Beginners need to feel the solid. They need foundations, Cartesian apodicticity, an ultimate ground. To be sure, "the Buddhist positive is threatening. It is no ground whatsoever; it cannot be grasped as ground, reference point, or nest for a sense of ego. It does not exist—nor does it not exist" (Varela, Thompson and Rosch 1992, 248–9). But the joy of the advanced is to abandon the foundational, to relinquish cognitive security, to release themselves to the *Abgrund*. The intricate edifice of our experience, its dormant and animate modes of materiality, its history and its culture, its values and its spirituality, is not demolished with the progressive rarefaction of its substructure. It simply floats, just as it is, without the least harm, in the buoyancy of absolute nothingness. *S'ūnyatā*, the openness, the uncontainability, of phenomena, is by no means the foe of *tathatā* (suchness), nor even its begrudging accomplice. As the measureless power of the sea upholds the ship, the inexhaustible buoyancy of emptiness is placed entirely at the service of suchness—without reserve. Were we intergalactic explorers floating weightlessly in the deepest reaches of interstellar space, we would be, and we could come to feel, no less secure than we are at present with our feet planted firmly on the trusted earth. For the earth, too, is afloat, as is the gyrating coagulation of planets and asteroids and dust with which it keeps company. And it is far better to release ourselves joyfully to universal buoyancy than to clutch at our petty handles of security at the cost of blindness to a universe adrift.

The book which you hold in your hands—not *the* book considered as a species or *a* book considered as an arbitrary instance, but *this very book*, this book here, now, *exactly as it is*—is bereft of a peculiarity which, for the most part, we naively assume it to possess, a feature the absence of which would, like the crumbling of sub-atomic foundations, change nothing, or perhaps, in a deeper sense, would change everything, since without it, this book detaches itself from our securities and begins to "float" right there in your very hands. This missing trait, which the tradition calls "own-being" (*svabhāva*), is the presumed self-existence which, for Aristotle—"that worst of sophists stupefied by his own unprofitable subtlety, the cheap dupe of words" (Bacon, 62)—and for the philosophical culture still attuned to his thinking, is definitionally inalienable from the notion of substance. Substance is—essentially—self-existent. And for at least this reason, the Buddhist tradition roundly repudiates the notion of substance in every one of its guises. "Whatever comes into existence presupposing something else is without self-existence (*svabhavata*)" (Nāgārjuna 1995, 7:16; cf. Streng 1967, 191). The reasoning is simple, and is resonant with the logic of Kripke's table. *This very table* could not have been made of ice *instead of* wood. To presume, on the part of *this table* a genuine alternativity, the real possibility that *it itself* might either be made of wood or ice is to presume that it is presently made of neither. Again, it is not that all the gaps are closed. Indeed, we follow Merleau-Ponty in championing the indeterminate, the ontologically lacunary, the ambiguous: and is understood, not privatively, not as, but as an entirely positive determination. Indeed, . But to the extent that the gaps are plugged, to the exact extent of the table's determinateness, the options are thereby foreclosed. It is not that the table *must be* made of wood, but that *if* it is made of wood, *it* (the very table made of wood) cannot, then, be made of ice. Buddhism extends this reasoning not only to the monadic attributes of a thing, but to all of its relations and modalities. *Another* book, *a* book, some book or other, might have been made of pure linen paper. But if *this* one was not, it could not have been. *Another* book, *a* book, might have been printed in India. But if *this* one was not, it could not have been. *Another* book might have been printed with Chinese calligraphy ink. But if *this* one was not, it could not have been. *All* the conditions and relations of a thing are constitutive. Absent its exact location on the bookstore shelf, absent even the particles of dust which find their home on its surface, "it," to put the matter paradoxically, would not be *it*. You would have in your hands another copy—not *this* one. Thus, the abolition of any condition, of any term of a relationship in which it stands, would *thereby* spell the abolition of this very book. Much is implicit in the "thereby." To say that *B* is *thereby* abolished with the abolition of *A* is to say that *B* is ontologically inextricable from *A*, that *A* is the condition for the very existence of *B*, and to say, moreover, that the being of *B* is so intimately bound up with *A* that, in effect, its existence *resides* in *A*, not in itself. Things exist, if you will, "outside of themselves." Being is ek/static, standing without. The out/standing existence of a thing resides, not *en soi* (for Buddhism, there is neither being-in-itself nor immanence), but (and we say this provisionally) *en autrui*. Not only is "[a] being which does not have its nature outside of itself . . . not a natural being" (cf. Merleau-Ponty 1988, 78), it is not a being at all. From the Buddhist perspective, nothing whatsoever is granted self-existence, nothing shelters its own existence within. Nothing exists *in se*; nothing exists *per se*. Phenomena arise in dependence upon other phenomena. And, as Nāgārjuna confirms, And

> Neither from itself nor from another,
> Nor from both
> Nor without a cause,
> Does anything whatever, anywhere arise"   (I:1, 1995, 3)

This extends to the very universal absence of self-existence labeled "emptiness" (*śūnyatā*). Ontological ecstasy is universal. Even emptiness is empty. "[T]he relativity of all things, is itself relative . . ." (Loy 1984, 443).

The displacement of an object's existence, its deferral to a thing or event or condition beyond itself, is not, however, a linear transmission, but a starburst of relinquishment. In Chandrakīrti's verse:

> Cloth is existent in its threads,
> The threads again in something else.
> How can these threads, unreal themselves,
> Produce reality in something else?"   (cf. Magliola 1986, 111)

The existence of this book, in the always lacunary specificity of its detail, depends upon its being printed by a particular press. But it also depends upon its being printed with a particular stock of paper, with a certain ink, and by a certain operator who happened to consume a particular cheese sandwich, with a particular slice of tomato and a particular dollop of mustard, for lunch. It depends, as well, upon the particular trees, felled by particular lumberjacks, in a particular grove with a particular soil density, humidity and reserve of nutrients, subject to particular atmospheric conditions, and enjoying a particular exposure to the sun. As Stcherbatsky explains, "[t]he effect itself, indeed, is nothing but the presence of the totality of its causes. If the seed and the necessary quanta of air, soil, heat and moisture are present in it, all other elements not interfering, the sprout is already there. The effect is nothing over and above the presence of the totality of its causes" (cf. Conze 1994, pp. 148–9). Minus *any single one* of these conditions, the book in your hands would have been different—not the *same* book altered, but *a different book.* The existence of this book is not merely "distributed" among its innumerable conditions, as if each were to receive a mere fraction of the estate, but bequeathed whole to each of its conditioning benefactors. *Each one* of these conditions is requisite for this book's existence. We have here a miracle more astonishing than the multiplication of a few loaves and fishes. For in relinquishing itself, in abandoning itself to its conditions, its "self" has been multiplied to infinity. To be sure, the book is nothing over and beyond its conditions. But its conditions scatter its presence everywhere. In the Buddhist vision, as for Whitehead, simple location is a pathetic, and also a pathological, fallacy. And more than this, it is a particularly virulent strain of the pathology of *avidyā* (blindness, lightlessness). The futility of the for-itself's fever to be God is thus redoubled. It is not that the in-itself possess the self-existence which we would vainly wrest for our own, but that *nothing*, neither consciousness nor its world, is thus endowed.

We know that everything—*everything*—is already destroyed, destroyed utterly and absolutely, ground to dust, and the dust ground to nothingness—and this without the least visible hint. We know that in the domain of the infinitesimal, sub-basement after basement has resolved into clouds of micro-dust, yet leaving the great cathedral of our ordinary lives unshaken, unchanged. And we must now see that the resolution of the particularities of our experience into their conditions, the magnificent starburst of ontological deferral, leaves no visible sign. This unimaginable conflagration in which the flame of self-relinquishment leaps from thing to condition, transforming in its explosive outrush each condition into a conditioned, and igniting then the more remote conditions in turn, until all of reality is ablaze, is insufficient to singe the wings of a humble gnat. *Nothing is changed!* To say, as we must, that the things of our experience are *nothing but* their conditions is, conversely, to say that all the conditions requisite for the manifestation of these things are present. With stark paradox, the presence of things is by no means abrogated by their absence. Presence and absence are the asymptotes of a regressive and a progressive analysis. The existence of *A* resides in its conditions, $B_1, B_2, \ldots$, and each of these conditions, in turn, defers its existence to a further radiance of conditions, $C_1, C_2, \ldots$ Were the analysis to terminate in a final, self-existent stratum of conditions, $Z_1, Z_2, \ldots$, the existence of A would be assured. Resting solidly upon the fundamental Z-stratum, A, though conditioned, would be no less secure than the Z's. However, no final member of this astonishing fireworks display—scintillae bursting into scintillae without end—is discernible. The profound deposition of Buddhist insight is that it has no end. And there is nothing upon which "the metaphysical drive to ground" (Salis 1988, 95) could vent itself. Each step of the regressive analysis is, though a vectorial indication, nonetheless a finite approximation. As Zen recommends, we must climb up beyond the end of the pole. Conze affirms that. After all, "theories are rooted in desires . . ." (Sangharakshita 1987, 37). Realization of the endlessness of ontological deferral is the great leap into emptiness.

Infinity, here, is not despair on the part of the finite; it is not the sense that however far we go, there will always be farther to go; it is not the exhaustion and tedium expressed in the hopeless *und so weiter*. It is the intuitive embrace of the entire approximative series and its contiguity with the asymptote of emptiness. With the transgression of each relative limit in the endless succession of purported limits, "the limit [opens] onto the limitless" (Hiley 1988, 106). Transgression "forces the limit to face the fact of its immanent disappearance" (Foucault 1977, 34). But we need not think of "the limitless" (emptiness) as the "number" that comes after infinity. Derrida has shown that This is, perhaps, what motivates Foucault's comment that, a line which "closes up behind it in a wave of extremely short duration" (35). Transgression thus returns us once again "right to the horizon of the uncrossable" (35). We come to see that the existence of our initial object, A, has been carried away forever, and resides nowhere. *A does not exist*. And this intuition easily generalizes itself: "There absolutely are no things" (Burtt 1955, 170). Or in Hui-neng's poetic voice, "[o]riginally, not one thing exists" (*ben lai, wu i wu*). Guenther is more abstract: Ontological dependence ensures that the "thing" is not the primal unit of ontic attribution. And infinite deferral ensures that no complex or totality or whole of "things" is either. Thus, Brand can write that "[t]rue being is not being object; there is, therefore, no truth of one being" ([1955] 1967, 204). The dynamic advent (*lai*) of conditioning which culminates in the present object "such" as it is has no ultimate ground. There is no First Cause, no *actus purus*, no *primum mobile*. The "*ben*" of "*ben lai*" (originally) is the infinite affordance of infinite deferral, not an absolute Thing, "Thing" writ large, in ontological capitals, standing as the Source, the *archē*, the *principium*, of the series. Suchness "comes" to us (*lai*), not out of time "immemorial," as if the Beginning had, like Atlantis, collapsed into the fathomless waters of forgetfulness, as if the primal event of "unforgetting" (*aletheia*) had been forgotten, but out of a time for which there is no First Event to remember. Without an anchoring First Moment, the "time" of this coming is not a temporal order, but a transordinal, and in an appropriate, if also paradoxical, sense, "timeless," medium of deferral. Presence is not the intimation of an absent, but memorable, Being, but the infinitely iterated testimony of there "being" no Being at all.

The world empties itself, empties itself even of "itself"—and of us—and there is utter void. Since "the Buddhists are interested in the *concrete* conditions of this *particular concrete* event" (Conze 1994, 149), Buddhism is sometimes claimed to represent a species of nominalism. But a Buddhist nominalism would be possible only if the unproblematic existence of particulars were admitted. And this, from the Buddhist point of view, is simply unthinkable. Buddhism affiliates itself with the nominalist rejection of ontologically independent essences or universals. But to assume that the elimination of eidetic universality leaves the world as a rattling gourd of separate and fully determinate particulars is a failure of imagination.

But we must be wary of taking the nonexistence of things as our *fundamenum inconcussum*, deriving, perhaps, a certain measure of comfort and security thereby, but also lapsing into nihilism. "The mode of repudiation or denial that is characteristic of nihilism is actually a very subtle and refined form of objectivism: the mere absence of an objective ground is reified into an objective groundlessness that might continue to serve as an ultimate reference point" (Varela, Thompson, and Rosch 1992, 240). There is an area of decided agreement between Buddhism and the Sartrean theory of *négatités*. While Buddhism will not allow that absolute nothingness is produced, nor does it accept Sartre's view that the for-itself generates the nothingness which shimmers between the shards of the shattered vase, it will agree that the phenomenal manifestation of nothingness (the thematic absence of the thing) is nonetheless conditioned. The absence of Pièrre arises *for us*, arises, that is, as a phenomenon, not solely on the basis of our anticipations. These expectations must collide with the fact that Pièrre is not here. Pièrre may have been delayed for a number of reasons. Suppose his great aunt, whom he dearly loved, had been afflicted with pneumonia. She would not have been stricken with pneumonia had she been younger and more resistant, and also had she not stubbornly refused the elixir of vitamins and herbs that Pièrre bought for her. Like the tales of Sheherazade, our story could continue without end. Absence has its manifold conditions as well to which it entrusts its burden of non-existence. And these conditions, in turn, have theirs. Leaping to the infinite, climbing beyond the pole, we see that nonexistence, endlessly deferred, is simply nowhere. *Nothing fails to exist*!

Nothing exists, and nothing fails to exist. All is empty (*śūnya*) and all is full (*tatha*). Buddhism recognizes three deleterious forms of craving (*taṇhā*)—each, in its own way, a condition of the painful underlying bourdon of the discordant psyche, the drone of suffering (*dukha*) vibrating through the busyness and fuss of ordinary existence, the very "level" (in Merleau-Ponty's idiom), *with* which, not *in* which we live, and move, and have our being—these three being the craving for sensory gratification (*kama-taṇhā*), the craving for existence (*bhāva-taṇhā*) and the craving for non-existence (*abhāva-taṇhā*). Phenomena pirouette before us, keeping their delicate balance for a brief instant, inclining, during their momentary performance, neither toward the one nor toward the many, neither toward unification nor toward reabsorption in the manifold. Both ways lead to death. Life is a balancing act. The Sartrean in-itself, positive, absolutely dense, and lifeless lies at the extremity of unification. Yet while the "avoidance of ellipsis by differential integration" which, for Heidegger, is "the properly spiritual task . . ." (Fóti 1992, 97) may, in its insistence upon recollection, be entirely admirable, it cannot be the task which Buddhism sets for itself. For the movement of integration, gathering, impels us toward oneness, toward plenary materiality, toward a lifeless "suchness" without emptiness. Fóti reminds us that, for Heidegger, the "labors of unification resist the self-relinquishing desire for annihilation (*Todeslust*) that . . . is often connoted by the figure of the streams flowing into the sea; they gather the richness of phenomenal presence into a 'phenomenology' " (56). The powerful Hölderlinian image is formative for the spiritual imagination of India as well. Surging through the river bed carved by karma over numberless kalpas, countless lifetimes, jīva at last empties into the boundless sea of Brahman, there to relinquish its illusory identity, there, at last, to "die" to the illusion of a separate individuality, a private ego. This expression of *Todeslust*, however elevated, however rarified, cannot represent the spiritual aspiration of Buddhism any more than the "labors of unification" which pull back from chasm of dissolution. For we would reach at the end only a spurious "emptiness" without suchness. Neither the formation nor the disintegration of individuality are to be pursued as ends-in-themselves. If existence and nonexistence languish, in the last analysis, for want of application, the craving that pursues them is a futile passion. We find, in the Buddhist tradition, a movement of suspension—non-attachment (*vairāgya*)—which is not, like the Husserlian epochē, a strategy or methodological ploy. It is not that, for the purpose of disclosing the domain of the phenomenal, we willingly forego the privilege of forming judgments concerning the existence and nonexistence of things—judgments which, in the nonphilosophical mode, we might naturally take to be true. The Buddhist epochē begins not with an artifice, but with a vision. It is not that, in a nonphilosophical context, we might naturally and reasonably apply the categories of existence and nonexistence, but that to do so is always unwarranted, always deluded, always a lapse into the somnambulism of *avidyā*. To take up the Buddhist epochē is not to *pretend* that things neither exist nor fail to exist, but rather to *see* that this is the case.

What remains unshaken by the Husserlian epoche, despite the voluntary relinquishment of prephenomenological judgments of existence, is the manifest *presence* of the things before us—the special object of *kama-taṇhā*. And we know that within the phenomenal domain opened up by the Husserlian epochē, existence and nonexistence break out once again. We may withhold our prior assumptions regarding the existence of this coffee mug. But whether the mug exists or not, it clearly *appears* to exist. The difference between "The mug exists" and "*It appears that* the mug exists" is, of course, the phenomenological appearance operator: "*It appears that* . . ." The embedded existential judgment remains the same. Presence, thus phenomenologically "reduced," has not somehow been sterilized of the virus of existence, but is its very breeding culture. Presence is overlaid with positive and negative significance, inducing modalities of desire and aversion, thus giving rise to the second-level desires for continuance and discontinuance of presence (existence and nonexistence), and ultimately motivating, through a species of theoretical wish fulfillment, the twin delusions of eternalism (endless continuation) and annihilationism (endless discontinuation). Presence is thus the matrix of delusion. Assuming annihilationism, nothing could arise. Assuming eternalism, nothing could pass away. The Buddhist insistence upon the radical impermanence (*anityā*) of all phenomena is thus more than a casual observation. It is an antidote. The epigrammatic pronouncement of Heraclitus that all things flow (*panta rhei*) subverts at a single stroke both eternalism and annihilation. Moreover, radical impermanence, disrupts even the passing continuity and discontinuity of presence. Presence becomes evanescent, evaporating simultaneously with its arising. Discontinuity—illustrated by a staccato sequence of disconnected pulses of presence—would, without retentive and protentive vectors of continuance, give no sense of flux, thus lapsing, impossibly, into eternalism. "[T]he world 'becomes' continually—it 'is' nothing" (Streng 1967, 37). Presence, conceived as static and unambiguous identity, conceived, that is, as the Sartrean in-itself, cannot withstand the insight of impermanence.

If emptiness—not simply the absence of presence, but, as we have seen, the absence *of absence* as well—is the abyss into which the regressive analysis plummets, then suchness (*tathatā*) is, conversely, the determinate evidence, the givenness of things *just as they are*, furnished by the progressive analysis. It is true that the existence of A resides in its conditions, $B_1, B_2, \ldots$, and that A, universally distributed, is nothing over and beyond these conditions. But inversely, it is also true that these conditions obtain. Self-existence aside, *A* is undeniably *manifest*. Buddhist ontology is an (anti-)ontology of emptiness. Buddhist phenomenology is a phenomenology of suchness. And to invoke once again a dark saying of the obscure Heraclitus, the way up is the way down. Historically, we find the dynamic of Mādhyamika dialectic wedded to the Yogācāra insistence upon meditative experience of *śūnyatā*. Indeed, as Sangharakshita maintains, wisdom (*bodhi*) "does not consist in the knowledge of, or union with, an Absolute, but in an understanding of, and a penetration into, the real nature of phenomena" (108). The thicket of complexly rooted and entangled contentions which have, through centuries of formulation, refinement and systematization, come to comprise the doctrinal body of Buddhism—the Four Noble Truths, the Twelvefold Chain, the Three Marks, and profusely more—represent the deliverances of Buddhist phenomenology, the Buddhist interrogation of the evanescent phenomena of our phenomenal world (*samsāra*). They represent the salvific saliencies intrinsic to phenomenal experience itself, the world-ensconced truths (*samvṛti*) discernible within a world-whole (*sam-*) imbued with lambent vicissitude (*vṛti*). The "higher truth"—though not a formulaic generality lodged at the pinnacle of abstractive ascent—the supreme (*pārama*) fruit (*artha*) of insight (*pramārtha*), is the realization of emptiness experienced when "the peace and silence of the Himalayas fill your whole being" (Sekida 1992, 219). At the palpating heart of the perfection of wisdom (*prajñāpāramitā*) lies the gem-like intuition of the *Heart Sūtra* that "[f]orm is emptiness; emptiness is form. Emptiness is not other than form; form is not other than emptiness" (Lopez 1988, 19). *Pace* Rorty, this intuition has nothing to do "familiarity with a language-game . . ." (1979, 35). It is a nonconceptual, unmediated openness. "Form," abbreviating the standard litany of skandhas, refers to manifest phenomena—manifest, but not the manifestations *of* a hidden reality. And we must not forget that "[t]he five Skandhas are not realities; the six objects of sense are by nature empty" (Suzuki 1981, 35). Devoid of own-being, thus devoid also of *ātman* (here, substantiality), holding nothing back, concealing nothing, occluding nothing, standing for nothing, pure show, manifest form is "not other" than emptiness, as the way up is "not other" than the way down. As Lopez sagely observes, "[t]here is a critical difference between form being empty and form being emptiness . . ." (58). Emptiness, the great abyss which makes possible the endless pouring of phenomena into their conditions, is not, of course, a "thing." Emptiness, absolute no/thingness, is not, then, an Atlas groaning under the weight of the world. While it conditions, it does not *ground*. "[A]n object of perception is swallowed up by the conditions which govern its presentation, and cannot be separated from them" (Conze 1994, 145). Setting aside intermediate approximations, phenomena release themselves into nothingness. Lucid perception of form is fringed with an awareness of horizonal release-ment into the void. And "to experience the world clearly, we must abandon existence to truth, truth to indication, indication to form, and form to void . . ." (Brown 1973, 101). For a thoroughly permeating intuition, form has abandoned itself completely into emptiness. Thus, "an object of perception is swallowed up by the conditions which govern its presentation, and can-not be separated from them" (Conze 145). Suzuki testifies that "[e]mpti-ness constantly falls within our reach; it is always with us and in us, and conditions all our knowledge, all our deeds, and is our life itself. It is only when we attempt to pick it up and hold it forth as something before our eyes that it eludes us, frustrates all our efforts, and vanishes like vapour. We are ever lured towards it, but it proves a will-o'-the-wisp" (1981, 60). Yet emptiness itself is empty. And though it might be the *final* condition of manifest presence—"final" in the sense of an asymptotic terminus—still it is not ultimate. For nothingness in its turn pours itself out, drains itself of its own nothingness—in Heideggerian parlance, *das Nichts nichtet*—and emp-ties itself completely into each manifest phenomenon, so that an intuition of emptiness is always the perception of form. Were any given phenomenon to be accorded self-existence, the universal abolition of self-existence would itself be abolished. Thus, emptiness is indebted to each manifest form, and repays this debt with the absence of absence which we call "presence." Form empties into emptiness, and reciprocally, emptiness empties into form. Thus, "[a] two-level world (of time and eternity) [is] dissolved within the dynamics of emptying—the emptying activity of highest truth" (Streng 1967, 38). The cyclical dynamic of emptying is elegantly expressed in Levin's words:

> Depicted in its archetypal form, i.e., as a circle, the hermeneutical gesture . . . is, of course, a welcoming, gathering into a whole; but the whole it makes is open, not totalized. . . . As a gathering which encircles, the hermeneutical gesture inevitably alludes to a center, something precious and worthy of protection. But the center is only *evoked* by the encircling: the gesture makes no move to point to it *directly* . . . there is 'nothing' in this center—nothing at all. In the center of the hermeneutical circle, 'there is' only emptiness, the presencing of an absence, the absencing of a presence. No origin. No goal . . . nothing is there to be grasped, nothing to be posited, nothing to be possessed, nothing reached. (1985, 164–5)

Every event of reciprocity, coconstitution, mutuality, every circuit of depen-dence—the interdependence of suchness and emptiness being the pertinent

instance—embraces at its heart a nothingness. We have called this nonorig-
inating, unattainable centrality "absolute" nothingness—that into which
the plenary and the vacuous equally dis/solve, the solution or re/solution of
all quandary. But while it illustrates the "operation of dissolving (*luo*)," its
work is not, *contra* Agamben, that of leading the relative phenomenon "to
its own **se*, to *suus* as to *solus*, dissolving it—*absolving it*—of every tie or alterity" (Agamben 1991, 92). Agamben claims that

> To think the Absolute signifies, thus, to think that which,
> through a process of "absolution," has been led back to its own-
> most property, to itself, to its own *solitude*, as to its own *custom*. For
> this reason, the Absolute always implies a voyage, an abandonment
> of the originary place, an alienation and a being-out-side. If the
> Absolute is the supreme idea of philosophy, then philosophy is
> truly, in the words of Novalis, nostalgia (*Heimweh*); that is, the
> "desire to be at home everywhere" . . . (92)

Caputo thus queries "how can you have an absolute relation to an absolute?
Would not the very relation and correlation dissolve the absoluteness. How
could anything be cor-related to what is ab-swallowtail Other, since the absolute absolves itself of all relation and correlation?" (1993, 80). But far
from the anchor which tethers the world-ship, absolute nothingness is
rather the boundless sea upon which we find ourselves adrift. It is delusion
to dream of the security of the home port. Absolute nothingness is absolute
homelessness. Yet we must recognize that even the interior nothingness
which centers reciprocal dependence, even "absolute" nothingness, is ontologically relative. As Streng explains, " 'emptiness' is represented neither by
the center (from which all points on the circumference radiate) nor by the
points at the end of the radius. Nor is it even the relationship between the
center and the circumference; but it is the recognition that 'center,' 'circumference,' and 'radius' are mutually interdependent 'things' which have no reality in themselves—only in dependence on other factors" (167). Emptiness
is always the "between." If the mind takes up residence in *any* relative absence, even the most abstract, the most nebulous, it forfeits the *Zwischen*.
But to lodge in the "between" as if there, at last, we had found the rock of
salvation is no longer to be "in between." In the words of Ryoho (1305–84
C.E.), "enlightenment and illusion are one. Do away with both, but don't
remain 'in between' either" (cf. Stryk and Takash 1963, 63–4). And in this
sense, authentic enlightenment occurs when consciousness neither bows to
pratītya-samutpāda, as if one's thoughts and perceptions were thus conditioned by extraneous conditions, nor rises above the law, observing it from
an aerial vantage point (*pensée de survol*) as an objectual theme of contem-

plation and point of attachment, but rather realizes, and thus *becomes*, the principle itself. In Hyakujo's pronouncement, "[t]he enlightened man is one with the law of causation" (Reps 1989, 91). Magliola tells us that "the authentic experience of *sunyata* runs a sort of Maoist 'continuing revolution' against focus!" (1986, 104), and as such is a "soteriological therapy, not an ultimate truth or ontological category" (Coward 1990, 145). "In Zen," as Herrigel remarks, "human existence as such is 'ek-static' and 'ek-centric', whether we are aware of it or not" (1960, 8). Or as Streng puts it, "*śūnyatā* is both relatedness and emptiness; it stands 'between' the absolute and the conditioned phenomena" (1967, 167). Like the Derridian *différance*, emptiness "erases its essentialization or phenomenologization" (Gasché 1988, 51). In its impish elusiveness, it beckons at the corner of the eye. But when one turns toward it—the chronic comportment of intentional consciousness—it has vanished. This is not to deny the Buddha's testimony that "[t]here is an Unborn, Unbecome, Unmade, Uncompounded; for if there were not this Unborn, Unbecome, Unmade, Uncompounded, there would be apparent . . . no escape from this here that is born, become, made and compounded" (cf. Conze 1978, 76). But this must not be conceived as an impermeable, impenetrable, indivisible absolute plenum of being, an "atom" in its original acceptation, or as a primal, irrelative, and, in Agamben's sense, "absolute," vacuity. We must not relapse into the prejudice which lulls "most Western philosophies" into representing "the 'uncombined' as equivalent to 'simple' . . ." (Streng, 37). Emptiness, no less than *différance*, "is older than Being itself," and "still more unthought than the difference between Being and beings" (Derrida 1982, 67). Like *différance*, *śūnyatā* "is not a source, it is not an origin. And that proposition follows, at the least, from this one: there simply is no simple. One could soon show that the concept of origin never operates without that of simplicity" (Brogan 1988, 85). The Uncombined is rather infinitely permeable, infinitely penetrable, infinitely divisible, and free from combination exactly because there is, within it, no/thing. It is pure "between." We would have no brief against Agamben's conception of the absolute were this medium of dis/solution considered as the authentic *suus*, the genuine *solus*, of each phenomenon, if it were recognized that "[p]ure solitude is absolute nonsolitude . . ." (Brogan, 85), if each phenomenon were to find it/self realized in selflessness, and if absolution were not the abnegation "of every tie or alterity," every specific modality of betweenness, but the realization of absolute relativity whereby the figural thing is resolved into horizonal betweenness. What Merleau-Ponty says of the unconscious, we must say of the realization of emptiness: "This unconscious is to be sought not at the bottom of ourselves, behind the back of our 'consciousness,' but in front of us, as articulations of our field. It is 'unconscious' by the fact that it is not an *object*, but it is that through which objects are possible . . . It is between them as the interval of the trees between the trees, or as their common level" (1969, 180). This extraordinary depiction of the unconscious is even more remarkable in conjunction with Merleau-Ponty's parallel depiction of reality. Both receive exactly the same characterization. Reality is not the screen upon which our views of things are projected, nor is it the views themselves. Rather, "the reality is their common inner framework (*membrure*), their nucleus, and not something *behind them*: behind them, there are only other "views" still conceived according to the in itself-projection schema. The real is *between them*, this side of them" (226). Like Merleau-Ponty, Buddhism finds no use for the preposition, "behind." *Behind* phenomena there is nothing—not even *nothing*. There is no sub/stance. There is only the abyss which gapes *between* the "trees" of our experience, *between* the constituents of the trees, and *between* the constituents of these constituents, until all is swallowed up and lost, until the authenticity of all is rediscovered in its utter relinquishment of self.

"Emptiness," as Nāgārjuna observes, is simply an alternative expression for "whatever is dependently co-arisen" (1995, 24:18–20, 69). The Buddhist *archē*, the *principium*—not oldest or first in the order of the later or the derivative, but rather transordinal—is the non-originary "principle" of *pratītya-samutpāda*. *Pāda*, cognate of the Latin *ped*, ancestral to our "pedal," "pedestal," "pedestrian," enacts the primal comportment of the foot: stepping, standing, arising (*utpāda*). But this standing is not the planting of the feet upon terra firma, the gesture of belligerent self-assertion, the vertical posture of solitary, isolated rectitude in contrast with the horizontal plane stretching beyond, the event of standing out or becoming figural. It is, rather, a *standing-together* (*samutpāda*). That no one stands alone is not a matter of courtesy or political etiquette, nor of frailty or infirmity, but of ontological dependence (*pratītya*). Each thing depends, for the possibility of its "arising," its coming-to-be, upon innumerable others. "Not one thing exists" (*wu i wu*; literally: [There is] not one thing). Each owes its being to all others, and, as we have seen, this ontological debt is stamped *paid*. For the existence of each resides in the other. No matter how powerful a thing is, its power is deferred to others; no matter how good, its goodness resides in others; no matter how intelligent, its intelligence is relinquished to others; no matter sacred or holy, its sacredness, its holiness, is absorbed in others. There is, then, a power, a goodness, an intelligence, a sacredness to the "originating dependently" which necessarily exceeds that which is manifest in any particular thing. Modifying the Anselmian formula, emptiness is that than which no[*thing*] greater can be conceived.

Emptiness is not, however, to be conceived as God. It is not an *ens realissimum*—in Nietzsche's words, "[t]hat which is last, thinnest, and emptiest . . ." (1968, 37)—but rather, the condition for the reality of any *ens*; it is not personal, but the condition for the flourishing of personality; it is not a creator, but the condition for the arising of all things. In the original discussion of Derrida's paper on *différance*, Brice Parain inferred concerning this odd nonconcept, nonword, that since "it is the source of everything and one cannot know it," it must therefore be "the God of negative theology . . ." (Brogan 1988, 84). Derrida's response is intriguing: "It is and it is not. . . . It is above all not . . ." (84). We have here a mirror of the analogous Buddhist response. Whatever temptations there may be to succumb to this identification ("It is . . .")—the familiar evasion of categorial and ontic attribution, for example—"it is above all not." No conception of divinity, no matter how rarefied, no matter how thoroughly purged of anthropocentrism, no matter how completely fumigated of the conceit of personality and creativity, no matter how self-consciously paradoxical, can enjoy adequation with emptiness. For "the 'purity' of sunyata is not purity and void considered as an object of contemplation, but a non-seeing, a noncontemplation, in which precisely it is realized that the 'mirror' or the original mind (of prajna and emptiness) is actually a nonmirror, and 'no-mind' . . ." (Merton 1967, 32). Concepts apply only (and at best) to *things*—"things," perhaps, as large as the *universe*, as vast as *infinity*, as nebulous as *indeterminacy*, or as rarified as *being*—but emptiness is not a thing, even a supreme thing. Like *différance*, emptiness is not a concept. In Nāgārjuna's words:

> The victorious ones have said
> That emptiness is the relinquishing of all views,
> For whomever emptiness is a view,
> That one will accomplish nothing   (1995, 13:8, 36).

To conscript Dufrenne's words for our own purpose, the Sartrean *apeiron* is, as we have seen, "not the negation of God, but a negative God (*un Dieu en négatif*)" (1973, 19–20). An ontology, like that of Sartre, ruled by binary exclusiveness must abnegate the conjunctive attribution of opposites: Nothing, for Sartre, can be *both* in-itself *and* for-itself. This "ideal synthesis," the systemic contoured absence of God, "is always indicated and always impossible" (1971, 792). It may be that "contrast elicits depth" (Whitehead 1978, 114). But inasmuch as binary differentiation requires a field, a ground, the "missing God" makes ineliminable reference to that which is deeper than contrast—the *ni-en-soi-ni-pour-soi*—and the God banished by binary exclusiveness is once again permitted by the very condition of binary exclusiveness. The ontology of emptiness is not in this way betrayed. To be sure, emptiness, like a universal solvent, exhibits its "dis-integrating character . . . toward all beings" (Streng 1967, 168), and in this sense welcomes them into itself. Emptiness is thus hospitable even to a purported supreme being, the greatest, mightiest, most venerable "Thing" of them all—but only at the cost of self-existence. Deity, if it exists, must, with all other beings, forsake its pretense to be a foundation unto itself. From the Buddhist point of view, the Sartrean category of the in-itself is not merely vacuous. The category is neither populated nor evacuated. It is incoherent. There is no genuine categorial distinction to be made. And if not, there is no binary exclusion at play. It is not that the in-itself-for-itself fails to exist, or even fails to exist out of systemic necessity. As an amalgam with the incoherent, it is simply unthinkable. Everything, every *thing*—gods and mortals included—bows to the principle of *pratītya-samutpāda*. Buddhism does not, then, permit in the night the God which it banished by day. The God of Sartre's theological imagination, the conscious source of itself which is given to pulling itself up into existence by it own bootstraps, is not unwelcome, not ostracized from our philosophical company. It is simply nonsense. Even emptiness—"itself" empty of itself—is radically indebted to each particular phenomenon. Even the absolute nothingness embraced within the reciprocal dependence of form and emptiness is devoid of "own-being."

    Though nothing prohibits a nontheistic metaphysic, a metaphysical vision without God seems somehow deprived, deficient, as if failing to conform to a prototype in which all of its resources are maximally utilized. A rudimentary metaphysic arises at the conjuncture of two conditions: first, there must be a framework of binary conceptual opposition; and second, one of the terms of that opposition, or a suite of such terms, must be elevated to a preeminent ontological or originary status. Buddhism is not, in this sense, a metaphysical view. Though admitting a purely local and circumscribed (intra-samsaric) sense of opposition, this opposition vanishes in the global appreciation like the obverse and reverse sides of the möbius strip. The Buddhist path begins and ends with *śila*—narrowly, morality, but in a more generous sense, attunement of our intentions to the good. But just as a line traced along a *single* side of the möbius strip will rejoin itself without shifting sides, though paradoxically appearing on "both" sides, the Buddhist wayfarer, while cleaving to the good, will traverse its opposite without wavering from the path. In this vein, Hui-hai can say that "[u]ltimate realization is beyond realization and non-realization. . . . Ultimate voidness is beyond voidness and non-voidness" (Blofeld 1972, 82). And in words that evoke the circuit of relinquishment of which we have spoken, the Buddha is represented as saying: "Beings, beings, O Subhūti, as no-beings have they been taught by the Tathāgata. Therefore they are called 'beings' " (Conze 1978, 101-2). Binary polarities have their proper work in our ordinary, "local," transactions. They have no universal utility whatsoever, and cannot, then, serve our understanding of reality writ large. Coward expresses the Derridian complaint that

> These opposites . . . have not been seen as equal entities. The second term is always put in the position of being a fallen or corrupted version of the first. Thus evil is the lack of good, absence is the lack of presence, error is a distortion of truth, and difference is an obstruction of identity. The two terms are not held in an opposing tension but are placed in a hierarchical order that gives the first term priority both in time and quality. (1990, 52–3)

The promotion of one pole to "cosmic" significance—ontological or originary priority—to the exclusion of its opposite is thus impossible. And Buddhism has no pretense to "metaphysical" profundity. "Metaphysical relations presuppose that there are already fixed entities and concepts which are then related. . . . The relational character of *différance* must be of another sort" (Brogan 1988, 32). And concordantly, Buddhism finds no place for the "fixed."

To say that no *thing* is greater than emptiness is not, of course, to say that emptiness is of unsurpassable greatness. All that a thing is—its being, its goodness, its power, its intelligence, its sacredness—is owed to its conditions, and these conditions efface themselves, in turn, in favor of theirs. "Emptiness" is the name for the possibility of this endless reversion and for the asymptotic resolution/dissolution toward which it unfolds. Any merit, any distinction, any excellence the thing might seem to possess, is due finally, to, emptiness. But as the rain falls upon the just and the unjust alike, so emptiness conditions not only the bright and the good, but also the demonic, the wicked, the destructive, the heinous. Evil, no less than good, owes its very possibility to *śūnyatā*. And if emptiness were to become, in an unproblematic sense, quite literally *good* in inheriting the goodness of what it conditions, it must also, and then inconsistently, become *evil*. The unintelligibility of applying this local incoherence to the global signals that emptiness cannot be conceived as *good* in the contrastive sense. To echo Hui-hai, ultimate goodness is beyond goodness and nongoodness.

"Beyond" does not, however, signal the Hegelian *Aufhebung*. In a passage of unusual lucidity, Derrida confesses that "if there were a definition of *différance*, it would be precisely the limit, the interruption, the destruction of the Hegelian *relève wherever* it operates" (1972, 40–2). Or as Caputo remarks, "[t]he strategy behind *différance* is to see to it that no thesis or *position* ever gets firmly enough into position to begin its course of opposition and composition. No dialectical relief is ever attained" (1993, 64). If "[t]he dialectic become *thesis*" is, in Merleau-Ponty's trenchant image, "embalmed"

(1969, 175), then a "good dialectic" must be mindful of the fact that "every *thesis* is an idealization, that Being is not made up of idealizations or of things said, as the old logic believed, but of bound wholes where significa- tion never is except in tendency, where the inertia of the content never per- mits the defining of one term as positive, another term as negative, and still less a third term as absolute suppression of the negative by itself" (94). Hegelian synthesis exemplifies a more advanced metaphysical schema in which binary exclusiveness is preserved (if also modified), but promotion to originary status, the "princely" position of the *principium*, the August aura of the *archē*, is conjoint. For Buddhism, there is no global unity of oppo- sites, since opposition vanishes in the global vision. If Sartre's ontology rep- resents the forced choice (either/or), and Hegel's represents conjunctive disparity (both/and), the Buddhist (anti-)ontology is, in Adorno's idiom, a "negative dialectic": a "neither/nor."

Bearing in mind the intimate embrace of identity in its most radical form (that of omni-qualitative fusion) and the Sartrean in-itself, Adorno's portrayal of the dialectic is especially poignant: "Objectively, dialectics means to break the compulsion to achieve identity, and to break it by means of the energy stored up in that compulsion and congealed in its objectifica- tions" (1973, 157). The pulverization of the in-itself requires, then, more than the ghostly antics of cerebral thought, though also less than the mus- cular application of hammer to anvil. If, as Adorno discerns, "the appear- ance of identity is inherent in thought itself, in its pure form. To think is to identify" (5); indeed, if "[w]e can see through the identity principle, but we cannot think without identifying" (149), then although the Sartrean phe- nomenological ontology is entirely reasonable in postulating the in-itself as a condition of our *thinking* about the deliverances of phenomenological in- vestigation, this very condition must be *seen through*. And in light of this "seeing-through"—the Buddhist *pra/jñā*—reasonability is transformed into absurdity.

In Corless's fortuitous phrase, emptiness is parsed as "analytic trans- parency." There is a paradox of considerable urgency that attends the "loos- ening up" (*ana-lysis*) whereby the parts and distinguishable features of a complex whole are brought to thematic givenness and whereby the whole *as such* thereby recedes into the experiential background. Subjecting Eddington's table to physical analysis, for example, we begin with the whole and end with a vespiary of particles. Or in Eddington's words, "[t]he plank has no solidity of substance. To step on it is like stepping on a swarm of flies. . . . My scientific table is mostly"—we would say: entirely—"empti- ness" (1935, 6). If our intention is to effect an analysis *of the (phenomenal) table*, we expect at the end what we posited at the beginning: namely, the phenomenal table. Instead, contrary to expectation, we find the "scientific table"—a phrase which clearly marks a concession to ordinary discourse. The scientific table is a nebula of micro-interactions, not a *table* in any humanly recognizable sense. The phenomenal table has disappeared, has become thoroughly transparent, upon analysis. For some philosophers, this apparent loss of the *analysandum* is troubling. For the Buddhist, it is lucid truth. Things disappear upon analysis because, once again, "[t]here absolutely are no things" (Burtt 1955, 170). Philosophers have, however, sought to retrieve the original whole within the rattling assemblage of dissevered parts. And there is an unobjectionable approach to this end. With exposure, the trees "come out," and the forest recedes. Sartrean decompression is an unquestionable phenomenon of our experience. But then decompression, the dynamic of saliency, is not analysis.

Or to take a different, but parallel example, one which represents the extraordinary contribution of Nāgārjuna, the definition, understood as an analysis of meaning, effects an entirely congruent transparentization of its *definiendum*. If "triangle" is defined as a plane, closed and rectilinear figure with three sides and three interior angles the sum of which is 180 degrees, we search in vain among its stock of essentials for triangularity. Two-dimensionality, rectilinearity, three-sidedness, and the like are each flatly distinct from triangularity. Triangularity is remainderlessly defined in terms of concepts which are clearly different from triangularity; its "identity" dissolves into difference. For "identity can never be anything other than the suppression of difference" (Dews 1988, 170). Triangularity "itself" has vanished in its definition. Or rather, its authentic selflessness (*anātman*) has come to light. Definition is not tautology, but rather, heterology. "[I]t does not indulge itself in the thought of a *to autos*, of something Self-same undergirding or overseeing what is happening" (Caputo 1993, 224). Adorno claims that "[a]ny definition is identification" (1973, 149). And if so, triangularity would be *identical* with a certain reserve of intrinsic attributes. Enigmatically, however, definitional "identity" siphons off all vestiges of a self/same *definiendum*. Definitional identity is, then, the repudiation of identity: not a *dis-*(or *dys-*)identification which leaves both terms intact, but the vaporization of an inalienable term which abnegates the ostensible relationship between "them." Remarkably, however, in the very disappearance of the "term" subject to definition, there is light. Dis/appearance is not, then, the extinguishing of the illumination of presence. On the contrary, presence is gross darkness. The relinquishment of presence—analytic transparency—is itself the effulgence of significance. Paradoxically, definition illuminates with meaning exactly by disrupting our fixation upon an ostensible locus of meaningfulness. Here, again, we have an analogous "Maoist

revolution." Meaningfulness is possible only to the extent that figural attachment is abandoned.

Sealed off from the world, incapable of immediate disclosure, a dictionary is always the site of potential circularity. We look up "existence" and
find it defined in terms of *being*; we look up "being" only to be restored to
the definition of *existence*. Not uncommonly, such loops and circuits are
both more extensive and more complex. '*A*' may receive the definition:
'... *B* ...'; '*B*' may receive the definition: '... *C* ...;' and thus forward.
Still, if, along the way, some '*Z*' receives the definition: '... *A* ...;' we
abandon hope of final intelligibility. Attempts to remedy the ailment of lexical circularity have included the desperate strategy of postulating a defini-
tive Z-level of simple, indefinable and intrinsically intelligible terms: the
ultimate building-blocks of our more complex forms of conceptuality. But
indefinability and intelligibility are, finally, incompatible. Meaning is possible *only* through the volatilization of typical of definition. Perhaps, indeed,
meaning *is* this volatilization. It is not simply that, purportedly simple and
indefinable terms are haunted by the specter of possible incomprehension,
but rather that incomprehension is constitutive of a term's reputed atomic-
ity, its ostensible inability to resolve itself into an aggregation of disparate
concepts. Moreover, comprehension is in no way served by repetition—the
only possible "definition" of an atomic concept. Perhaps, in some attenuated sense, "cat" means *cat*. But if, in the beginning our incomprehension is
genuine, to be offered the very same term in response to our solicitation of
meaning is to be left entirely in the dark. Paradoxically, then, "cat" cannot
mean cat at all.

Confining ourselves purely to the lexical domain, we have seen that
loops and atoms are incapable of rendering significance. What remains is
the infinite succession: '*A*' defined (in part) in terms of '*B*'; '*B*,' in terms of
'*C*'; '*C*' in terms of '*D*'; and thus without end. Each term in the chain is definitionally volatilized without circularity and without repetition. Each is
therefore meaningful. Of course, no physical dictionary, no circumscribed
aggregation of marks, could offer itself to such endless inscription. But perhaps intelligibility exceeds its inscription. We find here, in the conceptual
realm, a mirror-image of the infinite decomposability of the phenomenal. If
each term is meaningful, it is also transparent to definitional analysis. And
the interminable regression thus born becomes a field of emptiness. There
are, then, no "terms" to be defined.

Or perhaps, on the other hand, conceptuality does not exceed inscription. But perhaps, also, our dictionaries do no have to be so voluminous
after all. This would be the case if, contrary to the familiar Derridian dictum—*il n'y a pas de hors-texte* ["There is nothing outside of the text, or liter-

ally, there is no outside-of-the-text"] (cf. Norris 1982, 41)—there actually *were* an *hors-texte*, and if, moreover, significance consisted, not in such endless deferral, but in the word's somehow opening out upon, effacing itself before, the phenomenal. After all, "philosophy is not a lexicon . . . it does not seek a verbal substitute for the world we see, it does not transform it into something said . . ." (1969, 4). "Cat," then, would mean the extraconceptual, extralinguistic *cat*. The term would empty itself into the purportedly ontic (or at least phenomenal) domain. Of course, in this sense, meaning—not given by verbal definition—by-passes the dictionary entirely. Buddhism discloses "the fact that the terms of ordinary language do not express the real facts of existence" (Thomas 1953, 218). We have no need to deny a language-external reality. As Caputo insists,

> There is certainly something outside the text. . . . There must be, otherwise textuality would be a closed system, an internally coherent system, uninterrupted by anything else, anything *alter*—which would be to embrace everything that deconstruction resists. . . . *Différance* does not lock us up inside anything. On the contrary, *différance* is a doorway, a threshold (*limen*), a door through which everything outgoing (reference, messages sent, etc.) and incoming (messages received, perceptions, etc.) must pass. A threshold supposes both an inside and an outside. (Caputo 1993, 76)

We may, of course, wonder how we come to theorize about whatever internal or external alliance might bridge text and *hors-texte*, since our speculations regarding this affiliation constitute yet another text. But we should recall that *"the limit of language always falls within language; it is always already contained within as a negative"* (Agamben 1991, 17). What Merleau-Ponty says of the philosophy of reflection can be immediately transposed as a critique of the closure of textuality upon itself: "Once one is settled in it, reflection is an inexpugnable philosophical position, every obstacle, every resistance to its exercise being from the first treated not as an adversity of the things but as a simple state of non-thought, a gap in the continuous fabric of the acts of thought, which is inexplicable, but about which there is nothing to say since it is literally *nothing*" (1969, 44). Moreover, inasmuch as indicative meaning presumes the existence of its locus, the infinite porosity of the phenomenal deprives "cat" of significance. Meaning is inescapably a form of self-emptying—whether the recipient of this endowment is conceptual or phenomenal. We escape the emptiness of conceptual meaning only at the peril of falling into phenomenal emptiness. Fleeing phenomenal emptiness, we are caught in a ceaseless pattern of reverberation because we have not yet learned to float. Learning finally, to release ourselves confidently and joyously to *śūnyatā*, we enter into anechoic stillness. Meaning is everywhere, but nothing—no/thing—"means." All the bubbles which we took to shelter within themselves the delicate quintessence of significance have burst, and this fragrance imbues reality without inhering in a single thing.

Chapter 6

Making Nothing of Something

Nihilation—the repudiation of coincidence, the opening of an "impalpable fissure" in being (Sartre 1971, 124) which renders the "total plenitude," the "perfect equivalence of content to container" (120), porous and lacunary— is, to risk indelicacy, an ontological fantasy. As Flynn confirms, it is "revealed to consciousness *only* in the imagining act" (Flynn 1980, 106). Not only is imagination "an essential and transcendental condition of consciousness" (Sartre 1991, 273), specifically, of our consciousness (of) nihilation, but in its production of "the objects of negation, and of privation" (Flynn, 106–7), imagination shows itself to *be* nihilation. And if "[t]o imagine is simultaneously to produce an imaginary object and to make oneself imaginary (*s'imaginariser*) . . ." (Sartre 1971–72, 912n; Flynn, 108), then not only are nihilation and the *négatités* which arise from it fabulated, but also we who nihilate. And in postulating that "[f]or a consciousness to be able to imagine it must be able to escape from the world by its very nature, it must be able by its own efforts to withdraw from the world" (1991, 267), Sartre sets himself up for Merleau-Ponty's stinging comment that he seems to have "deliberately taken up a position in the realm of the imaginary" (1955, 262), and that he had decided to "enclose himself in words" (270). All the difference, all the articulation and salience, all the relation and structure, all the richness and diversity of our world are—incredibly—purely "imaginary." We do not *discover* the fissures, the gaps, the disparities, the distances, the absences which engender the extraordinary variegation of experienced reality, we *create* them—by imagining them. Or rather, we *do* encounter objective nothingness, en counter it as already eating away at the solidity of being—nihilation is an *ontological* act—but only *after* we ourselves have given birth to it. Sartre teeters unsteadily on the brink of idealism, and would no doubt succumb were it not for his "realism" with respect to the in-itself: the "screen" upon which our imaginative projections play. Sartre confesses a psychological penchant for realism "out of a taste for feeling the resistance of things, but most of all in order to accord to everything I saw its character of unconditional absolute: I could enjoy a landscape or sky only if I thought it was absolutely as I saw it" (1984, 83). And he can be assured of this, since the "as" is controlled by nihilation.

The purported event of nihilation is the indispensable condition for the arising of self-consciousness in all of its Sartrean modalities: the (reflective) consciousness *of* consciousness; consciousness of the summation, the pattern or *Gestalt*, of acts, states and dispositional qualities (the ego) thematized in reflection; and the prereflective self-presence—consciousness (of) consciousness—which enforces, in the non-positional mode, a subtle, impalpable, but nonetheless perpetually suggested and "haunting" hiatus between consciousness and itself—the "self" that it *would* be, both in the sense that consciousness is informed with a certain *nisus* to be what it cannot be, and in the sense that, like the peril of the moth attracted by a flame, the realization of this "futile passion" would spell the annihilation of consciousness. "In Sartre, consciousness is continually being frustrated by being thrown outside of itself, for consciousness can never achieve happiness or repose in itself. Thus, a Sartrean consciousness is denied the absolute" (Silverman 1988a, 302).

Buddhism never denies the self—*as appearance*. It never needs to. Appearance is appearance. And a Buddhist phenomenology finds much in Sartre's description of the self to admire. But admiration is not adoration, and if "[o]ntology is the interrogative word of adoration in the ear of . . . the Abyss" (Burke 1990, 83), Sartre stops short of hurling the apparent self into the void which devours all things, but at the same time, allows all things blossom, to borrow Dōgen's poignant phrase, like "flowers of emptiness." In Bataille's exuberant vision, "everything in me gives itself to others" (1988, 129). And if the task of phenomenology is to trace the efflorescence of constituted objectivity to its rootedness in the dark, rich interiorized illumination of preobjective experience, we must unearth the roots. Or rather than expose the tender down-shoots to the harsh light of analytic day, we must appreciate, sensitize ourselves to, the dark/bright soil in which they are suspended. Sartre's arrested ontology sinks no deeper than the in-itself, the primordially structureless infrastructure of nihilation. But the taproot of the self draws its nourishment from the nurturant ground of emptiness.

If "[t]here is not the slightest emptiness in being, not the tiniest crack through which nothingness might slip in" (Sartre 1971, 121), being becomes a plenary atom (*atoma*), not only undivided, but, in principle, indivisible, and incapable of porosity, fissuring. It becomes "individual" (*in-divisum*), "like a seamless garment, with a stitch or mark on it, unmarked by any genus or species, any category or class (*glas*)" (Caputo 1993, 74), and this thus ineffable, marking "a breach in the surface of philosophy" (73). Philosophy is fractured by the infrangibility of being. The indivisibility/individuality of being is ruled by a principle for what falls outside principles, a covering law for what law cannot cover, for a kind of out-law" (73). Being cannot be cut, cracked or bored into. It is not, and cannot be, the site of a hole or interstice. In short, as we have seen, Sartre harbors a quasi-Parmenidean conception of being. Being is a block, a plenum, intractable in its refusal of intrusion. And we have no doubt how Nietzsche would regard this Sartrean conception: "Evil I call it, and misanthropic—all this teaching of the One and the Plenum and the Unmoved and the Sated and the Permanent" (1954, 2). Unlike the Parmenidean *estin*, however, being is the content, the contentment, not of reason (*noûs*) but of preconceptual intuition. For rationality, which could scale reality only by digging its toes into the crevasses, would only slide off the smooth and frictionless surface of the in-itself. This effectively disconnects the easily assumed connection between rationality and the real. There is nothing on the part of the real which could validate the frolic, let alone the imposition, of rational categoriality. Thus, the nothingness which seems to pock being and pry it open is better represented in Sartre's frequent image as a "shimmer" playing on the superficial exterior. "*Non-being exists only on the surface of being*" (1971, 49).

Nothingness is, however, enfolded within a very different, and incongruous, poetic: that of the Sartrean *apeiron*. If being can "disintegrate," "deteriorate," "decompress," then it embraces within itself its own potential disruption, and internal vacuity is a condition of its own degeneration into the for-itself. If being is ineluctably plenary, nothingness can only dance, slide, perhaps ski, on its slippery exterior (if, indeed, Parmenidean being can *have* an "exterior"). But if nothingness can fester at its heart, then being cannot be Parmendean; and if being is, indeed, "opaque to itself precisely because it is filled with itself" (1971, 28), if it is "full positivity" (56), if "no more total plenitude can be imagined" (120), then, incongruously, it cannot fail to be Parmenidean. And we are left to wonder which is Sartre's true mentor: Parmenides or Anaximander? Is it *estin* or *apeiron* which models Sartrean being? The assumption of divisibility, disjunction, *differ[e]nce*—different, in this connection, from *differ[a]nce*—is that nonbeing, envisioned as an unstable and formless fluency which fills up the chasm, the interstice, thus opened up, indeed, *is*. And while Sartre will accept a nothingness which "is" exactly where somethingness is not, Parmenides will not countenance this admission. While both maintain remarkably similar *conceptions* of non-being, *nothingness* is, for Sartre, and is not, for Parmenides, instanced within the ontological catalogue. And if, as Sartre believes, being and nothingness exclude each other (or if, following Parmenides, they *would* exclude each other if, counterfactually, nonbeing had being), if they are genuine contradictories, then we cannot expect to find nothingness at the heart, but only at the surface of being. On the other hand, if 'being' designates the Anaximandrian *apeiron*, the archetic matrix of the twin-born in-itself and for- itself, and is thus "deeper," more originary, than either, nothing prohibits the worm of nothingness from gnawing away at its vital tissue. The in-itself may be impenetrable (unfit for worms), but what is true of the in-itself may not hold true of the precorrelative source of this onto-logical disjunct. If decompression makes implicit reference to a point of singularity, a point of maximum compression, from which detail and structure are flung in centrifugal abandon, then is the "space," the emptiness or nothingness which separates detail from detail, already enfolded within the singularity? If so, then being, the flash-point of this detonation, is already— always already (Buddhism would say, *infinitely*)—porous, and nihilation does not institute, but at best merely magnifies, its porosity. And if not, then being already—always already—floats within a nothingness which is at least coeval, if not more ancient, than itself. In this latter case, we would inherit the discarded Heideggerian envisionment of "nothingness surrounding being on every side and at the same time expelled from being" (1971, 51). Nothingness would be "that by which the world receives its outlines as the world" (51). Either being falls short of "absolute plenitude and entire positivity" (48), or the for-itself fails to be a merely accidental and occasional upsurge. If "Nothingness lies coiled in the heart of being—like a worm" (56), being is not absolute plenitude. But being, it seems, is also a "worm": "Nothingness carries being in its heart" (52).

Sartre repudiates the Heideggerian proposal: "we must be careful never to posit nothingness as an original abyss from which being arose" (1971, 48). For "[i]f we remove from this original emptiness its characteristic of being empty *of this world* and of every whole taking the form of a world, as well as its characteristic of *before*, which presupposes an *after*, then the very negation disappears, giving way to a total indetermination which it would be impossible to conceive, even and especially as a nothingness" (49). For Sartre, a purported "nothingness" prior to being—both devoid of being and anterior (either chronologically or ontologically) to being—is no genuine *nothingness* at all. "[N]othingness is subsequent to being since it is being, first posited, then denied" (47). Indeed, "being has no need of nothingness in order to be conceived and . . . we can examine the idea of it exhaustively without finding there the least trace of nothingness" (49). (Would it stress politeness to inquire here about the "worm"?) Though Sartre often uses the term 'being' to designate what we have called the *apeiron*, there is neither being (in-itself) nor nothingness prior to decompression. But in any case, the assumption that nihilation requires a solid, plenary block of being on which to operate sits uneasily with the vision of nothing-ness wriggling at the core of being. Nihilation, as Sartre understands it, is otiose.

Sartre, we have seen, is a closet metaphysician, proposing, in the dusk of the mythological "as if," an account for the for-itself—a "why?"—which, in the noonday glare of his developed ontology, he posits as systemically impossible. In a subtle litany, intoned throughout the pages of *Being and Nothingness*, "everything happens as if": "Everything happens as if in order to free the affirmation *of* self from the heart of being, there is necessary a de-compression of being" (27–8). It is "as if" insensate being were capable of comporting itself in a purposive way, "as if" it were capable of acting "in order to . . . ," and again, "as if" this mindless plenum were somehow capa-ble of the instrumentality requisite to make sense of Sartre's pronounce-ment that "the in-itself can not found *itself* without introducing the *self* of a reflective, nihilating reference into the absolute identity of its being and consequently degenerating into *for-itself*" (133). We know, of course, that the in-itself is devoid of an "itself," let alone a self. "[I]t is actually impossi-ble to say of the in-itself that it is *itself*" (156). It has no self in itself. Nor is it "itself" a self. But though the in-itself may, indeed (following the Anaximandrean line) degenerate, it *itself* does not degenerate. Unlike Hege-lian being, it is not "in its very depths the origin of its own surpassing" (47), or its own degeneration. The in-itself has density, not the depth of agential interiority. And nothing within it could accommodate the suggestion of an "origin." It *itself* cannot found itself—because it has none.

And if (waiving away this fatuous irritation) the in-itself were to "intro-duce . . . a nihilating reference into the absolute identity of its being," we must query the precise moment of this "introduction." *Before* the upsurge of nothingness, the in-itself cannot *do* anything whatsoever. It cannot found, introduce, nihilate or degenerate. It is lifeless, mindless, insensate material-ity without volition, without purpose, and without agency. *After* nothing-ness arises, there is, in Sartre's scheme, a purposive agent. But its agency presupposes the event of nihilation. Nihilation occurs, then, *after* Par-menidean plenitude and *before* the Anaximandrean degeneration which is consciousness, and is thus incapable of operating upon a plenary in-itself and of founding the for-itself through such an operation.

There is, here, a mimetic transfer from Husserl: egological agency is borne up by the "grace," the preegological givenness, the always-already-ness, of a passive-synthetic dynamism. And much, also, as Heideg-gerian Dasein—the being-there, being-on-the-scene, which *is* the questioning re[veil]ation, the [dis]closure, of Being—is understood as the "lighting" (*Lichtung*) of the "clearing" (*Lichtung*) which could not have cleared itself, so, likewise, the for-itself could not have instituted its own precondition.

Nihilation could not have been performed by the in-itself. The in-itself is not a performer. Nor could it have been accomplished by the for-itself. For the for-itself always comes too late. The event of nihilation has always already occurred. So we are left with a mystery. Who done it?

The infamous Heideggerian reply, though it has not escaped derision, seems at first somewhat more cogent than Sartre's crypto-metaphysical insinuation: Nothingness itself "noths" (*das Nichts selbst nichtet*). If the function of *das Nichts* is that of universal negation, then (assuming that it *has* a *Selbst* or an "itself") it would negate itself. The thicket of nothingness would clear itself. And, in an intriguing (not to say cogent) logical transformation, being could be understood as the nothingness of nothingness: that is, somethingness. Of course, if nothingness is devoid of identity (an "itself") it could not "noth" *itself*. But if we could speak of nothingness *itself* as universal, exceptionless (and therefore, *self-*) negation, then the clearing would be inevitable, necessary, and we would have granted too much. For surely, the being of Dasein is "thrown," accidental, factical—not ontologically guaranteed. But admitting the contingency of Dasein, we must also admit a certain selectivity on the part of *das Nichts*. It could not always and inevitably "noth" itself. The "noth-ing" of nothing by nothing itself would be an occasional event either initiated out of its own agency or triggered by . . . what? Who done it? If *das Nichts* is an agent, it is suicidal (or at least self-destructive). For if somethingness really is the negation of negation, it is born through the self-annihilation of nothingness. But then nothingness belongs to the preconditions of Dasein. And if purposiveness—illustrated in Dasein's instrumental comportment with respect to the *Zuhanden*—is, indeed, uniquely intrinsic to Dasein, it cannot be exhibited by *das Nichts*. *Das Nichts* is not endowed with the selectivity of self-abnegation requisite to accommodate contingency. Nor can it "commit" ontological suicide (or anything else). Again, the mystery: Who done it? In a moment of ingenuousness, Heidegger confesses that "it is quite incomprehensible why entities are to be *uncovered*, why *truth* and *Dasein* must be" (1962, 271). There is, and can be, no answer to the question of who (or what) "done it." The answer is honest, and exhibits a rare humility in the face of the unknowable. And it is, as Caputo comments, precisely what is exacted by Heidegger's own commitments: "The question 'why?' already belongs to the horizon opened up by truth. The happening of truth, of uncovering, is the condition under which it is possible to ask 'why?' so that the 'why?' will never be able to circle back behind truth and find the condition under which truth is possible. Truth is the condition of the why; the why cannot find the condition of truth. Truth happens, without why, before why" (1993, 231). Paradoxically, although its occurrence bespeaks its "possibility," *a/letheia*, the unveiling of Being which is Dasein, is *impossible* (or im/possible) in view of its priority to explicability. Nothing makes it possible. It just "happens."

Phenomenology has accustomed us to probing for the tangled roots of the judicative, the theoretical, the explicative, in the mire of the sheer, factical "givenness" of prepredicative experience. Givenness is a "gift" without "why?," uncalled for, not donated in response to our solicitation. It is "grace," unearned, undeserved, unrequired, undemanded, and sometimes unwanted. This is a gift, moreover, which we cannot refuse, and which, at the same time, *we* cannot receive. For it is there for us before *we* are. Heidegger's speculation concerning the "noth-ing" of nothing is a surreptitious, or perhaps simply compulsive, attempt to "circle back" behind the intrusive givenness of truth, behind the clearing of the clearing, behind the removal of the veil which is Dasein, and find the condition for the occurrence of that which gives sense to the very notion of 'condition.' This is an example of the error exposed by Niu-T'ou Fa-Yung (594–657 C.E.) in his declamation that "[t]he teaching of the truth is not the Truth" (Chang 1971, 20). We must rather practice "forgetting" which means "not circling back, cutting no eagle circles in the sky, no recircling or recycling, but just forgetting, just forging ahead and forgetting" (Caputo 1993, 111). But we have arrested Sartre, red-handed, if not red-faced, groping behind the inexplicable upsurge of nihilation, in a very similar act of circling back. Foreswearing metaphysics in his official posture (an unavoidable discipline for one who seeks to plumb the depths of human experience—*as given*), Sartre takes secretive refuge in a certain mytho- poetic which insinuates what a more candid metaphysic might simply assert: the in-itself founds itself, nihilates itself, and degenerates, because it desires to affirm itself, to institute *self*. An unadorned assertion of this sort would assault the very conception of the in-itself. But Sartre assumes that the same assertion embedded in the context of "everything happens as if" could dwell among his systemic assumptions in perfect peace. We cannot, without contradiction, assert that the in-itself seeks to become for-itself. This, for Sartre, is impossible—*in principle*. But "everything happens *as if* the in-itself sought to become for-itself" could avert logical collision only if the "as if" deprived its imbedded assertion not only of truth but of possibility as well. For to assume even its possibility is to collide with its impossibility in principle. Though "[i]t seems impossible to get beyond the 'as it were' (*gleichsam*)" (Caputo 1993, 74), the "as it were," the "as if," must render its internal assertion impossible, and must, then, be read as affirming that "everything happens as if the impossible actually occurred," as if, that is, the impossible were possible. In an interview with Leo Fretz, Sartre confides that "[t]here should be an ontology—*which we cannot create*—wherein one can see how the in-itself has produced the for-itself . . ."

(Fretz 1980, 226; emphasis added). Inability, in this case, may simply be an index of the futility, perhaps the incoherence, of the attempt. But while I relish the paradoxical and the playful turn of phrase as much as anyone—only a Sartrean could read that the for-itself "is defined . . . as being what it is not and not being what it is" (1971, 28) without closing the book—I can find no other natural employment for "the possible impossible" than in designating the given. And the event of nihilation, motivated by the mythic pursuit of selfhood on the part of the in-itself, occurs, of necessity, *before* the conscious reception of implosive givenness. But there are also occasions on which the mythic framework is lifted, and "impossible" assertions are made with a straight face: "The in-itself can not provide the foundation for anything; if it founds itself, it does so by giving itself the modification of the for-itself" (130); and "the in-itself is nihilated and absorbed in its attempt to found itself" (133). The im/possible has become simply impossible. Sartre contradicts himself. The insensate cannot make an "attempt." Mindless materiality is incapable of "founding" or "giving." And although the brute in-itself "can not provide the foundation for anything," it seems, nonetheless, to found itself. And the only way to avert the evident threat of incoherence is by assuming that the in-itself *itself* (if it *has* an "itself") is not "anything." Being is not, of course, a thing. But certainly, "Being is" (29). And this plunges Sartre deeper into incoherence, since his claim that "the in-itself can not provide the foundation for anything" is intended to repudiate its founding, not of particular things, but of an evident non-thing: the for-itself.

Sartre rejects the view that "the real is suspended in the heart of possibilities" (1971, 53), that the actual is simply the fortunate recipient, selected from an indefinite roll of pre-subsisting contestants, of the honor of actualization. Phenomenological givenness renders possibility subsequent to actuality. "The possible appears to us a property of beings" (149). It is a way in which the actual could (possibly) be, a subjunctive declination from the actual. To be explicable, an event must first be possible. And there is consequently no recourse to the "why?" of the given beyond its sheer, actual givenness. It just *is*. It is absurd. In the searching intuition of Angelius Silesius, the rose blossoms "without why" (cf. Heidegger 1957, 69).

Buddhism is quite comfortable with the "just is," recognizing no "beyond," "beneath," or "behind." But the "unit," if you will, of just-is-ness is not the rose, not a particular actuality, but the entire field of conditioning in which the rose surrenders its being to sun and soil, and they in turn exist ecstatically, outside themselves, in their conditions. The rose may be clipped from the bush, and the bush severed from its roots; but ontological deracination is not a possibility. The rose "is" the deep and tangled confusion of its ontological indebtedness. The roots go deep, deep beyond measure, deep beyond our knowing, fathomlessly deep. The rose, then, is not a totality, but a whole. It has no "outside," no limit which one can reach in order to gain an objective, external point of vantage. And though it has a certain integrity, it is a "unit," a *one*, only by courtesy. It is uncountable, nonobjectifiable. And it is the rose in *this* sense, as a context without boundary, as a network without limit, that "just is." And in this expansive sense, "the world lurches from moment to moment, that each new moment is a new start, a *leap* (*saltare*), a gratuitous exultant event . . ." (Caputo 1993, 40). Substance is a misguiding and ensnaring delusion which anchors our futile efforts to cling, barnacle-like, to experience which we construe as "positive." But the Buddhist portrayal of the "just-is-ness" (*tathatā*) of our experience is at the same time profoundly qualified by the vision of *pratīya-samutpāda*. Just as "not one thing exists," not one thing is given. A "thing" is always an individuated saliency which rises against a background of subdued experience through a certain repulsion or negation. And "suffering is, according to Buddha, what is individual . . ." (Bataille 1988, 22). The figural thing *is-not* its contextualizing ground. But in Sartrean terms, the ek/stasis of the figural saliency is an internal negation. And the purported "being" of the figure is deferred to its ground. Thus, there *are* no things. And just as the growing of the tree is nothing over and above the presence of the moisture, soil nutrients and sunshine which condition it, the upsurge of (intentional) consciousness is likewise resolvable into the plethora of factors which support its being. Tracing out the conditions of a phenomenon (and consciousness, in this sense, is, of course, a phenomenon) is not an explanation but a description. It is not that consciousness arises *because* of its conditions, but rather, that its existence is factored out among its conditions. It *is* its conditions. There *is*, then, no consciousness (in itself). And thus, it "itself" is not given. This does not, however, jeopardize the "suchness" (*tathatā*), the exactly-as-it-is-ness, of the phenomenon of consciousness. It is not that consciousness is unmanifest, but rather, that it *itself* is unmanifest, since it has no "itself." Nothing, no stable, substantial, identifiable "thing" is manifest. But this is true without altering the manifest character of experience in the least. What is altered, however, is the *way* in which experience is enjoyed. And this "way" is the Way to liberation.

The Sartrean in-itself is, then, neither *in* itself nor in *itself*. An "itself" is an identity—a character, a "style," a *Wesen*—which, through a certain abstractive intention, can be wrenched away from its ingredience within an ontological integrity, thus standing forth as a saliency blossoming upon an experiential plain. The "itself" would, then, be the voice of its ground, the characterizing expression of that openness which conditions its being. The sonority of this voice, its resonance and fullness, is the remission of anechoic silence. But unlike that of the mythical Echo, whose voice, "[i]n the end . . . is nothing but the words of others," the appeal of the abyss is by no means "the death of the living voice" (Salis 1988, 85). The Sartrean in-itself does not *have* a "what," it *is* its "what." Nothing "about it" gives it style or determinacy. It *is* its own style. There is nothing—no determinate "thing" (not even "itself") *in* itself, since all within is fused together—without rift, and without the possibility of saliency. It is "the inherence in itself without the least distance" (1971, 27). The in-itself is not the site of its own expression. The figure/ground distantiation is inoperative, as is the disjunction of *noēsis* and *noēma*. The in-itself is "the noema in the noesis" (27), or the utter pervasion and saturation of noēsis by noēma, the remainderless engulfment of noēma within the quasi- spatiality of noēsis. If the in-itself "speaks," it is either thunderous or silent, resonant or quiescent in its indissoluble plenitude—but affording no occasion for representation. It may "give voice," but it does not give *its* voice—not to an elect representative, and certainly not to "itself."

Ventriloquism is rather the province of the for-itself: "the consciousness which says *I Think* is precisely not the consciousness which thinks" (Sartre 1972, 45). And in the ontologically first instance, at the level of the prereflective *cogito*, projection is the attribute of that self-presence which is the ontological modality of the for-itself. "Presence to self . . . supposes that an impalpable fissure has slipped into being. . . . Presence is an immediate deterioration of coincidence . . ." (Sartre 1971, 124). The "fissure" which qualifies self-presence is the disintegrity of the in-itself and "itself." The for-itself is the vocalization of the in-itself through "itself." And its message is one of affirmation. The in-itself *in itself* is mute, "an affirmation which can not affirm itself" (27). Merleau-Ponty outlines a sense of assertoric priority which does not devolve into voicelessness: "beneath affirmation and negation, beneath judgment . . . is our experience, prior to every opinion, of inhabiting the world by our body, of inhabiting the truth by our whole selves . . ." (1969, 28). This residence is at once both "affirmation"—positivity, the materiality of the general element of flesh—and "self-affirmation": the flesh speaks. In our always-taken-for-granted insertion in the world, there is no requisite "to choose nor even to distinguish between the assurance of seeing and the assurance of seeing the true, because in principle they are one and the same thing . . ." (28). Implicit, here, is a commentary upon Sartre's quasi-Cartesianism. For a view which segregates subjectivity from objectivity, the in-itself, as the domain of objectivity, is cognitively insecure, the site of detached presences which, while convincing in their display, may be treacherous in their distortion, or worse, of eidola vanishingly remote from their home in "the true." But there are two ways in which "seeing" and "seeing the true" may be interfused. One, of course, belongs to Merleau-Ponty. Vital experience is the immediacy of the true. Authentic perception offers no distinction between appearance and reality. Indeed, it "is not even an act, a deliberate taking up of a position; it is the background from which all acts stand out, and is presupposed by them . . ." (1962, x–xi). The Buddhist view, for which "not one thing"—no *res*, no *objectus*—exists, though not dissociating the real and the manifest, posits, as the only meaningful sense of objective truth (*samvṛti*), the simple presence of the object— the object *is* as, in the most comprehensive sense, it *appears* to be—and is thus aligned with Merleau-Ponty. But in the ultimate acceptation (*pāramārtha*), the discriminate object corresponds to nothing real. As Streng reminds us, "Since there are no intrinsically different objects of knowledge, the distinction between 'mundane truth' and 'ultimate truth' does not pertain to different objects of knowledge, e.g., the world and ultimate reality. It refers, rather, to the *manner* by which 'things' are perceived" (1967, 39). The Ultimate is not an object. "The Ultimate Truth to which the term *nirvāna* points is that it is without any designation; in actuality there is no 'it' and no designation . . ." (75).

For Sartre, the for-itself is the enactment of "the affirmation *of* self" (1971, 27), an affirmation liberated "from the heart of being" (27). The affirmation *of self* is what the in-itself would express, and would express through "itself," were it only to have an "itself." Yet *per impossibile*, were this counterfactual discharged, *it* (the in-itself) would not be "it": the in-itself would have been transformed into the for-itself, and also, as such, would no longer *be* what it is. The transformation is, in the Aristotelian option, either accidental or essential. If accidental, the in-itself becomes furrowed with nothingness, thus vitiating Sartre's Parmenidean proclivities. If essential, a novel modality of being is born—porous being—and immediately supplants the "absolute plenitude" of Parmenidean being. Thus, the in-itself "is the foundation of itself in so far as it is *already no longer* in-itself . . ." (130), and nihilation is no longer the "making nothing" of being, but its replacement. Or else (a final alternative hardly consistent with Parmenidean logic) prenihilated being—the *ni-en-soi-ni-pour-soi*—remains as the impossible referent of the twin born in-itself and for-itself, and nihilation is the event of giving birth. Neither gestation nor parturition is consonant with the immutability and indivisibility of Parmenidean being. And the *apeiron* is, in turn, inhospitable to plenary positivity. The in-itself *is* itself so thoroughly that its "self" dissolves within it. "It is this self. It is itself so completely that the perpetual reflection which constitutes the self is dissolved in an identity. . . . In fact being is opaque to itself precisely because it is filled with itself" (28). The for-itself "has" a self, but can *be* itself only "*in the mode of not being it*" (68). Sartre's ontology, resonant here with the Buddhist, precludes the possibility of an innocent and unproblematic identity of consciousness with the self, or what Lacan vividly designates as "the deceptive obviousness of the notion that the self-identity which is supposed in the common aware-ness of the ego has anything to do with a presumed instance of the real" (Lacan 1966, 69). For Sartre, "the subject can not *be* self, for coincidence with self . . . causes the self to disappear" (1971, 123). Being-self is always being-at-a-distance.

Sartre is (perhaps understandably) indecisive regarding the agency re-sponsible for nihilation. If "everything happens as if the For-itself by its very nihilation constituted itself as "consciousness of _____" (1971, 295), then it would seem that the for-itself does the nihilating. But if, on the other hand, "the in-itself can not found *itself* without introducing the *self* of a reflective, nihilating reference into the absolute identity of its being and consequently degenerating into *for-itself*" (133), it would seem, on the con-trary, that the in-itself—wholly out of character for the stolid and inert—en-acts nihilation. The alternatives are equally ruinous. Nihilation is an impulsive upsurge, not the performance of an antecedent agent. If an order of antecedence is at all intelligible here, one must say that the event of nihi-lation predates the for-itself, that *nihil* comes about as a result of the sponta-neous occurrence of "*nihil*-ization." Sartre confirms that "in order to nihilate itself, it must *be*. But Nothingness *is not*" (57). The conclusion is in-escapable: nothingness cannot nihilate itself. The Heideggerean resolution is thus foreclosed. One gathers a consistent impression that Sartre intends the nothingness of consciousness to be, not the languid consequence of an unrehearsed ontological exuberance, but an episode indistinguishable in its dynamism from the advent of nihilation. And it thus becomes difficult to see how the for-itself could "do"—instead of *be*—nihilation. After all, nihila-tion is barely distinguishable from decompression. And the for-itself is neither the effect nor the witness of decompression. It *is* the event of de-compression. And of course, the intrinsic torpidity and lifelessness of the in-itself could not predict its capacity to stir itself even to rot. If nihilation is conceived as an occurrence intermediate between the plenary fullness of the in-itself and the vacuity of the for-itself, the event of evacuation which at the same stroke pulverizes the one and introjects the other, then it falls to Merleau-Ponty's remarks regarding mediation. Assuming the Parmenidean proclivity of Sartre's thought, we can echo Merleau-Ponty's insistence that, "in the absence of all difference, there would be no mediation, movement, transformation; one would remain in full positivity" (1969, 92). Differ-ence, rupture, *écart*, has no part in Parmenidean being. If nothingness is more, however, than a simple "flickering" on the surface of being (1971, 42), a superficial glint or twinkle, if it is rather a fissuring, a rupturing of an otherwise integral plenitude and positivity, an ontological disaster—"a loss that cannot be incorporated into a 'result' . . ." (Caputo 1993, 29)—it must be, for the in-itself, a cataclysmic transmutation. It would take more vibrancy than dead matter could summon to bring about the fracturing of being. The for-itself serves as the agent of its own nihilation. In Merleau-Ponty's presentation, "there is no self-mediation either if the mediator is the simple or absolute negation of the mediated: the absolute negation would simply annihilate the mediated and, turning against itself, would annihilate itself also, so that there would still be no mediation, but a pure and simple retreat toward positivity" (1971, 92). And in this case, the for-itself could loose itself in its object only if its self-negation were, by contrast, relative. And it is hard to reconcile the nonpositional self-awareness which holds consciousness back from the brink of utter absorption in its object with a description of consciousness as a "non-substantial absolute" (17). Thus, "[i]t is . . . ruled out that the mediation have its origin in the positive term, as though it were one of its *properties*—but it is likewise precluded that the mediation come to the positive term from an abyss of exterior negativity, which would have no hold on it and would leave it intact" (1969, 92). Sartre's oscillation on the issue of agency is, however, not entirely inappropriate. Pronouncements such as the ones quoted above are usually couched in the quasi-mythic "everything happens as if . . ." modality which intimates a certain bracketed metaphysics. Though repudiating Husserl's transcendentalism, Sartre is not, in his resort to metaphysics at the junctures of failure, significantly remote from Husserl who, "[i]n the facticity of the constitution of the world, that is, in the impossibility to explain it from the transcendental subjectivity, . . . saw the starting-point of metaphysics proper" (Kern 1964, 298). The reduction is not air-tight. Metaphysics seeps into Husserl's thought through the vents provided by the givenness of the given. And as Heidegger urged, facticity "does not submit to neutralization" (Caputo, 25). Indeed,

This, perhaps, is what accounts for Tsung-mi's preference for transparentism. And our own efforts at *Gelassenheit*, at loosening the metaphysical grasp, letting both transparentist and translucentist seemings be, letting them go and relinquishing them, have, paradoxically, only succeeded in reinstating transparentism. But if it is true, as Levin attests, that "'[t]hinking,' spellbound by the authority it wields during the rule of metaphysics, is itself part of the problem" (1985, 60–1) then for at least this reason, we may not need to take these reserved speculations with ontological solemnity. And at a deeper level, it may be that Sartre wavers before the alternatives because he senses that neither provides a coherent account and that nihilation is more adequately depicted as the twin birth of the in-itself and the for-itself from the womb of the *apeiron*, the "neither."

For Sartre, "[t]he *self* . . . represents an ideal distance within the immanence of the subject in relation to himself, a way of *not being his own coincidence* . . ." (1971, 123–4). The self is a rent in an otherwise seamless fabric, a rupture in the plenitude of self-identity. In Reb Lema's poignant admonition, "[d]o not forget that you are the nucleus [*le noyau*] of a rupture" (cf. Derrida 1978, 67). The self is not a positive entity standing separate and aloof from the stratum of immanence. Thus, "the *self* cannot be apprehended as a real existent" (Sartre 1971, 123). It is rather "a way"—a way of not being in-itself. It is a way of "escaping identity while positing it as unity" (124). The self is not this event of positing, but is, as it were, the way in which an "absolute cohesion without a trace of diversity" comes to appear as "a synthesis of multiplicity" (124), the way in which the in-itself exposes its porosity and interior degradation. Much as a flame in a windless room is, despite its incessant dynamism, relatively still, so, also, the event of nihilation is "a perpetually unstable equilibrium" (124). And the self is, if you like, the form of this upsurging, its modality, its "how," or what Sartre calls "a perpetually evanescent relation" (140). The self is thus questionable to the exact extent that the notion of nihilation is called into question. And we have found ample reason to do so.

But if the in-itself represents the dissolution of self, without remainder, without distance, without the disruption of "having"—if "[i]t is this self" (1971, 28)—then "self," in Sartre's employment, splinters into ambiguity. There is "self" in a quasi-nominal sense which is liquidated in the medium of being, and which, on the Anaximandrean reading, can be recovered from being through nihilation. And there is "self" as a mode, a modality, a way, a relation, relationship or relationality. "Self" is used as a monadic term of nihilation, and "self" is used as its dipolar *modus*. If "[t]he characteristic of selfness (*Selbstheit*) . . . is that man [*sic*] is always separated from what he is by all the breadth of the being which he is not" (51), then the self is the *separation*, not the *separated*, and there is no separation in the in-itself, dissolved or otherwise. And the understanding of self as an isolate distilled through nihilation repudiates its dipolarity. We can cheerfully grant to Sartre the two distinct senses of a word without crying equivocation. But in freeing "the affirmation *of* self from the heart of being (27), it is not clear that the self at "the heart of being" (the monadic self) is the self thus liberated (perhaps, the relational self). If the liberated self is monadic, then the self affirmed and the self dissolved within the medium of being are one and the same, and affirmation has no purchase upon the ontological status of the self. Yet "affirmation *of* self" has, indeed, rung a crucial ontological change. The self affirmed has, in the prereflective *cogito*, become a presence, the ectoplasmic haze which permeates consciousness and, in a primordial way, separates consciousness from itself—not to say "from its *self*." But what we are "not to say" is significant. To evade the circularity of understanding "self" as that which separates *from self*, we must disjoin the "itself" and the "self" of consciousness. Consciousness *itself* would be consciousness *qua* consciousness, consciousness considered under the aspect of *what it is*, and thus, consciousness surmounting itself sufficiently to make of itself its own landscape. *Would* be. But then, there is no consciousness *itself*. There is nothing which consciousness *is*. It neither is, nor does it have, a "what." It rather transcends its "what" with each pulse of its life. It is constituted by the event of *not-being* "what" it is—or what it simply *would* be, were it not to nihilate "what" it is. Sartre observes that "to affirm that the consciousness (of) belief is consciousness (of) belief is to dissociate consciousness from belief, to suppress the parenthesis, and to make belief an object for consciousness; it is to launch abruptly on to the plane of reflectivity" (121). To speak of consciousness *itself* is thus to abolish nonpositional self-awareness, the prereflective *cogito*. A consciousness *itself* would not, then, be structured by presence to self. Thus, there can be no disjunction of *self* from *itself*. But if, on the other hand, affirmation signals an ontological transformation (or perhaps an ontological genesis or supplantation), then the self affirmed is distinct from the self beyond (or prior to) affirmation. But then the "affirmation *of* self" would have no efficacy in releasing the self at "the heart of being." If the "two" selves are *one*, we lose interiority; if two, then nihilation—which conditions affirmation—has nothing to do.

Self, in Sartre's usual acceptation, is not the Cartesian *res cogitans*, the agent, situated, perhaps, "off stage," which performs the acts of consciousness. Sartre rejects "the self as a little God which inhabits me and which possesses my freedom as a metaphysical virtue" (1971, 81). Consciousness *is* its own spontaneity, and Sartre finds no need to reduplicate the spontaneity of consciousness with that of an agential ego. Self is rather that which is left behind in the event of self-transcendence. It is the snake skin which the for-itself perpetually sheds with each momentary quiver of its inconstant life. The self is the springboard, the *point d'appui*, which confirms the movement of transcendence in the direction of its future, the condition for its *not-being* "what" it is. The self is "what" consciousness is—in the mode of *not being* it—the essence which it cannot simply exemplify, but ever repudiates in the freedom by which it realizes its own adventual possibilities. The self is its shadow, its past. Its present is always a transcending of its past. The self is "the existence in-itself of the For itself" (1971, 184–5). And "the self-as-being-in-itself is what human reality lacks . . ." (1971, 138). "It is the self which would be what it is which allows the for-itself to be apprehended as not being what it is . . ." (138). Consciousness cannot *be* itself—nor can it be its *self*. Self is a deposit of essence transacted in each act. Sartre appreciates Hegel's pun: "*Wesen ist was gewesen ist*" (72). Consciousness does not simply *have* an essence (in the present tense). Its essence is rather "what has become" (*was gewesen ist*). Thus, "[e]ssence is everything in the human being which we can indicate by the words—that *is*. . . . every application of the formula 'that is' to man [*sic*] causes all that is designated, *to have been*" (72). As Merleau-Ponty affirms, "[i]n the very measure that I see, I do not know *what* I see . . ." (1969, 247). And while the for-itself can never be severed from its shadow, neither can the two coincide. A fabulated Peter Pan, parted from his shadow, could only reside in "Never, Never Land"—a domain which welcomes the *en-soi-pour-soi* with equal hospitality.

Despite common remonstrations to "be yourself," to "be what you are," the pretense of self-coincidence, "the sincerity which aims at itself in present immanence" (Sartre 1971, 110), is in bad faith. Sincerity aims to "bring me to confess to myself what I am in order that I may finally coincide with my being; in a word, to cause myself to be, in the mode of the in-itself, what I am in the mode of not being what I am" (110). We find in the *Transcendence* a preview of Sartre's later conception of *mauvaise foi*. It is, he writes, "as if consciousness hypnotized itself before this ego which it has constituted, absorbing itself in the ego as if to make the ego its guardian and its law" (1972, 101), as if, in other words, consciousness simply and unproblematically *were* "what" it is. The for-itself *is-not* (nihilates) the in-itself. Thus, the gravity of its pretense exceeds the opprobrium of self-deception. Bad faith is, finally, bad ontology. While consciousness ineluctably enacts the "futile passion" to secure its fragile being by becoming its own ontological foundation, it is self-deceptive pretense to suppose that it could, except in the mode of *not* being what it is, straightforwardly, *be* "the impossible synthesis of the for-itself and the in-itself" (1971, 140). Sartre tells us that "every effort to conceive of the idea of a being which would be the foundation of its being results inevitably in forming that of a being which, contingent as being-in-itself, would be the foundation of its own nothingness" (128). The in-itself-for-itself "would be its own foundation not as nothingness but as being and would preserve within it the necessary translucency of consciousness along with the coincidence with itself of being-in-itself. It would preserve in it that turning back upon the self which conditions every necessity and every foundation. But this return to the self would be without distance; it would not be presence to itself, but identity with itself" (140). The in-itself and for-itself are not, of course, separate Cartesian substances. "Consciousness has nothing substantial . . ." (17), but is rather the evacuation of substantiality. Still, there is something Cartesian implicit in the exclusiveness, the reciprocal repulsion, of the two modalities of being. It is a systemic necessity of Sartre's ontology that the modalities do not overlap. Nothing is both in-itself and for-itself. If "[t]he act of causation by which God is *causa sui* is a nihilating act like every recovery of the self by the self, to the same degree that the original relation of necessity is a return to *self*, a reflexivity" (128), we must see that, for Buddhism, necessity is not truth. As the being of beings is deferred to conditions beyond them, so, also, is the truth of truths. A proposition which is true in virtue of "itself" is, then, not true at all. For Buddhism, as for Adorno, "[t]ruth is, rather, a field of force" (1983, 72).

Yet "[e]verything happens . . . as if the in-itself and the for-itself were presented in a state of disintegration in relation to an ideal synthesis. Not that the integration has ever *taken place* but on the contrary precisely because it is always indicated and always impossible" (Sartre 1971, 792). Sartre refers to this unrealizable synthesis—always indicated as the site of a detonation to which, in phenomenological principle, we have no intuitive access—as "a missing God" (792). And if, as Sartre insists, "it is necessary to draw the consequences of [God's] absence right to the end" (1975, 352), we know that the "end" has not been attained until the absence of God is recognized as systemic. To say that God is "missing" is to affirm that nothing within the domain of our intuition answers to the conception of a for-itself which is, at once, in-itself. "[T]here is no consciousness *of* this being . . ." (1971, 141). God's absence simply *is* the categorial repulsion of for-itself from in- itself, the systemic impossibility of their overlap. Sartre is clear that the exclusive disjunction of for-itself from in-itself does not import an unproblematic atheism, but rather banishes the incoherent ideal of self-founding consciousness from the province of our experience. "Shall we say that it [God] does not exist? Those contradictions which we discovered in it prove only that it can not be *realized*" (140). God remains, however, oddly "necessary," since "without this being . . . consciousness would not be conscious—*i.e.*, lack" (141). This is not to say that God is, in a classical theological sense, a necessary being. But the existence of God is as indispensable as the analysis of consciousness as lack—a deliverance entirely upset by Sartre's countervailing claim that "God, if he exists, is contingent" (129). Yet the desire to be God, to realize the unrealizable, to find repletion in that which is lacked, is constitutive for consciousness.

But a distinction can only be drawn upon a field which subtends it. And "[i]n the shunyata experience, the attention is on the field rather than on its contents" (Guenther and Trungpa, 1988, 27). As Buddhism teaches, we must sensitize ourselves to the intrinsically undistinguished ground which bears the imprint of our discriminations. The ground is cloven into for-itself and in-itself. And this very cleavage, this cleft, is the absence of God. But the blade which divides has two inalienable sides, two sides which, in their integrity, cannot be divided. The cleft separates in-itself from for-itself. But in the cleaving, the "two" are indissolubly *one*. And the sword "combines in itself" their "incompatible characteristics" (Sartre 1971, 140). The incoherent ideality which Sartre is pleased to call "God" is, then, the condition for ontological disjunction. Otherwise put, Sartrean dualism entails a contradiction. And we might thus be left with a certain implicit theism, were we not, finally, to look to the ground. For ultimately, there could be no cleavage, and thus, at least functionally, no cleaver, without that which is cleft. That which takes the sword into itself, opening itself in division, and subtending the cleavage, is not the *en-soi-pour-soi*. It is not the "Both." And it lies too deep to be one or the other. It falls to neither side of the divide which it accommodates. The ground is rather the "Neither": the *ni-en-soi-ni-pour-soi*. The Neither is that which allows both, and allows *the Both*, to be. It is not that a Buddhist sensitivity to the condition for discrimination—emptiness—repudiates God. Buddhism is *non*-theistic, not *a*-theistic. Rather, God is deprived of ultimacy. The Both could not *be*—could not be that which divides the ground—without the Neither. The "sword," the incongruous ideality which amalgamates in-itself and for-itself, is seen to be conditioned, and thus, incapable of functioning as God functions within a typical theism. A "knight" played as a pawn is not a *knight*—regardless of its evident visual similarity to other knights. And likewise, in the game of theology, a "God" deprived of its role as the ultimate and unconditioned foundation of reality is not a *God*. This is a functional atheism, if you like. But just as an aberrant "knight" conscripted to serve as a pawn is not thereby deprived of existence—the chess piece does exist—so, also, a functional atheism need not deny the conceptual counter thus functionally transformed. "Human reality is a perpetual surpassing toward a coincidence with itself which is never given" (139). And while God "haunts non-thetic self-consciousness" (141) as its constitutive, if ineluctably absent, locus of reference, the *en-soi-pour-soi* is never a telic finality. The Neither permits the Both. But the Neither is also in/different to the existence of the Both. The conatus of consciousness is fulfilled, then, in its finality and ultimacy, not in a contingent, if also systemically anomalous, upsurge, but in emptiness. Desiring to be Self-Thinking Thought, the thinking of the Sartrean for-itself is nonetheless separated from itself as thematic consciousness of thinking by an unbridgeable chasm. "[T]he consciousness which says *I Think* is precisely not the consciousness which thinks" (1972, 45). And Sartre would agree, I think, with Lyotard's larger suggestion "that each thinking consists in a rethinking and that there is nothing the presentation of which could be said to be the 'premiere.' Every emergence of something reiterates something else, every occurrence is a recurrence . . ." (1990, 8–9). And inasmuch as consciousness seeks ultimacy, it seeks not to realize a simultaneous self-lucidity and opacity, vacuity and absolute density, but rather an intrinsic detachment from both. Enlightened mind is neither the for-itself, defined by means of nihilation, nor is it mindless plenary materiality.

Emptiness is not an absence, a privation, a pocket of vacuity at the heart of an otherwise compacted being. Emptiness is like boundless space which, while not yielding "place" to its solid inhabitants, nonetheless yields to them their being. Space is not dis/placed by voluminous objects. It does not part to allow them "room" (*Raum*), does not abandon its "realm" in response to intrusion. For nothing can intrude upon space. Nothing can displace it. Serenely, quietly, without the least quiver of abrasion, without the slightest breath of disturbance, space simply pervades its spectral denizens. Objects pass through space like immaterial ghosts. Or is it space which thus passes through them? The one gives no resistance to the other. Sartre's ontological scheme makes no explicit appeal to the capaciousness without which the solidity, density and compression of the in-itself would be impossible. Yet if being in-itself is to be envisaged according to the "myth of the plenum" (cf. Wyschogrod 1990, 208–17), a compaction of identity so utterly dense as to resolve the "self" of self-identity into distanceless fusion, there must nonetheless be space for this solid volume. Or else, if space is compacted within this originary singularity, then being is always already porous; and again, we witness the uneasy oscillation in Sartre's thinking between two incompatible models of being. But in any case, Sartre seems unaware of the "space" which his ontology requires.

We have spoken of the "ground" (*Grund*) of ontological disjunction which is riven by the Both. And the ground does part (or does *seem* to part) in response to the sword. It is reft, bereft of its seamless integrity. And this rift is the contour of the missing God. This *Grund* must, then, have its *Abgrund*—or must come to light as being its own *Abgrund*. "The groundlessness of Being, if we must speak of it, is the groundlessness of the ground that continues to surrender to the radical interrogation that it nonetheless sustains" (Johnson and Smith, 1990, 90). A sponge floating in a pool of water is permeated by its aqueous medium. From the "fluid" standpoint, as it were, the sponge makes relatively little difference. The water is (in this case, relatively) in/different to the presence of the sponge. Yet from an external vantage point, the water *seems* to terminate at the surface of the sponge, thus *appearing* to be excluded by the suspended object. Similarly, the ground of dis crimination *seems* to assume the contour of the Both, *seems* to con/form to the missing God, and thus, *seems* to be riven, furrowed, indented by the trenchant presence of the sword. Since the gaze is halted by opacity, and since, accordingly, we cannot see *through* the luminally exclusive density of the object, and thus, cannot register the space which pervades it, the object *seems* to exclude space. The space within the cup *seems* severed from the environing amplitude of universal space. The vessel, the solidity which conditions its internal hollow, *seems* to institute a dualism of "inside" and "outside," "self" and "other." But this seeming is conditioned by a naive and unenlightened conflation of presence and exclusion, manifestation and expulsion. Yes, discriminations can be made. And yes, the ground—envisioned under the aspect of this confusion—can be riven. And yes, again, reality does, indeed, seem to accommodate discrimination. But no, the *Abgrund*—envisioned, now, with the realization that opacity does not disrupt, does not rupture the seamless medium which pervades it—is not subject to discrimination. *An sich*, the abyss cannot be cleft; *für uns* (for the unenlightened), it serves as the medium of conceptual cleavage. The ground of discrimination is, then, the *Abgrund für uns. Grund* and *Abgrund* differ only phenomenologically, not ontologically. The enlightened see it as it is. The unenlightened see it as it appears to a mind immersed in confusion—as a rarified ethereal fluid displaced by the serried and imporous solidity of the object.

Emptiness has no capacity to baffle ingress, to preclude or deflect. It is not solid, dense or thick-set. Nor is it a merely relative nothingness, a fault which opens up in primordial solidity. Though "negative" in the sense of being permissive, open, insolid, it is no less "positive" in the sense that it denies nothing at all. It neither nihilates, nor annihilates, neither "makes nothing" of something, thus creating absence, nor simply destroys, creating nothing at all. Without friction, abrasion, or negation, it allows all things to be exactly as they are, in their rich and vivid suchness (*tathatā*). If nihilation is an ontological fiction, it is, nonetheless, at least a prima facie phenomenological datum. The spacious largesse of the Abyss is not challenged, threatened or disrupted by its voluminous occupants, and finds no need to repudiate them. Likewise, the meontic phenomenology of Buddhism holds no brief against the (merely apparent) nihilation which conditions the (merely apparent) disjunction of the in-itself and the hollow which it encloses. Sartre is not so much wrong as insufficiently comprehensive. The engine of nihilation rolls well on Buddhist tracks so long as its ontological freight is decoupled.

I recall with delight a conversation which I had with my friend and teacher, the Most Venerable Ratmalane Somāloka, as we entered an ice cream shop in Waikiki. We had been talking about (what else?) emptiness, and now, in the white heat of existential anguish, confronting the endless array of flavors, the great wisdom poured forth. Emptiness, my friend proclaimed, is a thing's *not being what it is*—and this from a Buddhist monk almost entirely innocent of the drama, hyperbole and paradox of Sartrean rhetoric. What struck me was the inversion. Is it not "things" which are exactly what they are? And is it not consciousness which is alienated from itself in virtue of *not-being* the very self (in-itself) which it lacks? But no. All phenomena—both the wall of opacity which is erected around each seemingly separate consciousness and which, it is claimed, absorbs its intentional interest, and the space apparently enclosed within this confinement—are not what they are. If enclosed space—the cavity, the vacuity, the hollow, the chasm—is, though undeniably phenomenal, nonetheless lacking in ontological credentials, we can say no less for the opacity and solidity which conditions it. "Absolute" space cannot condition relative vacuity, but is seamlessly continuous with all seemingly enclosed spaces. And the seeming solidity of the enclosure is no solidity at all for space. For space, all is spectral, wriathlike. Both chasm and precipice are unreal. Each conditions the other. Thus, neither is self-existent. And both are innocent of a "self" or "itself." If "not one thing exists," if "there absolutely are no things," then the nubilous enwrapment which consciousness clutches about itself is also empty.

But the not-being-what-it-is which, according to my friend, informs the domain of objectivity can be understood more searchingly in terms of the "rupture of immanence" elucidated in *Mind as Mirror* (cf. Laycock 1994, 173–80). If openness to quality is phenomenologically indistinguishable from qualitative pervasion, if, against a murky ground, the bright, pellucid crystal of Tsung-mi's trope cannot be discriminated from a darkened crystal, then immanence fissures into transcendence and brings about "the fracturing of the immanence of transcendental consciousness, its exposure to its repressed 'outside' " (Dews 1988, 17). For any purported item of immanence—an objectuality which localizes the claim of coincidence between *being* and *appearing*—there is always one "appearing" too many. And the difference which prizes apart the two appearings shatters immanence at its core. Congruently, Adorno posits that "[w]hile philosophy of immanence . . . can only be ruptured immanently, i.e., in confrontation with its own untruth, its immanence itself is untruth" (1983, 25). Nothing simply *is* as it appears. This is not a "hermeneutic of suspicion"—though even this seems preferable to Rorty's "mechanics of weightlessness" (Caputo 1983, 679)—but a phenomenology of "wariness"—provided that we hear in that word the etymological overtone of "awareness."

Consciousness intends, at/tends, foreshortening its infinitely variable focal length to converge at the heart of its object. Its proflux is absorbed in the dark interior core, the negativity, of opacity. Phenomenology, as typically understood, seeks the roots of our articulated and objectivated experience in prearticulate, preobjective positivity. Our cognitive interests are fulfilled, as it were, in being silenced. For as Merleau-Ponty knew well, the sonority of language "lives only from silence; everything which we cast to the others has germinated in this great mute land which we never leave" (1969, 126). Buddhism does not seek to realize the privation of sound, but rather the vastly resonant emptiness which conditions sound by permitting us to listen "through" it. Husserl's "X" centers a radiance of modal presentations. But what might seem a starburst is more authentically a black hole. The intentional object engulfs all intentional illumination. And if consciousness is envisioned as a beacon of light pouring forth into the abyss of presence, we must also see that its source, in its pretense of melding being and appearing, provides an "unquestionable answer" in response to the interrogation of reflection. Buddhism fractures the delusory integrity of a being which pretends to be without enfolding its own undoing. No being simply *is* its own appearing. There are no unquestionable answers, but only questions opening beneath questions without end. And "[w]hat is questionable can sometimes be worthy of thought, and what is unthinkable can sometimes be glimpsed as that which thinking is about" (Mehta 1987, 15). Neither is there an anechoic vacuum which swallows up the interrogative demands of consciousness. Emptiness is the assurance that all answers are answerable to questioning, and all questions meet with the responsiveness of answering. If consciousness looks-*at*, awareness looks-*through*. Kant theorized that all seeing is seeing-*as*. Husserl, following Brentano, deepened the Kantian proposal with his postulation that all seeing is (in an ontologically uncommitted sense) a seeing-*of-something*. And Buddhism replies to both in its recognition that authentic *seeing* is unimpeded by the "something" which, for the phenomenologists of presence, would otherwise stop up the gaze.

Seeing-through is not an adjustment of focus. It does not involve a merely partial transformation of attention. For to attend, now, to the ground in preference to the former figure is simply to constitute another object with its own horizons, its own context. Background becomes foreground with its own background. Rather, "[t]o direct attention to 'a thing' is the first step in the direction of affirming a self-sufficient entity" (Streng 1967, 37). A seeing enabled by pure transparency, a transparency which in no way calls attention to "itself," which, in phenomenal presentation, *has* no "self" to attend to, is focused, as it were, at infinity. It converges upon no object, no matter how remote. It is a beacon of illumination pouring forth without obstruction into the fathomless abyss. There is nothing—no *thing*—to see. Its light is neither absorbed by opacity, nor remitted by reflectivity. In Bataille's effervescent exposition, "[t]here is in divine things a transparency so great that one slips into the illuminated depths of laughter beginning even with opaque intentions" (1988, 33). Phenomenality is constituted by focal foreshortening, by convergence. Were we, conversely, to look straight through an object as if we were looking beyond it, or, indeed, as if it did not exist, we might at first become aware of it a relatively indistinct haze of quality, a vague medium still announcing itself as presence, but opening nonetheless to what lies beyond itself. Consciousness, not absorbed in its presence, but impeded by it, would not yet have achieved the infinite outlook, the attitude of non-convergence. When even the ectoplasmic haze of qualitative presence has been transformed into pure medium, the infinitary posture is attained, and the "object" simply resolves into emptiness. "[E]mptiness," Lispector writes, "is a medium of transport" (1988, 106). Every level of articulate structure is "fuzz" for the level beneath it. The diffusion which we take delusively as irrefrangible presence fractures into clarity and distinctness with the advance of analysis. Lured by clarity (L. *claritas*), light, we witness level after level of haze, confusion, indistinctness vanishing into lucidity. And if we are not to posit a terminal stratum of obfuscation—refuge for those who seek security in the phenomenal, but gross darkness for the profoundly incisive in/sight, pro/gnosis, *prajñā* which Buddhism cultivates—we also know that to open the gaze beyond the blearing fog of presence is to open to an illumination which has neither source nor target, but is rather the clear luminescence of emptiness.

Consciousness, for Sartre, perpetually surpasses itself toward "the self-as-being-in-itself" which "human reality lacks" (1971, 138). Buddhism concurs with the "futility" of the passion to be "filled up." But it also sees that awareness exhibits no such "desire." Sartre was unable to explode the myth of opacity. Desire, for Sartre is "a lack of being" (137), and is constitutive of our finitary mode of mindfulness. This assumes, however, that our interests are best served by being immured in the opacity—presence, immanence, or experiential plenitude of one sort or another. Buddhism bears witness to the an "explosion" which occurs by itself. There is no substance, no "X," no core of opacity, nothing to absorb the light of awareness. Nor is there an origin (*origo*) which would determine the intentional "orientation" of a ray of consciousness. Awareness is not a directional "ray," but a luminescence, a glow. It is not a shaft of illumination which traverses space, but rather the spatiality of emptiness aglow with its own diaphaneity.

At each point, all of space is accessible. Each point is the exact center of space. Each point is, without the least shadow of impedance, utterly hyalescent. To see "it" at all is to see *through* it. "It" is not self-effacing, but entirely devoid of self-presence, entirely devoid of the gossamer, ectoplasmic mist of manifestation which could be called "itself." And all other points are "there," at the center, without distance or mediation. In the immediacy of its receptivity, it mimics, if only ironically, the quintessential function of phenomenological immanence. But it does not appear *as it is*, since it *is* nothing at all. Or rather, its being is exactly the utter absentation of being, and thus, the decisive "emptying" of self which, on the other hand, mimics the function of phenomenological transcendence. Its immanence is exactly its transcendence. Its immediacy is exactly its mediation. Or as Merleau-Ponty discerns, "[t]he immediate is at the horizon and must be thought as such; it is only by remaining at a distance that it remains itself" (1969, 123). And "[m]ediacy is . . . a directive to cognition not to comfort itself with such positivity" (Adorno 1983, 24). Each point is constituted by its "not being what it is." But it is not troubled or "haunted" by the purported presence which it absents, the being which it lacks. For nothing is lacking. All of space is "there." It is not defined by deficit, by an opacity which, de jure or de facto, would otherwise be its content. It is not the absence *of* what should or would be present. It is not a hole or hollow deprived of repletion. It is, in fact, already full. But this fullness is the im/mediate repletion provided by all it receives. And in its receptivity it is utterly open to all that is utterly open. It is "full" of emptiness. The "presence" which it welcomes is utter absence. The "opacity" which it enjoys is utter transparency. The being which it embraces is utter non-being. It is not defined *against* fullness or presence or opacity, but *according* to them. It is not founded upon the nihilation of being. Nor, like the Sartrean for-itself which trembles at its own solidification, does it seek to found itself by becoming solid being. It rather "floats," without foundation or support—and certainly without the purported buttressing provided by "itself."

Chapter 7

The Myth of Repletion

A hole invites repletion. Or rather, as Sartre would amend, this invitation is issued, not of itself, but in virtue of transcendence. "An incomplete circle does not call for completion unless it is surpassed by human transcendence. In itself it is complete and perfectly positive as an open curve" (1971, 136). To "transcend," in this peculiar sense, is to surpass the positive in the direction of the possible: the possible positive. Vacuity cannot be intuited *as such* were it not the site of possible suffusion. Were we incapable of envisioning the positivity which, counterfactually, *could* be there instead, our world would own no holes—nor would there be even the surface of an indentation. There would be no "negative space." And in fact, to press Sartre beyond himself, inasmuch as the concavity of an open curve is constituted by the imaginary solid which would fill it, even the curve is not, in itself, purely positive.

Given imaginary repletion—positivity in the mode of the possible—the hole does, however, appear as the welcoming occasion for a filling. To say that it *can* be filled up is to say (at least) that we can imagine it filled. Filled, however, it is no longer a hole. Indeed, filled, "it" *is* no longer at all. For the hole, repletion is annihilation. If the hole were its filling "in the mode of identity, the ensemble would become an in-itself" (Sartre 1971, 147). "Its" identity is constituted precisely by its lacunary openness. Thus the hole exhibits a curious ambiguity. The hole is open. It "invites" filling. It *is not* that which would fill it. But in Sartre's frequent idiom, it *has to be* this fulfillment. It exhibits a certain impatience, a certain appeal, for repletion. The hole seems to exist for the sake of being filled up—as if its own deepest desire, its destiny, were to concretize the imaginary presence which, while satisfying its inner passion, would, at the same time, effect the destruction of the hole as a passion for positivity. Yet as Kierkegaard advises, "the ultimate potentiation of every passion is always to will its own downfall . . ." (1985, 29).

And desire, represented as just such "a lack of being" (Sartre 1971, 137), is the invocation, sustained by a passage to imaginary repletion, of that which would fulfill/annul it. The vacuity of desire is, however, self-referential. Desire desires itself as desiring (cf. 137), and resists its annihilation through fulfillment. It desires the repletion of the in-itself without loosing itself as for-itself. There is no authentic [satis]faction, no making-full. Or rather, satisfaction would not satisfy the desire of desire to *be* desire. As Sartre attests, "that coincidence with self which is satisfaction, where thirst knows itself as thirst at the same time that the drinking satisfies it, when by the very fact of its fulfillment it loses its character as lack while making itself be thirst in and through the satisfaction" (154). Consciousness desires to be God. And indeed, "the aim is the thirst passed on to the plenitude of being, the thirst which grasps and incorporates repletion into itself as the Aristotelian form grasps and transforms matter; it becomes eternal thirst" (154). The fragile for-itself, a frangible vessel subject to the unpredictable upheavals and vicissitudes of conditions which could swamp it, fill it, absorb it remainderlessly into the lifeless in-itself, seeks not merely to moor itself to its object, but to secure its being against the ever-grinning specter of mortality by becoming its own foundation. The agonizing irony, however, is that, *per impossibile*, were this project to be realized, and were the for-itself actually to become, and thus, finally, to *be*, its own foundation, consciousness would be extinguished. Death attends the project of averting death. In a word sharpened to indignity, "it is metaphysical to struggle against oblivion . . ." (Lyotard 1983, 132). Being-unto-death is ineluctable. And paradoxically, we authentically *live* only to the extent that we abandon the project of securing our life by becoming *causa sui*. In Loy's transposition of the Platonic dictum, "life-and-death are the 'moving image' of nirvana" (1988, 234).

The envisionment of consciousness as a lack, an occasion of possible repletion, assumes what we have called the "Anaxamandrian" distillate of Sartre's unstable conception(s) of the in-itself. For a being which refuses penetration, which is absolutely dense, absolutely plenary, and which is so as a matter of ontological principle, could not, without forsaking its principled density, fissure into crevasses of nothingness. Lack, however, is said to constitute "*in its being* the being concerning which it makes the denial along with the being which it denies" (1971, 135). It is depicted as an internal negation—"a type of negation which establishes an internal relation between what one denies and that concerning which the denial is made"—and, of all internal negations, it is "the one which penetrates most deeply into being" (135). Impenetrable being, being which is "full positivity" (56), would thus be inhospitable to lack. Lack could at best display itself at its surface, but could in no way afflict the Parmenidean in-itself in its very being. Thus, in evolving his theory of lack, Sartre has implicitly taken a stand on the sense of the in-itself which he is willing to countenance. Nothingness is no longer in exile, "expelled from being" (51). And we are left to marvel at his pronouncement (typical of many others) that "[t]here is not the slightest emptiness in being, not the tiniest crack through which nothingness might slip in" (121).

The internal relation constituted by lack im/plicates the cavity or interstice which calls for filling ("that concerning which the denial is made") and the absent presence, the possible positivity, which would choke it ("what one denies"). The hole, or "that which misses what is lacking" (Sartre 1971, 135)—what Sartre calls "the existing"—could not, then, exist *as such* without "that which is missing or 'the lacking' " (135). And to complete the analytic "trinity" of presupposed conditions, the impossible *telos* of the hole—filled openness, negative positivity, the vacuous plenum—is "a totality which has been broken by the lacking and which would be restored by the synthesis of 'the lacking' and 'the existing'—this is 'the lacked' " (135). Though a filled hole is not a hole, and repletion annihilates at a single stroke both the openness and *its* specific satis/faction, Sartre persists in regarding the state of [full]fillment as "synthesis": "each particular for-itself (*Erlebnis*) lacks a certain particular and concrete reality, which if the for-itself were synthetically assimilated with it, would transform the for-itself into *itself*" (147). However, the purported "synthesis" would, in principle, fail to preserve the integrity of its analytic moments. The totality which is the lacked is ruptured through excavation, the displacement of solid content. But a properly filled hole is not a *hole* at all. In [full]fillment, cavity and content are not merely inseparable. Nor are they merely indistinguishable. The hole simply vanishes, and along with it the duality which an ostensible "synthesis" would preserve.

What the hole would welcome into itself, the earth which has been removed, and which it constitutively lacks, is "of the same nature" (Sartre 1971, 147) as the earth which suffers excavation. "What the crescent moon lacks in order to be a full moon is precisely a fragment of moon . . ." (147). The heap of earth removed through excavation (the lacking) is the possible [full]fillment of the pit. Indeed, "[w]hat is given as the *peculiar lack* of each for-itself . . . is the possibility of the for-itself" (147). But just as certainly as the hole could not exist without the heap, the for-itself could not appear as the actual removal of the in-itself. Unless "the lacked" also designates the preexcavated state, the hole involves, not a trinity, but a quadruplicity of analytic factors—the fourth (our addition) being the earth prior to displacement, what we might call the "unlacking." Sartre's language of "synthetic assimilation" (147) confirms our reading that the unlacking is not the lacked. Nihilation transforms the unlacking—not the lacked—into the lacking. Or rather, through displacement, a "portion" of the unlacking becomes lacking. But even this is inadequate. For prior to displacement, the portion of earth displaced did not exist at all—*as a portion*—any more than a bead of spray hurled into the air by the sea's ebullience existed—as an individuated drop—prior to the upsurge which gave it identity. And thus it is for every primordial institution of the portion, every portioning which is not a reapportionment, every displacement which is not antecedently a placement. The transformation of "stuff" into a portion of stuff—earth into a heap of earth, water into a drop of water—involves the original application of the measure (etymological cousin of *mens*: mind). [Mens]uration is the primal *écart* whereby unbounded materiality is given limits. And this delimitation, this rupture, of the unlacking is the negativity of the hole. The existing and the lacking are com/mensurate, the earth removed is exactly sufficient to fill the hole.

Given Sartre's Parmenidean proclivities, we would expect the in-itself to be insufficiently porous to welcome the shovel. Nihilation, on this reading, could not be excavation. Yet, again, we find Sartre settling into a more Anaximandrean outlook in his proposal that nihilation is the original lapse of coincidence, the event of refusal whereby identity with a "portion" of being-in-itself is repudiated. Nihilation is exactly the *écart*, the delimitation, the measuring, the portioning, the displacement of which we have just spoken. Nihilation is, then, and could only be, excavation.

The for-itself is "haunted" by the lacked, by the distanceless fusion of negativity and positivity, emptiness and its utter suffusion, which lures it as its welcoming and annihilating God. The moments of this purported synthesis are preserved in their distinctness only by enactments of consciousness which construe the present dissolution of duality in light of its preterit institution. But this construal, the insistence upon prolonging, in the hermeneutic mode, a past which has now vanished, is always delusory. A fresh-filled hole is, of course, distinguishable from land not yet excavated. And this gives a certain cogency to the discrimination of lacked from unlacking. But the loose, particulate texture of the new fill bespeaks a porosity, an intricate lattice of fissures and interstices, not present in the original state. The new fill gives itself as laced with veins and pockets of vacuity. But to this extent, the new "fill" is not, properly, or completely, a *fill* at all. Were it thoroughly filled, its graininess and texture would resolve into density and solidity, and the new fill would be indistinguishable from the original state, the lacked from the unlacking. Ontologically, nothing—aside from the processes of excavation and repletion and the intervening duration—

distinguishes the lacked from the unlacking. Thus, a "synthesis" which preserves the duality of the existing and the lacking is always misplaced.

We have seen Sartre pendulate between Parmenidean and Anaximandrean conceptions of being-in-itself, and have noted a consequent instability in his conception of nihilation. And we are prepared, at this point, to
attest a similar oscillation between two very different conceptions of nothingness. Consciousness is, for Sartre, a "hole of being at the heart of Being"
(1971, 786). In the analogue, the hole is de/fined by its tellurian medium,
by the terrene positivity the negativity of which it simply *is*. "Somethingness" is environmental, and nothingness is interior. A certain unicity informs interior nothingness. It is *a* cavity, *a* vacuity, surrounded by the
plenary materiality which it *is not*. But nothingness, in this sense, is irrelative
to its embracing somethingness. As the very absence of the latter, it is not be
conceived as a positive relatum. And, of course, since relation of any sort assumes the anterior "de-structuring of the in-itself" in which "in-itself is nihilated and absorbed in its attempt to found itself" (133), neither is the
preexcavated unlacking a possible relatum. The existing is not *related to* the
unlacking, it is its very absence. There is, however, an alterior conception.
The work of the measuring, portioning, negatively determines a certain remove of removal, a distantiation which prizes existing apart from lacking.
Our former quadruplicity—Sartre's three conditions of lack together with
our unlacking—must be supplemented by a fifth factor, the new quintet
now recognizing the seamless, impartite capaciousness—the remove—
which permits the event of excavation. As the *différe[/a]nce* of lacking from
existing, nothingness in this second sense is dipolar and relational. It is an
internal negation (thus, relation) between "what one denies" and "that concerning which the denial is made" (135). The hole and its excavated content
cry out for one another, cannot exist without one another. The unlacking
can, however, exist without the existing. Dipolar nothingness thus depends
upon unitary nothingness, and the latter, in turn, upon the unlacking.
Nothingness-as-privation is imaged by the hole, the bubble in being.
Nothingness-as-remove is well-represented by a line segment the length of
which "intervenes . . . by virtue of the negation of an absolute, undifferentiated proximity" (54). Nonetheless, "[w]e can in fact give the *segment* as
immediate object of intuition, in which case this segment represents a full,
concrete tension, of which the length is a positive attribute and the two
points A and B appear only as a moment of the whole. . . . Then the negation, expelled from the segment and its length, takes refuge in the two
limits . . ." (54). Similarly, although excavation, dis/placement, is conditioned by a negation of the "absolute, undifferentiated proximity" of being-
in-itself to itself, this very event of removal can become an "immediate
object of intuition," a tension, the limits of which are the hole and its exca-

vated content. The for-itself does not *differ* from the in-itself, it is the very *differing* from the in-itself that Sartre describes as "an expanding de-structuring" (133). It is not the product, but rather, the very event, of decompression. Consciousness is not removed from its nihilated object. It rather *is* this very removal. It is intrinsically dipolar—not that it bridges subject and object, but rather, that it implicates the nihilated object and the very evacuation of the latter's being. The monadic, irrelative nothingness of the hole is at best the consequence of dipolar event of removal. And if the "decompression of being" frees "the affirmation *of* self from the heart of being" (27–8), if excavation creates the hole, then dyadic nothingness is ontologically prior to monadic nothingness, and we cannot, then, construe the for-itself on analogy with the hole. Either consciousness is a hole in being or the event of hole-making—but certainly not both.

However, despite the assertion that nothingness "is the foundation of itself in so far as it is *already no longer* in-itself . . ." (Sartre 1971, 130), it founds itself *as nothingness*, and not *as being*. Being-in- itself—as nihilated— "can found its nothingness but not its being" (133). The earth removed "founds"—ontologically conditions—the hole. "This missing For-itself"— the lacking—"is the Possible" (153). The lacking is the condition for the possibility of the existing. It is the "the self-as-being-in-itself" which "human reality lacks" (138). The for-itself lacks *itself*—not because the "itself" of the for-itself fails to exist, but because it is displaced. The "self" of the for-itself is always untenanted, always vacant. Or rather, it is always displaced, distantiated from, the vacancy of the for-itself. "Nothingness is always an *elsewhere*. It is the obligation for the for-itself never to exist except in the form of an elsewhere in relation to itself, to exist as a being which perpetually effects in itself a break in being" (126). Here nothingness is defined, not against the environing contour of the originally unlacking, but against the lacking. Of course, a hole is as much the privation of the ground as the absence of earth which has been removed. Sartre insists, however, that "while the For-itself *lacks* the In-itself, the In-itself does not *lack* the For-itself. There is no reciprocity in the opposition. In a word, the For-itself remains nonessential and contingent in relation to the In-itself . . ." (145, n. 12). The hole lacks its "portion" (Gr. *moira*, fate) of the unlacking. To be "portioned-out" is the destiny of the unlacking. And this befallment, being nonessential, contingent, is thus fateful. The hollow result of the event of portioning-out is thus factical, "a memory of being" (133)—but no less factical, no less inessential, no less contingent, than the consequent accretion of the lacking. The undisturbed earth does not insist upon excavation. But the lacking could not exist without the existing, the earth removed without the hole from which is removed. To identify the in-itself with the lacking is to assume the very reciprocity-in-opposition which Sartre is concerned to deny. On the other hand, to identify the in-itself with the unlacking is to deny the foundational character of the in-itself—its role as the possibility of the for-itself—which Sartre is concerned to affirm.

We have spoken of the hole "as such": as the site of possible repletion and as ontologically conditioned by the lacking. And this is understandable in view of Sartre's thesis that "what is given as the *peculiar lack* of each for-itself and what is strictly defined as lacking to precisely this for-itself and no other is the possibility of the for-itself" (1971, 147). But the "as such" intrigues me. For unlike a butter knife which (optionally) can be "seen," naively, without mediation, or seen *as such*—self- mediated, apprehended in light of its "own" quiddity (*tode ti*), its own "what-ness"—the hole is seen *as such* or not at all. Construal *as* the absence of possible presence is constitutive for the curious quasi-object which we call a hole. There is nothing analogous to seeing the butter knife *simpliciter* prior to seeing it *as* a butter knife, since, prior to the imaginal intuition of its possible content, there is, for us, no hole. Not only does the entertainment of possibility (requisite for the consideration of concept, and ultimately of essence) found the presentation of the hole, it is ingredient in this presentation. The hole *is*, and is necessarily apprehended *as*, the site of possible repletion.

The attribution to the hole of an "as such" is, however, attended by a decisive dissonance. Sartre tells us that "[w]hat the for-itself lacks in order to be made a whole with itself is the for-itself" (147). The for-itself lacks *itself*. We cannot speak of consciousness "itself," certainly not of consciousness *in* itself. For it does not *have*, but constitutively *lacks*, itself. If "consciousness as such" bears the freight of "consciousness as it is *in itself*," it could be countenanced only on pain of despoiling Sartre's axiomatic assumptions concerning the nature of the for-itself. And if "consciousness as such" assumes that consciousness unproblematically exemplifies its essence, we must remind ourselves that the for-itself does not have, but rather transcends, its essence. It is not *what* it is. Nor is it in any way to be identified with its "whatness." It lives its life in successive disengagement from its essence, and cannot, then, be considered "as such." But if the hole can only be seen as such, it turns out to be a singularly unpromising trope for the vacuity of consciousness.

And what, moreover, is a "site," if not a place, a bounded space, and thus, if you will, the "hole" which gapes within a framework of imaginary solidity? Is the very notion of hole, then, not hopelessly circular? The rent in materiality, the gouge in positivity, which we call the hole is ineluctably constituted as a "site": the *site* of possible positivity. The hole *is not* (we might almost say "nihilates") the possible positivity which it lacks. The hole is rather the *site* of possible positivity. The Latin *situs* holds etymological suggestions of leaving, thus vacating. And the result of e[vacu]ation is the vacuum. There seems to be no way of defining "hole" except (circularly) *as a hole*—that is, *as such*—or at least in terms which feed from the metaphor of the hole. We could only define the hole *as a hole*: the hole is a hole for possible positivity. But the for-itself is not, and in fact, constitutively lacks, the in-itself. Should "hole" prove indefinable, or definable only tautologically, it would succumb to Nāgārjuna's dialectical axe and prove meaningless as well. And if meaningful, then either the image of the "hole in being" is unsuited to provoke insight into the nature of consciousness or we must be able, without incoherence, to speak of "consciousness *as such*."

The single word, "*anātman*" (Pali: *anatta*), enfolds the relentless drive of Buddhist thought to uncover and deconstruct the last vestige of self (*ātman*). Nothing "has" self. Nothing rests passively and complacently "in" the self that it would have. All phenomena lack themselves—the very "selves" which the excavated heap of other phenomena would (if it could) provide. Nothing, then, is *in* itself. Nothing exists *as it is*. Nothing exists, and nothing can be presented without delusion, *as such*. To speak of the object *as such* is to assume a certain coordination of the aspects under which it is seen and features which are *intrin[sic]* to it, which belong to it by nature, which, pursuing the etymology of the word, stand beside (L. *secus*) the interior, which penetrate most deeply into its being. It is just this interior being which Buddhism repudiates. If its intrinsic features are expressive of this core, the object is ek/static, outside itself; its nucleic being resides among its attributes. But this is hardly a case of intrinsity, since purportedly intrinsic features would not stand in proximity to the interior, but rather, to the extent of their expressiveness, would themselves harbor the interior. The ob/ject "thrown" (*jectus*) "toward" (*ob-*) us blossoms in a starburst of exteriorization. The being of the object would be "fragmented whole," as it were, factored out among its potentially numberless expressive attributes without falling into division among them, each attribute expressive of the entirety of the object's being. *Zero*, of course, is the only number which can be divided by any number and still maintain its integrity. Ecstasy entails emptiness—not intrinsity. To say, moreover, that intrinsic qualities are merely "beside" (*secus*) the central ontic point of the object, is to regard them as surface display, glitter. The intrinsic reverses itself and becomes extrinsic. We thus have little choice but to regard the interior being of the object as the site of inherence. And, once again, with its openness, its receptivity, the "site" reveals itself as a vacuity, a hole. The in-itself can be regarded "as such," then, and, indeed, could have a "self" or "itself," only by surrendering its plenary density and becoming an interstice, a gap, a hole. Intrinsic qualities would float in an interior void. Or—and this comes, perhaps, to the same thing—these qualities would conceal the hollowness within. And since (being intrinsic) they could not be indifferent to the interior, they would, to that extent be expressive. Again we witness the autodeconstruction of the very notion of intrinsity—and thus, the "as such." It is not that all qualities prove extrinsic, instead. For extrinsity can be no more intelligible than intrinsity. And since one interior emptiness is indistinguishable from the next, to regard the butter knife *as such* is to observe its ostensibly "intrinsic" properties bobbing upon a limitless sea of emptiness.

The early Theravāda tradition conceived local space as "lack of matter" in which "there is nothing to be seen or felt." Depicted as "the gaps, interstices, vacua, holes, apertures, etc., which occur between . . . objects," it is "finite, visible and conditioned" (Conze 1962, 164). From the beginning, Buddhism has offered an analysis of the hole not unlike Sartre's. *Samsāra—realitas*, the domain of *res*, ontic modality of manifest phenomena—is structured by *pratītya-samutpāda*. Every occurrence, every ontic upsurge, is like a sheaf of wheat erected through dynamic op/position, each straw both leaning upon and supporting others. Entrusting its being to others, each is empty (*śūnya*), devoid of own-being (*sva-bhāva*). Each is a void, a pocket, a bubble. Each is lacking all the others. And each, like the Sartrean for-itself, would be annihilated were the lacking of the lacking not ineluctably constitutive. The "arising" (*utpāda*) of phenomena depends—ontically—upon the evacuation of self. The suffusion (Sartre's "synthesis") of the existing by the lacking, its [full]fillment, would cause the phenomenon simply to vanish. Lacking, in this case, is not an ontological, but an ontic privation. Each being defers its being to a constellation of other beings—not to Being. While Sartre posits an asymmetrical relationship between existing and lacking—"[t]here is no reciprocity in the opposition" (1971, 145, n. 12)—Buddhism insists upon symmetry. "[B]eneath this level of opposition lies a sea of tranquillity in which all things are complementary rather than contradictory" (Blyth 1976, 14). Each straw in the sheaf both leans and supports. Each phenomenon drains itself kenotically into all others, and, in turn, reposits the being of others within "itself" (the very "self" which it reciprocally offers up). Each is both vacuum and suffusion, hole and content, existent and lacking. Like the line segment which can be viewed as the "negation of an absolute, undifferentiated proximity" and as "a full, concrete tension"—"[t]here are two forms, and the condition of the appearance of the one is the disintegration of the other . . ." (1971, 54)—each plays both roles: the empty and the full.

There is, of course, an ontological dimension of excavation. While, for Sartre, nihilated being is depicted as the excavated content of the hole, it is nonetheless *Being*, and not a particulate dust of *beings*, which is removed. Buddhism recognizes no irrefrangible density. Solidity is a myopic haze which a more trenchant vision (*prajñā*) would resolve into finer structure, the elements of structure at each successive level similarly proving nebula of indistinctness. Dis/placement involves removal—through space—to an alterior place—a meted and "destined" portion of space delimited by environing positivity (manifest nebulousness). We cannot understand the event of excavation (and thus, the hole) without reference to the space between places, the space which separates/unites the original site of portioning and the site of consequent deposit: the remove. Or rather, the site of portioning is co-occurrent with the primal event of portioning. Prior to portioning, there is no site. There is only the unlacking which lacks for nothing. The remove arises in the very enactment of excavation, and is thus a derivative nothingness. Deeper than, anterior to, the remove, prior to the hole and the deposit, is a spatiality of authoritative subtlety, an ultimate, unsurpassable vacuity which Sartre expressly repudiates. Nothingness, for Sartre, is not "an infinite milieu where being is suspended" (1971, 56). Yet without the emptiness which grants permission to being, neither the lacking nor the unlacking, neither the existing nor the lacked, could enjoy any ontological reputation whatsoever. The hole is formed in the earth. But the earth is not boundlessly extensive. It drifts like a speck of dust through the measureless amplitude of interstellar space, its apparent solidity wholly transfused, wholly permeated, wholly compromised, by the boundless abyss. The in/difference of space is not contempt for the insignificant, the vanishingly small, but is rather an index of its affordance of being, its refusal to op/pose, or equally, its unrestricted affirmation of position. Space is that which, in principle, cannot range itself *against* anything, which can have no enemies, which is concordant with all, and which, because it does not resist also cannot be resisted. Its pure permissiveness is its suffusion, its permeation, of the seemingly solid. Nothing is so dense, so plenary, that it can exclude that which, in principle, cannot but welcome it.

Solidity, the principle of expulsion, can act only upon the solid. The domain of the solid, the plenary, is the modality of reciprocally external existence, existence *partes extra partes*. Any suggestion of an ostensible partite structure on the part of the solid would fling part from part as dramatically as a visible explosion. It is the impartite integrity of the in-itself that defuses the detonation. And if the Sartrean vision of a being of infinite density, "an indivisible, indissoluble being" (1971, 15) which "is itself indefinitely" (29) is not to be supplanted by the Buddhist recognition of bottomless deterioration, dis/integration, division, dissolution, we cannot understand the "perfect equivalence of content to container" (120–1) or the "coincidence with itself" (123) as insinuating the least shade of internal relatedness. Self-coincidence, self-identity, self-equivalence, would seem to posit the shadow of duality separating the in-itself *from itself*. This is clearly not Sartre's intent. But if its terms are in no way discriminable, the assertion of identity not only looses its point, but verges into meaninglessness. To be significant, a statement of identity must search the subtle crevasse between identicals, pry them apart, and yet declare them one. "Within identity there is yet difference" (cf. Chang 1971, 230). The blur, the nebulous fusion and dissolution of detail which wafts above articulated structure, is, from the Buddhist vantage point, the "one" which the manifold *are*. Thus, ironically, the very meaningfulness of Sartre's characterization of the in-itself deprives it of density, indivisibility. The condition of meaningfulness for Sartre's ontological proposal is that it be false.

But Sartre's understanding of space is redeemingly insightful. Space is the medium of decompression: the metastasis which institutes, in place of the fusion and indistinctness of identity, the perspicuous detail of its terms. When "the continuous background . . . bursts into a multiplicity of discontinuous elements" (1971, 254), it is space which affords this fulguration. Or rather, space is the volatility of continuity. "It is precisely this perpetual evanescence of the totality into collection, of the continuous into the discontinuous that defines *space*" (254). If "the world . . . appears as an evanescent totality" (254), space is its "instability," its ideal capacity to "disintegrate into external multiplicity" (254). Spatiality is "the disintegrating relation of the world to the *thises*, of the *thises* to the world" (272). Space is "the permanent passage from continuous to discontinuous" (254), and "results in the pullulation of the *thises*" (255). Space, then, is neither the continuous (the world-ground) nor the discontinuous (the figural "thises"), but the possibility of dehiscence. If "the world appears always ready to open like a box," space is this readiness. Space is not the "box," nor its differentiated contents. Nor is it the event of opening. It is rather the virtuality of opening. It is not dehiscence, but its delitescence. "Space is neither the ground nor the figure but the ideality of the ground inasmuch as it can always disintegrate into figures" (254).

The flowers of discontinuity bloom in the soil of the continuous. But we must query Sartre's assumption that the "thises" were *already there* prior to efflorescence, that they "*already were* (there in the heart of the undifferentiation of the ground) what they are now as a differentiated figure" (1971, 254). Thinking of space as "pure exteriority" (254)—his Kantian idiom, not for a form of intuition, for space "can not be a form" (255), but for the possibility of exteriorization—Sartre seems to assume here that things maintain their reciprocal externality even though, in virtue of remoteness, their visible articulation lapses into a haze of indistinctness. With evident paradox, Sartre avers that space "is a moving relation between beings which are unrelated" (254). There is no doubt that the flowers "come out." But Sartre seems to have no reason, beyond a visceral realism, and no phenomenological warrant, to suppose that visibilia drawn inward from their vanishing point, from their junction of dissolution in the ground, were *already there*, and there as "what they are now." While Sartre's prospect accords well with the Buddhist, he has unwittingly given over too much to a position which he officially rejects. For to declare that figural objects stand forth—ex/sist—exactly as they were when lost in the indiscrete tumble of prethetic experience is to suppose that the lapse of difference, the deliquescence of detail, which characterizes the ground is a purely phenomenal, and not an ontological, disposition. But if space is the virtuality of decompression, we should expect the originary state of compression, the liquidation of *différe[/a]nce*—the in-itself—to be treated with enhanced ontological reverence. Buddhism quite naturally regards the in-itself as a myopic blur, a failure of clarity occasioned by egological convergence. But if, for Sartre, the continuity of the ground is (as for Buddhism) a product of nearsightedness, if the "this," in all its actual detail, is already (though imperceptibly) *there*, then decompression is not the deterioration of the in-itself, but the making-apparent of a disintegration which has always already taken place. The in-itself is empty, not full. And Sartre has tacitly abandoned his ontology.

The nihilated object stands at the extremity of the remove. It is remote. And at the limit of remoteness, the object merges into the world-ground, or is rather drawn from this ground, showing that the world (as final continuity) is a merely apparent wash of indetermination. Again, Buddhism concurs. But ironically, the realist proclivity illustrated in Sartre's discrimination of the *real* "differentiated figure" from the *apparent* "undifferentiation of the ground" volatilizes the real. Though the world "is revealed simultaneously as a synthetic totality and as a purely additive collection of all the 'thises' " (1971, 253), the already-thereness of the figure, the real collectivity of "thises," purports that the "syncretism of undifferentiation" (254)—an unlikely stand-in for "synthetic totality"—is empty of ontological status.

Of course, space "can not be a *being*" (Sartre 1971, 254). "Space," as Puligandla discerns, "is able to accommodate all objects equanimously because it is itself not an object among other objects" (1985, 56). But the inference that "[s]pace does not allow itself to be apprehended by concrete intuition" (Sartre, 255) is alien to the spirit of Buddhism. To be sure, space is not a contingent absence which, in principle, could be brought to sensuous givenness. Nor is it an ineluctably absent presence. Its modality of absence in no way contrasts with presence. It is neither an accidental nor an essentially fateful befallment that its purported "presence" remains beyond intuitive fulfillment. It *has* no presence, but continuously evades presentation in its disengagement from the presentable. The abyss conditions the hole. It is not an interstice which could be congested with hyletic givenness. Nor again, is it a being in any way capable of sensuous opalescence. The fixation of mind which destines a portion (*moira*) of space to determinacy,

transforming it, thus, into a qualitatively discriminable, *place* (though discriminable only in virtue of "its" environing positivity), assumes, but does
not thematize, space. A place is a being. Space, as Sartre tells us, "*is not*, but
it is continuously spatialized" (255). It perpetually disengages itself from
the individuable things and places which inhabit it. To be thus "spatialized"
is to refuse coincidence with, and in a more expansive sense, to "nihilate,"
not only the in-itself, not only the articulate forms of being-in-itself which
arise, in their concretion and relatedness, on the basis of the originary nihilation of the for-itself, not only the *négatités*, the intuitable absences, which
condition concretion and determinacy, and not only the for- itself as the individuated "hole" in being, but every specified, every discriminated, every
individuated being, in-itself and for-itself, and every determinate modality
of being.

Sartre passes almost imperceptibly from a conception of conscious
nothingness which arises through the ebbing of integrity, the effluent withdrawal of identification with the in-itself, to a situated, thus modalized,
withdrawal, a "*qualified* negation" (1971, 277). Consciousness is not merely
the nihilation of being, but the nihilation of being *in a particular way*. We
are holes, not space. Affirming the seamless continuity of hole and space,
Buddhism will not abandon this distinction without comment. The apparently bounded space within the cup is not different from the space which
surrounds it. Individuation, though undeniably apparent, and thus, phenomenologically warranted, finds no place in Buddhist (me)ontology.
Insofar as the task of phenomenology is understood as that of disclosing the
experiential ground for philosophical claims, ontology exceeds phenomenology. That alone which is specified and qualified in determinate ways is
subject to the "concrete intuition" which Sartre withholds from space.
Space effaces itself. Or rather, at the precise site at which it calls attention to
its "face," its "self," it has been transmuted into place. Its *clarity*—a word
whose telling ambiguity integrates luminosity and luminal mediation—is
exactly its perpetual eluding of concrete intuition. And to this extent, Sartre
is assuredly correct. But while space is not a concretion of quality, and has
nothing to offer to an intuition which demands specificity, determinacy, as
a condition of its operation, it does not follow that space is beyond the pale
of a pure, nondiscriminating intuition (*prajñā*) which, while revealing, reveals no-thing at all. In Suzuki's presentation, "the functioning of Prajna is
discrete, and interrupting to the progress of logical reasoning, but all the
time it underlies it, and without Prajna we cannot have any reasoning whatever. Prajna is at once above and in the process of reasoning. This is a contradiction, formally considered, but in truth this contradiction itself is made
possible because of Prajna" (1981, 55). The eye, open and functioning normally, does not cease to *see* when the lights are turned out. Nor, were it to

gaze off to infinity, would the eye fail to see, even though its vision did not converge upon an opacity. As Hui-hai discerns, "[t]he nature of perception being eternal, we go on perceiving whether objects are present or not. . . . whereas objects naturally appear and disappear, the nature of perception does neither of those things; and it is the same with all your other senses" (Blofeld 1972, 48). It is just that there is nothing (no *thing*, no specificity, no determination) which space is *like* (though our awareness of space may be *like* our awareness of anything at all). And as Blake perceives, "[i]f the doors of perception were cleansed, every thing would appear to man as it is, infinite" (1975, 197). Sartre is deeply insightful (though not evidently correct) in his recognition that being-in-itself is available to consciousness in the preconceptual moods of nausea and boredom. As an objectless affect, a mood is a certain pervasive tincturing of consciousness. But what, then, of the "null-mood," the absolutely unimpeded clarity of consciousness, unqualified by affective coloration? Much like silence (the null-sound), the null-mood, though illuminating, will illuminate—make *clear* (luminous and transparent)—nothing at all. And our intuition of space is similarly clarifying. The inverse of immanence (the identity of being and appearing), space is the interliquation of being and non-appearing, of light and its medial openness. The intuition of space is the clarifying openness to clarity.

The abyss, which is "clear" to a clarifying intuition, is, if not phenomenologically, then ontologically undivided from the hole. The sides of the cup, the apparent density of the surrounding earth, do not interrupt the unbroken continuity of space. Space offers no impedance to the solid. "Opposition and resistance can only arise between one object and another, but not between space and any object" (Puligandla 1985, 56). But neither is it disrupted by massive positivity. However, a decisive shift from Sartrean commitments is brought about by the determination to take the abyss as a condition for the hole, and thus, to take it with ontological seriousness. For Sartre, the hole, the bubble in being, unequivocally "is," although it *is* as a privation of being. The hole is defined against its environing positivity. What it *is* is exactly its *not being* the density which surrounds it. The issue which separates Sartre from the Buddhist outlook concerns the way in which this definition functions: phenomenologically or ontologically. Buddhism would happily concede that what the hole *appears* to be is an absence of massive presence. But what it *is*—ontologically—is the abyss. It is, then, a condition of the *appearance* of the hole that the hole does not exist. While being-in-itself (grounding and presupposed by the for-itself) is the primal category of Sartre's ontology, the in-itself is, for the abyss, no more than ectoplasmic *Schein*. And the for-itself, limited and individuated consciousness, is continuous with the abyss. The hole, then, as the site of repletion by the unreal is likewise unreal. In its ontological integrity, it is final reality. As conceptually circumscribed, it is unreal.

The hole is the site of possible repletion. The abyss cannot—in principle—be "filled." Were we to grant to Parmenides the conception of being as absolute spissitude—a spissatus of such utter opacity and density as to blot out every vestige of clarity—a being unique and incomparable, and thus without relation, spatial or otherwise, to another beyond itself, a being, then, which would pervade the abyss devouring every morsel of vacuity, every pore, every follicle, every stoma, every follicular gap—even still, this absolute plenum could not *fill* the abyss. Repletion is annihilation. A sated vacancy ceases to exist—at least inasmuch as its negativity is defined against the positivity of its satiation. The abyss remains serenely in/different to ful[fill]ment. It does not thirst for satiety. Nor does it offer the least resistance to that which would inhabit it. It welcomes its content without preying upon it. The vacua of Sartre's ontology are predatory. Though Sartre renounces "that primitive illusion . . . according to which to know is to eat—that is, to ingest the known object, to fill oneself with it (*Erfüllung*), and to digest it ('assimilation')" (1971, 258–9), the pursuit of repletion never arrives at the first bite (let alone digestion). Like hungry ghosts, they are unable to consume their prey—or would be able to do so only at their own ontic expense. To describe their predation, we must speak in the subjunctive: *per impossibile*, the hole *would* lapse from being *were* "it" (a problematic reference) to achieve satiety. There is, however, no question of filling the abyss, not because it is unbounded, for we could imagine a boundless plenum, but because that which would fill it is ineluctably spectral, wraithlike. Whatever densities, whatever solidities, there may be, pass through space without impedance like a will-o'-the-wisp evaporating through a solid rampart. Nothing "occupies" space as an army might occupy a defeated nation. Space cannot be forced, for it offers no resistance. Space is neither absorbed nor displaced by plenary presence. It *lets-be*, and is the condition for the wraithlike "being"—the apparent reality and ultimate non-reality of the massive and voluminous.

For Sartre, "[t]he existence of space is the proof that the For-itself by causing being 'to be there' adds *nothing* to being" (1971, 254). What does the affirmation that this cup, this telephone, this book, *exists* add to its being-there? Sartre's intentionally ambivalent reply is "nothing." Being is not thereby fattened by a supplemental quantum of presence, an ancillary modicum of positivity. There has, however, occurred a subtle modulation of the ontological fabric of our world. "It is the for-itself in its presence to being which causes there to be an *all of being*" and "*this* particular being can be called *this* only on the ground of the presence of *all* being" (250).

Intrinsically devoid of allness and emergent particularity, space is nonetheless the dwelling for the *all* and the *this*. Allness is not a discernible feature of
being. It is not positive. Still, *all* is transformed, in the twinkling of an eye,
when envisioned as "all" (a primal instance of originary portioning). There
could be no locus of attachment, and no totality of such loci, without the
thematic positing of existence. Space *lets-be*. And the Buddhist withdrawal
of both ontic assent and ontic denial bears witness to Hui-neng's ringing
proclamation: "Not one thing exists. It is "the 'madness' of the *epoché* . . ."
(Rovatti 1988, 133) that attunes the mind to that spaciousness which,
while constellated with presences, is in no way disrupted by them.

Sartre assimilates quantity to spatiality. "[S]pace and quantity are only
one and the same type of negation" (1971, 264). Both are defined as "pure
exteriority" (254, 263). Space is "a totality which is dispersed in relations of
exteriority" (270). And while we would demure at regarding the abyss as a
"totality"—it could be totalized and submitted to ac/count—only if it
sported an "outside," thus regressively presuming a space for this exterior
display—there is acuity in Sartre's view that space conditions dyadicity. We
would append only that space also conditions monadicity. There could be
neither "two" nor "one" without space. Space, then, is not *one*, and also not
two. It is numberless, transordinal, in[sub]ordinate. But Sartre's characterization of exteriority as a "relation-of-absence-of-elation" (283) signals a
dramatic divergence from Buddhist insights. Dōgen admonishes us to "let
go of all relations" (cf. Menzan 1988, 104). Exteriority is understood in
terms of in/difference. The "this," the figural locus of positional consciousness, "defines its place by revealing itself . . . as indifferent to other beings.
This indifference is nothing but its very identity, its absence from ekstatic
reality . . ." (Sartre 1971, 288). The holographic, *ineinander* figuration
which imbues the Buddhist vision of dependent co-arising (*pratītya-
samutpāda*) renders ontological in/difference unthinkable. All phenomena
are ek/static, existing in deferral, beyond themselves. Nothing is endowed
with *being* simpliciter. But in Thích Nhât Hạnh's telling idiom, all things
"inter-be." Emptiness is relational being. No being is "indifferent," since
being (being inter-being) is constituted by difference. Setting this aside, the
language of "indifference" may find a certain aptness after all. While remoteness may be a predicate of separated units of positivity, it is misleading
to posit the same with respect to purportedly "separated" points or portions
of space. With progressive removal, the detail and articulated structure of
the object lapses into indistinctness, its very identity lapsing, finally, into the
continuity of the *Weltboden*. Nothing similar to this occurs in the clarity of
our intuition of space. Space is not intrinsically busied with detail which
could "lapse" into disindividuation. A point is not a *this*, "a point of singularity which punctures the surface of the reproduction . . ." (Derrida 1988,

264). To see "it" at all is exactly to see *through* it. Its being *is* its diaphaneity, its translucid disclosure of what lies beyond it. Its "self" is its self-effacement in deference to the different, the other. This relation, this mode of related-ness, is, in an evident sense, ontologically sensitive to difference. It is the re[veil]ation of the different. But in an equally valid sense, since the being of the point is its revealing, in the revealing of the point, the revealed and the revealing are indiscriminable, in/different. The remote, posited as such in association with remote positivity, is, paradoxically, absolutely proximal. The point of the point is that location is perlocation, and perlocation is co-(l)location.

Science, the witness of empirical repeatability, is inevitably limited, and limited especially in its failure to countenance the nonrecurrent, thus non-idealizable, nonquantifiable, nongeneralizable, a default which elucidates Lyotard's claim that "empiricism cannot be understood through empiri-cism" (1991b, 38). The unique is alien to science, and thus scientifically un-intelligible. Thus, physical explanation can never be complete. For science, the real is the repeatable. Or in Baudrillard's words, "[t]he very definition of the real becomes: *that of which it is possible to give an equivalent reproduction*" (1983, 146). Scientific reality thus assumes the antecedence of the "re-": "the real is not only what can be reproduced, but *that which is always already reproduced*" (146). There is no original, no first instance. Or as Foucault says, "representation no longer exists; there is only action" (1977, 206). There are reproductions subsequent to reproductions without end. And in this sense, "it is reality itself that disappears utterly in the game of reality . . ." (Baudrillard, 148). And Buddhism disparages "the vulgar prejudices of those who, from mere tribal sluggishness, are convinced that 'Western', i.e., Judaeo-Christian and scientific, modes of thinking are the unfailing stan-dards of all truth" (Conze 1962, 10). Only repeatability affords control. Thus, if there is a nonscientific *scientia*, a knowledge of the un repeatable, then—respects to Foucault—knowledge cannot simply be conflated with power. Indeed, "ignorance is a necessary condition for doing science" (Puligandla 1985, 105). And the knowledge of the emptiness, the condi-tioned arising, of phenomena is exactly an envisagement of their freedom from law-governed regularity. Because the wake of conditions which give rise to a phenomenon is augmented with each arising, and because phe-nomena arise as an expression of the entire wake, there is no question of repetition. A phenomenon simply *is* its wake of conditions. But with each augmentation, there is the generation of a radically novel wake. Phenomena are "out-laws"—beyond lawful regularity—and are not, then, subordinate to technological power. If "[m]en pay for the increase of their power with alienation from that over which they exercise power" (Horkheimer and Adorno 1972, 9), then alienation is a symptom of *avidyā*, a blindness to the implications of emptiness. While Sartre is no unqualified opponent of science, a certain modest disapprobation is felt in his description of scientific practice: "the scientist is concerned only with establishing purely exterior relations. . . . the result of this scientific research is that the thing itself, deprived of all instrumentality, finally disappears into absolute exteriority" (1971, 275). Merleau-Ponty concurs in his claim that "science began by excluding all the predicates that come to the things from our encounter with them" (1969, 15). Contemporary physics might welcome the discarded vision of materiality as constituted in fluctuations of vacuity. Sartre regards this "reabsorption" as qualitative impoverishment. For him, "the quality is the presence of the absolute contingency of being, its indifferent irreducibility" (258). Quality is resistance to recurrence, impedance to idealization. Quantity, on the other hand, is an "ideal nothing in-itself . . ." (263). Quantity and quality are not, then, on friendly terms. The latter could be absorbed into the former only at the sacrifice of its own being. Science strips human experience of uniqueness and unrepeatability, of contingency and inexplicability, leaving in place a system of abstract idealizations, a system which explains, yes, but a system, nonetheless, which explains only the explananda which withstand scientific reduction to quantity. Still, there is a glimpse of another construal in his repudiation of Husserl's view of quality as a "fulfillment" (*Erfüllung*), as if it were possible, without obliteration, to fill the vacuity of consciousness. Quality is rather "the giving form to an emptiness as a determined emptiness of that quality" (258). Quality is a modalization, a modification, a fluctuation, of emptiness. It is at least pertinent to attend to Sartre's admission of the possibility of an experiential re/duction to the empty, the spacious. Far from the familiar "nothing-but-ism" which would consign folk psychology, folk phenomenology, folk ontology, to the land of whispers, this "leading-back" would not be an abandonment of that which is "lead," but a retracing of the dynamic of its sap, its quiddity, its structured appearing to the *tathāgata garbha*, the immeasurable, unquantifiable "womb" of the surpassing-toward-suchness. Suchness, in Buddhist terms, is already enfolded in emptiness. And to this extent, Sartre's view is resonant. But the reduction—scientific or, in the Buddhist case, ontological—represents, for Sartre, the relinquishment of quality. There seems, however, to be little guiding this view apart from stipulation. Sartre posits that "[q]uality is nothing other than the being of the *this* when it is considered apart from all external relation with the world or with other *thises*" (257). Naturally, if our awareness of quality prescinds inevitably from spatiality, the intuition of space is non-qualitative. Quality would vanish in a reconstruction which acknowledges only the "relation-of-absence-of-relation." From the Buddhist vantage point, however, the "this" cannot be considered apart from all relation with the different. Confined to the Sartrean understanding of external relation, Buddhism would regard this concept as vacuous. There *is* no external relatedness in this sense, since being is inter-being, and ontological in/difference is without illustration in our experience.

Sartre is nowhere more insightful than in his compelling portrayal of the originary "synaesthetic" dimension of experience—though the fact that "[w]e eat the color of a cake, and the taste of this cake is the instrument which reveals its shape and its color to what we may call the alimentary intuition" (1971, 257) has nothing to do with the knitting-together of already articulated strands of sensory input. Still, in his description of this prearticulate *aisthesis*, there is a salient intimation of *pratīta-samutpāda*. "The fluidity, the tepidity, the bluish color, the undulating restless of the water in a pool are given at one stroke, each quality through the others; and it is this total interpenetration which we call the *this*" (257). Thus, Sartre can write that "every quality of being is all of being" (258). And "[i]n this sense a quality is not an external aspect of being, for being, since it has no 'within,' can not have a 'without' " (258). Indeed, "quality is *the whole of being* . . . It is not the 'outside' of being; it is all being . . ." (258). And while we might wonder how Sartre's repudiation of the inside/outside distinction squares with his assertion that the figure "holds the ground *within* it [emphasis added] as its own undifferentiated density" (260), we can only admire the perspicuity of his vision of interpenetration. He is pure crystal in his recognition that "the yellow of the lemon is not a subjective mode of apprehending the lemon; it *is* the lemon" (257). There is no ponderable massiveness, no substratum, no "undifferentiated ground" which does not "wholly penetrate" the figural "this" (260). "There is therefore no substantial form here, no principle of unity to stand *behind* the modes of appearance of the phenomenon; everything is given at one stroke without any primacy" (272). And Sartre's antisubstantialism is in perfect consonance with the Buddhist rejection of *ātman* in all of its dis/guises.

What Sartre seems to miss is the relativity of the discrepancy between internal and external relations. It can be convenient, useful, interesting, even vital, to regard the terms of a plurality as bearing their outsides to one another in stolid disaffection. We *can* regard them as mutually indifferent. And the fact that we can regard them this way instead of seeing them as implicates of an integrated totality is itself a tribute to *pratītya-samutpāda*. Still, we cannot derive an ontology from accidental modes of apprehension. It would be an audacious and unwarranted leap to pass from the *possibility* of regarding a multiplicity of "thises" as irrelative and reciprocally indifferent to the ontological appropriateness of doing so, and thus, in his sense, to a positing of the "in-itself." Sartre is, of course, right that being-a-group-of-three is not a property of the members of the group taken severally (1971,

263). But he circumvents the possibility that this numeric determination might be "a concrete property of the group" with insouciant haste. And he passes with even greater abandon to the conclusion that "[t]he relation of quantity is therefore a relation in-itself but a purely negative and external relation" (263). "Three-ness" does not, of course, belong to singularities. And were Sartre right that it does not also belong to totalities—triplets, in particular—numerical quantity might well be "isolated and detached from the surface of the world as a reflection (*reflet*) of nothingness cast on being" (264). Sartre modulates into a Parmenidean key with his tacit assumption that nothingness does not bore into being, but only shimmers at the surface. And this is incongruous with his deposition that quantity is a mode of spatiality and the conjoint poetic of the hole which assumes a non-Parmenidean construal of being. The "hole in being" is a portion of space devoid of density and positivity. Much as emptiness is empty even of "itself," quantity, as a mode or specification of spatiality, is "finally exterior to itself" (264). But if the vacuous site of possible repletion is a portion of space, we cannot concur that quantity/spatiality is "a purely exterior relation between the thises" (264).

Chapter 8

The Possibility of the Possible

The hole needs only to *have been* dug. With one exception, its pluperfection, assuming the closure of a prior event of excavation, posits no further advent. Were the world flash frozen after the excavation, were all occurrence quelled, were all to lapse into breathless stillness, there would still be holes. There *would* be, that is, assuming the prospect of a thaw. For if the hole is the site of possible repletion, then despite the statuesque quiescence of a frozen world-scape, at least one further event must, if inconceivably remote, even if never actual, at least be possible: that of repletion. Like the portioning-out of the unlacking, repletion is an absolute (irrelative) event. Excavation is not excavation *of the hole*. The hole is rather the result of excavation. And repletion is not the filling *of the hole*. It is the event which annihilates the hole. In themselves, excavation and repletion, though they designate a referent which is not "there"—in the one case, the hole prior to excavation, in the other, the hole subsequent to repletion—do not directly operate upon the hole. The hole is a relative phenomenon suspended precariously between two absolute events: creation and destruction, nihilation and annihilation. To be hospitable to the hole, the world could be, but could not *necessarily* be, purged of happenings. The hole is founded in the past completion of excavation and the possible, thus, possibly adventual, befallment of repletion. In a cryogenic world, the adamantine crystals of frozen events must thrill with the suspense of the possible. In a world in which nothing can "[hap]pen," there could be no holes. Holes would be [hap]less. Holes require happen-stance, the per[haps].

The deposit formed by excavation is, of course, contemporary with the hole. Both occupy the same present. Yet while the lacking fits the existing like hand in glove, the one "transcendent and complementary" (Sartre 1971, 147) to the other, complementation is, in principle, never achieved. "Hand" could be inserted into "glove" only at the peril of abolishing the "glove." We can no more speak of the repletion *of a hole* than we can speak of the death *of a living being*. "Dead animal," contradicting in the predicate what is affirmed in the notion of an animate being, a being endowed with *anima*, is simply a solecism, referring, at best, to the a perceptible *requiem* for a once living being. And "filled hole," though it may serve as the memorial for the once yawning chasm, is likewise self-contradictory. "Human-reality is free because *it is not enough*. It is free because it is perpetually wrenched away from itself and because it has been separated by a nothingness from what it is and from what it will be" (568). But the lacking is not only wrenched from the unlacking, it is transposed into a different temporal register. It becomes adventual. The "missing For-itself" becomes "the Possible" (153). While "all negation is ekstatic" (266), exhausting itself in its denial of the other, it is not simply that the existing has its being outside of itself, in its complement, its "self." It is not merely [ek]static, standing contemporaneously *beside* itself. It is also *ahead* of itself. Its "self" is always a project to be realized. For Sartre, "I *am* not the self which I will be. . . . I am not that self because time separates me from it" (68). Nihilation (excavation) institutes "a temporal form where I await myself in the future, where I 'make an appointment with myself on the other side of that hour, of that day, or of that month' " (73). In its assumption of contemporaneity, the static image of the hole and its deposit becomes (at best) unhelpful, and at worst, deeply misleading. Possibility—"the *peculiar lack* of each for-itself" (147)—lures the for-itself into the future like the proverbial carrot dangling from a stick just beyond the ass's nose (cf. 277–8). As Sartre comments, "we run after a possible which our very running causes to appear, which is nothing but our running itself, and which thereby is by definition out of reach. We run toward ourselves and we are—due to this very fact—the being which can not be reunited with itself" (278).

The upsurge of the for-itself institutes a dramatically novel logic of modality. "I didn't know your house was as large as it is" invites the flip rejoinder: "How could it be otherwise." But the amusement conceals a perfectly sober Sartrean point. It is not that the in-itself maintains its properties *of necessity*. Rather, the very sense of its contingency provides that—*given* the contingent and inexplicable ensemble of qualities which it presently enjoys—*it* could not be otherwise than *it* occurrently is. Indeed, *it* is (it *is*) "what" (the interpenetrative multiplicity of its qualities) it is. We have seen that "the yellow of the lemon . . . *is* the lemon" (257). *Given* that the lemon is yellow, *it* (identical with its yellowness) could be no other color. *Given* that the house is exactly as large as it is, *it* (identical with its largeness) could be neither smaller nor larger. Properties are embraced by the figural object, the "this," with a contingent necessity: *Given* its yellowness (a purely contingent endowment), the lemon could not, without effecting the rupture of its self-identity, fail to be yellow.

This is evident from what Sartre affirms concerning the (loco-) motion of the "this": "If a *this* were to be transferred from one place to another and during this transfer were to undergo a radical alteration of its being, this alteration would negate the motion since there would no longer be anything which was in motion" (286). For the in-itself, qualitative stability in motion is a condition of self-identity. With the for-itself there arises a being which repudiates its own quiddity, evading it, transcending it, leaving it behind, with each pulse of its profluent life. It never simply *is* what it is. Like a snake shedding its skin, it perpetually discards its essence. Given its peculiar "whatness," the in-itself could not be other than it is. Under the same assumption, the for-itself could not fail to be other than it is. In Lyotard's concomitant declaration, "I am no more than what I already was, and I am no longer it. Life signifies the death of what one is, and this death attests that life has a meaning" (1984, 7). The ontological divide concerns what is to be done with a being's qualitative endowment: coincide with it or elude it; have it or transcend it?

But if "[m]otion . . . supposes the permanence of the quiddity" (Sartre 1971, 286), can the essential aspects of the "this" ever undergo change? Sartre tells us that "[m]otion is in no way similar to becoming; it does not change the *essence* of the quality; neither does it *actualize* the quality. The quality remains exactly what it is; but its mode of being is changed" (289). There is, then, a way of undergoing temporality which leaves the essence intact (motion), and a way of undergoing temporality which alters the very essence of the "this" (becoming). Both modalities of temporal engagement are equally possible. And Sartre seems little concerned with the threat of incoherence which the conception of *becoming* presents. The thirteenth-century Zen master, Dōgen, saw clearly, however, that firewood does not *become* ash, winter does not *become* spring, life does not *become* death. Or as Nāgārjuna discerned long before, "[y]outh does not age in the strict sense and milk does not turn into butter. . . . youth is youth, age is age, milk is milk, and butter is butter" (Inada 1970, 91). Resistance to becoming does not import the foolish and empirically untenable view that the one is not *followed* by the other. There is supplantation—not becoming. The terminus of becoming is being. If A were to *become* B, then at the end of the process of becoming, A would *be* B. If firewood were to *become* ash, then at the closure of the event of burning, the firewood, with all of its essential properties intact, would simply *be* the ash which ensues. And this is patently absurd. In the end, if something has *become*, it has *come to be* exactly what it *is not*. And this idiosyncracy is officially reserved for the for-itself. Sartre's admission of becoming on the part of the in-itself can only ensure the vacuousness of his prime ontological category.

From a Buddhist point of view, the particularity of the "this" is sustained by a radiance of conditions, each of which is ontologically requisite, and each of which absorbs within it the very being of the particular. *This* ragged, yellowing, marked and annotated copy of *Being and Nothingness* would not be manifest—here, now, exactly *as it is*—had it not been moved to its present location. The *this* could be seen as unaffected by motion only by prescinding from its radical particularity. *A* book might well be moved from shelf to desk without altering in the least anything which we think when we think of *a* book. *This* book could not be. Motion is, then, essential to this particular. And Sartre's assumption that only its mode of being, but not its quiddity, is affected by motion either neglects its particularity, or absorbs its particularity into universality.

Moreover, if the *this* is equally capable of motion and becoming, if both are equally *possible*, it is not clear how a general notion of possibility could apply to both. Sartre's view that possibility is "a concrete property of already existing realities," that "[i]n order for the rain to be possible, there must be clouds in the sky" (1971, 150), is, from our point of view, unobjectionable. Actualities do not bob, like so many fragments of ice, on a vast warm sea of possibility. Rather, possibilities are tethered to the actual as the alternative modes of being which the actual could assume. "[T]he real is anterior to the possible" (1984, 37). To speak of "something" undergoing substantial transformation is, through incoherence, to withdraw the locus of possibility. *What*, exactly, enjoys the possibility of such change? No[*one*]thing is to be found at the beginning and at the end. No[*one*]thing becomes. As Bergson says, "There are changes, but there are underneath the change no things which change: change has no need of a support . . . movement does not imply a mobile" (1946, 173). And should we assume that the segments of this process, the "before" and the "after," undergo becoming, the problem would simply reproduce itself indefinitely by mathematical fission. And if becoming cannot be attributed to any[*one*]thing, to any *this*, neither can its possibility. No[thing] has the possibility of becoming. If becoming is possible, it is not the possibility of any *thing* at all. And if, as Sartre claims, "[t]he possible appears to us as a property of beings" (1971, 149), the notion then lapses into deep mystery.

Or perhaps we should take a cue from Aristotle, and envision quidditative transformation as a surface modification which invokes the depths of potentiality. In the lightless depths of *hypokeimenon*, all is still and unchanging, undisturbed by the superficial formal vacillation which would make of one and the same "stuff" (*hylē*) indifferently a golden statue or a golden vessel. If the possibility of becoming is not to be lodged in the substance, might it, then, inhere in the hyletic potentiality which becoming [in/e]vokes? Setting aside the not insignificant quibble of how an Aristotelian could know of *hylē* when it is form, not matter, which is transcribed onto the soft wax of the passive intellect, we might well wonder how an unchanging hyletic substratum could be rein/formed. Not only is it incapable of becoming in virtue of its sheer lethargy, its in/difference to form seems incompatible with its being in/formed at all. In what sense is [in]formation an operation [per]formed upon the *protē hylē*? If materiality remains in/different, unaffected, then "it" is not sufficiently passive to be the subject of an operation of in/formation. Moreover, if *one* and the "same" portion of gold—and we can only wonder at the criterion of "sameness" here—becomes *two* entitatively distinct golden figurines, *hylē* would seem, then, to be intrinsically numberless. And we have no right to assume an underlying sameness throughout substantial change. Indeed, "since these existents constitute one order of being, the changes which they undergo cannot be fairly described as 'substantial' " (Kasulis 1993, 160).

The Aristotelian coincidence of matter and potentiality founders, also, upon the wisdom of Dōgen. Since (presumably) the "same" matter can assume an indefinite number of successive forms, matter is understood as the potentiality for form-taking. Substantial becoming is an operation which leaves the hyletic depths untouched: one and the same fund of *hylē*, indifferent to form, is now differently in/formed. But if firewood does not *become* ash, there is no question, once again, of a unitary materiality underlying substantial change. Dōgen speaks of the "total exertion of reality." We may speak equivalently of the remainderless exhaustion of potentiality. To be exactly what it is requires the discharge of all of a thing's potentiality. There is no potentiality "left over" for the *this* to *be* something which it *is not*.

Sartre himself derides the notion of potentiality as "a *magical* conception" (1971, 150). Accordingly, "[b]eing-in-itself can not 'be potentiality' or 'have potentialities' " (150). Though it may be the locus of *possible* precipitation, "[t]he cloud is not 'potential rain' " (150). The shimmer of potentiality is cast upon an in-itself which is Laodicean with respect to this curious ontological spellcraft. Though "[t]his inkwell *can* be broken" (270), "[i]n itself the inkwell is neither breakable nor unbreakable; it *is*" (270). And its apparent frangibility "is entirely cut off from it, for it is only the transcendent correlate of *my* possibility of throwing the inkwell against the marble of the fireplace" (270). This is not, perhaps, the place to carp over the tacit substantialism of a screen-and-image model of "magical" projection. But it would be possible to recognize potentiality as "the transcendent correlate of *my* possibility" only in the attitude of reflection. And we must always be wary of according to reflection the power of ontological desideration. The theme of reflection displays a clarity, articulation and thematic presence which are altogether lacking in the lived, prereflective apprehension. And this proud acquisition may turn out to be a phenomenological impoverishment—certainly, if the atmospheric vagueness of the prereflective presence is an authentic attribute, and not the blur produced by excessive proximity. The issue of whether potentiality is a shadow cast upon the in-itself by our possibilities or an integral strand in the fabric of reality cannot, then, be left to reflection.

Sartre's analysis of potentiality supplements the Husserlian theory of apperception. For Husserl, the selective perspectival slant at which the object announces itself is the conduit of the object's luminous, compelling sensuosity, its rich, intricate concretion. But the object *as a whole* is given in perception, and not merely the radiant countenance which it turns toward us. However indeterminate and lacunary the imaginal anticipation, we "take" its ungiven profiles in the subjunctive mood. Apperception, as Husserl calls it, is our counterfactual access to the sides not immediately presented. We are *not* standing on its opposite side. But we can still anticipate what the object *would* look like *were* we to see it from there. The other sides are hyletically *absent*, but could be brought to presence. Sartre tells us that "the world is revealed as haunted by absences to be realized, and each *this* appears with a cortege of absences which point to it and determine it. These absences are not basically different from potentialities" (1971, 273–4). The absences of this phantom procession inhabit a subjunctive domain, the world of the "could be" which Sartre does not clearly delimit from that of the "will be." To be sure, that which is "to be realized" can achieve realization only in the future. But nothing ensures its realization. And, indeed, it may never be realized. Sartre conflates the tense of realization with the ontological modality of potentiality. This confusion underwrites his pronouncement that "[p]otentiality on the ground of the future turns back on the *this* to determine it" (270). It would be less misleading to say that the *this* is determined in the concreteness of its multifaceted presence by a potentiality which, while actualized (if at all) in the future, is grounded in the subjunctive, the mood, and, if you like, ontological mode, prepared by epochetic suspension of ontic positing. The subjunctive is, in Sartre's phrase, the domain of "being-beyond-being" (268). But "the full moon becomes the potentiality of the crescent moon" not through ecstatic investment in "the future full moon" (268), but through a questioning entertainment which inclines neither toward affirmation nor toward negation. If "the flower is a potentiality of the bud" (268), it is so even if the bud never flowers. Potentialities may arise in our encounter with the world without the least expectation of eventual actualization. Potentiality does not entail eventuality. And this disrupts the cogency of Sartre's deposition that "[i]n order for the *this* to be entirely deprived of potentialities, it would be necessary that I be a pure present, which is inconceivable" (270). If potentiality is not the echo of our own possibility resounding from the future, but a reflux of our own projected capacity from the world in brackets, then the exclusive insertion of my presence in the present should not despoil the potentiality of the *this*. The *this* is disclosed, not "as coming to itself from the future" (266), but as rejoining itself from the subjunctive.

In a passage of surpassing convolution, Sartre weaves a theological strand through his discussion of potentiality: "The possibility that consciousness exists non-thetically as consciousness (of) being able not to not-be this is revealed as the *potentiality* of the *this* of being what it is" (1971, 266). The in-itself simply *is* what it is without the luxury of being *potentially* what it is. The inkwell neither possesses nor lacks the potentiality to be itself: it *is*. Yet its "being-what-it-is-ability" is *revealed*. It *appears*. Or rather, it is the form, the *Auffassung*, under which a certain possible consciousness is manifest. If quidditative potentiality is disclosed within our experiential world, then a non-thetic "consciousness (of) being able not to not-be this" must be *possible*. We must, that is, be capable of abrogating nihilation (not-being this) and must, at the same time, be capable of a non-thetic awareness which subtends this abrogation. The possible consciousness which Sartre has in mind could, it seems, be no less than divine: the in-itself-for-itself. The annulment of nihilation is the annulment of the for- itself. The continuance of non-thetic awareness is its (inconsonant) preservation. Quidditative potentiality, "the *potentiality* of the *this* of being what it is," assumes the possibility of God—assumes, that is, the possibility of the collapse of the ontological bifurcation which Sartre labors so assiduously to instil. This possibility is metasystemic. If the for-itself is "haunted" by the specter of God, this menace appears from beyond the scheme of Sartrean duality. The logical urgency of the divarication is intrinsic to Sartre's systematic ontology. But at the same time, the extrasystemic "possibility" of the collapse is indicated, from within the system, as a meta-systemic threat. The seeds of its undoing are planted in the for-itself's desire to be God. And it is this menace which is revealed as "the *potentiality* of the *this* of being what it is." Without "the missing God," the "this" *would* be, but *could not* be, what it is.

If possibility is anchored in the actuality of the *this*, it would seem that the *this*, in turn, is moored at the bulkhead of probability. "Those potentialities which refer back to the *this* without being made to be by it and without having to be—those we shall call *probabilities* to indicate that they exist in the mode of being of the in-itself" (Sartre 1971, 270-1). However, if probabilities are, with Sartre, to be regarded as potentialities, then service as the correlate of possibility cannot be an invariant feature of potentialities. Unlike possibilities which are "possibilized," "probabilities are not 'probabilized' . . ." (271). And if probabilities "exist in the mode of being of the in-itself," if they are "*in itself* as probable" (271), there is a salient exception to the thesis that "[b]eing-in-itself can not 'be potentiality' . . ." (150). And with these graphic irregularities, we can only wonder what possibility in its most general sense might amount to. Less charitably, though with greater fidelity to the precision of Sartre's expression, we might simply have to ac-knowledge the inconsistency.

Sartre's ruminations on our interrogative emplacement within being disclose a more searching conception of possibility, one which presents it-self as prior to the excavation of the hole: "[t]here exists . . . for the ques-tioner the permanent objective possibility of a negative reply" (1971, 36). It is unclear how much a "permanent objective possibility" might have in common with a probability. But clearly, this possibility, the possibility of thwarted expectation, baffled efforts of investigation, is not the product of possibilization. It is, in fact, a crucial condition for the upsurge of con-sciousness, and thus, for the positing of its praxiological possibilities. Were the "negative reply" not an ever-present prospect, were this possibility, in fact, never present, consciousness would always, and necessarily, find what it was looking for. Dis[covery], dis[closure], would turn out to be the im-mediate, effortless, and inevitable correlate of the investigatory will. Seeking and finding would not be mediated by the impedance of the in-itself, the "coefficient of adversity." And consciousness would not represent an outrushing transcendence in the direction a world of objects inde-pendent of, detached from, resistant to, our voluntative involvements. Consciousness, that is, would not confront, would not found itself in, would not nihilate, and would not be *of*, the in-itself. The *possibility* of fric-tion, resistance, adversion, the negative reply, is constitutive of the ontolog-ical sense of the in-itself. "Will needs the world and the resistance of things" (1984, 37). In Sartre's intriguing description, "[i]n a dream, there is no dis-tinction between wanting to drink and dreaming that one is drinking. So the mind, victim of its omnipotence, *cannot* wish. It cannot even wish to wake up. It will only dream that it does wake up. For it to be itself again, the real must invade its dream in some way. Thus the dreamer is bound hand and foot by his absolute power" (37). "Let a genie give me power to realize my desires there and then, and at once I fall asleep . . ." (38). And thus it would be, also, for an omnipotent Deity who "meets no inertial resistance." An omnipotent God is "dreaming." "He is imprisoned in himself and can-not will anything. Divine omnipotence is tantamount to total subjective servitude" (37). Here we find a current of possibility which runs deep, in-deed. The exact inverse of the Heideggerian "ownmost possibility"—the possibility of having no (further) possibilities—the possibility of obstructed desire and exploded expectation, without which there could arise in our world no *négatités*, no ontological infrastructure for discrimination, no discriminate objects, and thus no footing for consciousness, is a condition for the (possibility of) having any possibilities whatsoever. And once again, we must pin the label on this effort to reach behind possibility to the possibility of possibility. The label is "metaphysics"—a practice from which Sartre wishes to separate his own ontological project. Young children are extraordinarily gifted metaphysicians. "Why?" is pursued by "why?" without end—long after the adult intellect is willing to satisfy itself with a settled explanation. "It just *is*" is of no avail. My own children met this expression of helplessness with "*Why* is it just is?" It was clear from that point on where the deeper philosophical wisdom lay. And I continue to this day to sit at their feet. As Gasché says of elucidation, interpretation is a totalizing comportment, since it is based upon "an operation of decision-making in a totalizing perspective" (1987, xv). It is not that I wish to exhume, from an archaeological stratum beneath the possibility of the negative reply, yet a deeper possibility of the possibility of the negative reply, and thus forward to the annoyance of all. But conversely, assuming that the possibility of the negative reply is basic—not more profoundly based—it is not evident to me why the manifold praxiological possibilities which offer themselves for realization could not also dispense with a deeper basis. Why—in addition to possibility—do we need the possibility of possibility?

Permanence, which Sartre describes as "[t]he first potentiality of the object . . . the correlate of the engagement, an ontological structure of the negation," is said to come to the object "from the future" (1971, 266). As the unbroken continuity of the *this* which subtends present eruptions of givenness and purports their continuance beyond the now, permanence "is not a purely established *given*, but a potentiality" (266). The present object is an invariance constituted, in part, of perpetually shifting patterns of absences which, in their appeal "to be realized," require prospective continuity. Once again, however, while the "appeal" can find response only in the dimension of deferral (a presently "realized" absence—an evident solecism—would be a presence), we cannot envision realizations as blowing up out of the future like leaves in a gale. Realizations are not "there." They are not projectiles hurled into the present. If not yet realized—not yet transformed into presences—absences are not *will-be*, but rather *would-be* realizations. A "realized absence," like a dead animal, like a filled hole, like the in-itself-for-itself, is an internally conflicted notion. Yet in relegating realization to the "will-be," Sartre assumes the eventuality of a present in which an absence *is* realized. He assumes, that is, the future presence of an absence. And this assumption undermines the postulation of any significant difference between presence and absence. Future absences are presences waiting for realization. And realization then becomes the forwarding of a presence into the

present. Presence is transtemporal, omnitemporal. And the present becomes the window past which the parade of presences pass successively in
review. If presence is indistinguishable from absence, if absences are presences which have not yet arrived, then absence cannot beckon us into the
future, and does not, as a consequence, require an underlying permanence.

Transtemporal continuity, invariance throughout the opalescent
ephemera of fluid time, is, in Husserl's acceptation, the hallmark of ideality,
or in Sartre's present idiom, of the abstract. Indeed, "permanence and the
abstract are only one" (1971, 267). But an attentive disentanglement of the
"will be" from the "would be" invalidates the passage from the "cortege of
absences" which constitute the object to a presumed continuance of the object beyond the present. Absence does not, of itself, entail permanence. Nor
does it entail ideality. Were the "filling" of empty intentionality, the "realization" of absence, inevitable, an event fully formed, running toward us to
throw itself into our arms, we might acknowledge these entailments. But
we have neither the prescience nor the commitment to predestination or
preformism to certify this view of the future. To the extent that "I apprehend it as permanence—*i.e.*, as essence," the *this*, Sartre informs us, "is already in the future although I am not present to it in my actual presence but
as about-to-come-to-myself" (280). Presence to the absent, the event in
virtue of which the absent as such is brought to presence, is always "about-
to-come." The empty intention is a possible filled intention, and is thus rel-
egated to the future, which, for Sartre, is the home of the possible. There is,
then, no present presencing of the absent. In this way Sartre avoids the inconsonance of a present realization of the presently absent. But the incongruity breaks out again in the dimension of the future. For in the future
perfect—"a sort of *hypothesis.* . . ." (Derrida 1986, 48; cf. Fóti 1992, 104)—
when the event of realization will have been completed, we have (will have)
a future present in which the absent is realized: that is, no longer absent.
And a future contradiction is no more acceptable than a present one.

Sartre testifies to the diacritical interinvolvement of the abstract and the
concrete: "the concrete is concrete only in so far as it leans in the direction
of its abstraction, that it makes itself known by the abstraction which it is"
(1971, 267). The language of this passage echoes, if faintly, a deep insight
of Buddhist dialectical deconstruction: Mādhyamika. Being resides in phenomenal condition. And conceptual meaning resides in *definiendum*. If an
object depends ontologically upon a given condition, there is a clear sense
in which it *is* that condition. And in tandem, since concretion is unthinkable
without abstraction, concretion *is* the abstraction. Symmetrically, we must
add, abstraction pours itself out into concretion as well. In the diacritical
dyad, the being of A is referred to B, and that of B to A. But A cannot sustain the being of B without being B in an absolute (non- relative) sense. Yet

if *A were B simpliciter*, *A* would not depend upon *B*. Thus, the being of *B* must be counter-referred to *B*. Neither *A* nor *B* can sustain the being of *B*. Its being is homeless, tossed like a hot potato between *A* and *B*. Or better: being is a certain "energy" which circulates in the "between" (emptiness), the ontological insistence upon non-duality. Being is inter-being.

Seminally, Sartre affirms that "[f]ar from abstracting certain qualities in terms of things, we must on the contrary view abstraction as the original mode of being of the for-itself . . ." (1971, 267). The for-itself *is* the episode of decompression, the combing-out of the matted, tangled, indeed, quite strictly "con/founded" qualitative [con]fusion denominated the "in-itself." The [dif]fusion of quality is, then, the interpolation of negativity into "a quasi-affirmation in which the affirming is coated over by the affirmed," an authentication which "exists without any inner finitude in the peculiar tension of its 'self-affirmation' " (283). The for-itself is the separation of strands of quality which, in the in-itself, are dissolved in identity. The opening of qualitative divergence is the "abstraction" of which Sartre speaks, and it is not difficult to see why Sartre would claim that the abstract "is necessary for the upsurge of the concrete . . ." (267). As a category of experience, the concrete is clearly indebted to the abstract. Indeed, "the abstract haunts the concrete as a possibility fixed in the in-itself, which the concrete has to be" (261). And we have here a striking revisitation of a theme put forward at the very beginning of *Being and Nothingness*: in phenomenology, the essential, the eidetic, the abstract, is "no longer opposed to being but on the contrary is the measure of it" (1971, 4). But if the concrete is, indeed, a category of experience, if, that is, the concrete is to be discriminated from the in-itself, then we must wonder how successfully Sartre has overcome the dualism of being and appearance. It is Sartre who endorses Nietzsche's repudiation of "the illusion of worlds-behind-the-scene" (4), and it is Sartre who scowls at the conceit of a "being-behind-the-appearance" (4). But it is also Sartre who speaks of nothingness as a "shimmer" on the surface of being, and of time as a superficial run-off. If, as Buddhism will also insist, what you see is what you get, if there is no "behind," then the disjunction of the in-itself from the concrete is illegitimate. "True philosophy," Merleau-Ponty tells us, "does not go 'behind' . . ." (1988, 39). To be consistent, we must not pry the phenomenological apart from the ontological. Yet the rescue of consistency in this instance opens qualms over another possible incoherence. For if the in-itself *is* the concrete, we must wonder how, without sacrificing the ontological primacy of the in-itself, Sartre can claim that the abstract (the for-itself) "is necessary for the upsurge of the concrete . . ." (1971, 267).

Moreover, if the abstract is uniquely and essentially the invariant, the concrete is then the varying, the impermanent. Nothing in Sartre's ontology prepares an expectation that concrete *reality* might have its being *in process*, that impermanence may be its ontological modality. On the contrary, only the for-itself can "become" in the sense of *coming to be* that which it is not. (Even this "be[coming]" is a "coming" without "being"—the for-itself perpetually eludes co-incidence with what it "is" in the mode of not-being it.) In fact, "that glass or that table . . . do not endure; they *are*. Time flows over them" (1971, 281). Enduring is not an enactment on the part of the in-itself. Time happens *to* the in-itself. It is "the means offered to everything whatsoever to be in order to be no longer" (Merleau-Ponty 1964c, 317). The in-itself is impassive. Though not, as the "concrete" must be, dynamically profluent, the in-itself is also not perduring. Since "in permanence nothing comes to differentiate what is from what was" (Sartre, 291), the passage of time must be disrupted by an upsurge (*jaillissement*) or arising (Sanskrit: *utpāda*) which breaks the monotony of undifferentiated continuance. "The *present* dimension of universal time would . . . be inapprehensible if there were no motion" (291). But beyond the epistemic issue of apprehensibility, there would *be* no time without the disruption of permanence. But if the in-itself is the unchanging river bed, and if time, the measure of which is motion (or at least change), is a surface run-off, the for-itself has a great deal of accounting to do. "Permanence," Sartre tells us, "will appear . . . as the pure slipping by of in-itself instants, little nothingnesses separated one from another and reunited by a relation of simple exteriority on the surface of a being which preserves an atemporal immutability" (281). And if space is frangibility, the readiness to shatter into grains of externality, Sartre is here "spatializing" time. This Bergsonian complaint is enlivened in some degree by the resolution of the temporal into the atemporal. And again, in Sartre's claim that "[t]ime is pure nothingness in-itself" (293) we find even more compelling evidence. For quantity, which Sartre assimilates with spatiality, is described in precisely the same way: an "ideal nothing in-itself . . ." (263).

The for-itself desires to be God. But in arrogating to itself the responsibility for all objective motion, it has already enthroned itself in the heavens. Whether it is change as the "alteration of the quality of the *this*" which is "produced . . . in a block by the upsurge or disintegration of a form" (1971, 286) or the change of location that we call (loco-)motion that conditions our sense of the passage of time, change—the qualitative, relational or spatial *différe[/a]nce* between nonsimultaneous moments—can have no purchase upon the in-itself. "[T]he unchangeable *this* is revealed across a flickering and an infinite parceling out of phantom in-itselfs" (281). Time is a frenzied tarantella danced out upon a featureless ballroom floor, an indeterminate plane without the least irregularity. And inasmuch as the "floor" (the in-itself) is taken as *real*, time, its experiential conditions, and its fluid phenomena (the "dance") are all *unreal*. It is not that Buddhism would take up the opposite cause, though as a description of the *res* of our experience, impermanence is an incontrovertible feature of *realitas* (the domain of *res*: *saṃsāra*). Rather, the antisubstantialism of Buddhism repudiates every sense of the "behind." Sartre claims that "[t]he For-itself directs the explosion of its temporality against the whole length of an immense and monotonous wall of which it can not see the end" (280). But we must rejoin that the "wall," that which underlies the variegated frivolity of time, is an ontological fiction. There is no contrast between the underlying, the "behind," and that which is projected upon it. Impermanence is not therefore "unreal" in contradistinction to a "real" permanence which underlies it. It is simply phenomenal—beyond affirmation and negation.

Still, Sartre claims that "[m]otion has the exact value of a fact; it participates wholly in the complete contingency of being and must be accepted as a given" (Sartre 1971, 286). Perhaps we should say a "taken." For the in-itself can do no "giving." It *does* nothing at all. Nor does it even "endure." If motion is a brute "fact"—"something that philosophy is forced to swallow while being unable to digest" (Caputo 1993, 76)—it is so in the original sense of *factum*: that which is made. It is a temporal configuration which *we* constitute—a *captum* which is not a *datum*—and for which *we* must take final ontological responsibility. But if "[a] world without motion would be conceivable" (Sartre, 286), we must either deny that the event of conceiving occurs as an discontinuity within an otherwise frozen world (appealing, perhaps, to a transcendental domain which lacks consistent correlation with the consecution of mundane events) or else we must regard this "conceiving" as mysteriously transtemporal or atemporal—an "event" which never (in the pluperfect) occurred, is not (in the entirety of its duration) occurring now, and will never (in the future perfect) be completed. Sartre is right that "we can not imagine the possibility of a world without change" (286), but he seems to discard the solid insight thus attained by hedging "except by virtue of a purely formal possibility . . ." (286). If we *could* imagine an unchanging world in virtue of "a purely formal pos sibility," and could imagine our imagining in correlation with it, then the event of imagining would be either metamundane or atemporal. A "formal possibility" inaccessible to intramundane, temporally intrusive events of conceiving or imagining, could only be noumenal. For Buddhism, however, "[n]oumena do not exist. Only *dharmas* exist and support *dharmas*" (Sangharakshita 1987, 120). And having no conception of such a possibility, we would have no warrant for positing it.

Moreover, the atemporality or metatemporality displayed by the "formal possibility" is of questionable coherence. And we must also query the cogency of asserting that "[t]he pipe, the pencil, all these beings . . . whose permanence is wholly indifferent to the multiplicity of profiles," beings that are "transcendent to all temporality," are nonetheless "revealed in temporality" (Sartre 1971, 281). If being "in" time entails being temporal—could it mean otherwise?—then, as Dōgen clearly saw, the conception of the atemporal as a fixed and impassive boulder, a monolith of atemporality, ranging itself against the white-waters of temporality is a simple contradiction. To salvage consistency, we must determine a sense of "being-in" (while not, perhaps, being "of") which permits noncontradictory residence to the atemporal within the temporal. Perhaps we should take Sartre at his word. After all, he stops short of claiming that the pipe and the pencil are *in* temporality. They are rather *revealed* in temporality. The nuance is vital, and brings to mind its *locus classicus* in the Platonic doctrine of time as the moving image of eternity. The atemporal, like the full moon serene in its quiescence, casts an image upon the roiling waters of time, and through the ebullient arabesque of dancing, multiplied reflections is revealed "in" time. For Sartre, however, the story is somewhat more involved. "The cohesion of Time is a pure phantom, the objective reflection (*reflet*) of the ekstatic project of the For-itself toward itself and the cohesion in motion of human Reality" (293). If the atemporal is an image revealed "in" time, time is in turn a reflection revealed "in" (upon) the in-itself. Indeed, in Sartre's ontological perspective, "the *lapse* of time disappears, and time is revealed as the shimmer of nothingness on the surface of a strictly atemporal being" (294). Time is an illusory apparition. And while the distinction between a surface variability and a "deep" invariance, a superficial impermanence and a real and underlying permanence, collides with Sartre's vocal disavowal of sub/stance, it also leaves his analysis of human existence as engagement without ontological ground. The absences which constitutively "haunt" the *this* are "voids to be filled" (274). They appeal to us prethematically as urgencies, exigencies. "They are *tasks*, and this world is a world of *tasks*" (274). But if the temporal realization of absences—the presencing *of the absent* which we have already come to see as conceptually flawed—is now itself regarded as phantasmal, if the event of realization, the engine of time, proves unreal, then human engagement is also a phantom. Moreover, the "instrumental-thing" (275) "both rests in the quiet beatitude of indifference and yet points beyond it to tasks to be performed which make known to it what it has to be . . ." (274). A good trick! The lethargy of the in-itself would hardly predict the vigorous exercise of "pointing." But we would be happy enough to see the do-nothing do something if we could only determine what *we* are pointing to when we designate the *this*. We can forgive a harmless figure of speech. It is the absence which appeals for repletion. Still, however the trope is precised, if the "pointing" of the *this* is convertible with the appeal of the absent, then the *this* must be constituted of its absences.

On the other hand, if the *this* does, indeed, rest in the "quiet beatitude of indifference," there is nothing within it either to point or to appeal, and, in its constitution, it is absent the absences—the tasks—which would make it instrumental. It is a thing or an instrument, but not both.

A parakeet may take its reflection for a rival bird, and may, in this way, prove no less astute a phenomenologist than those of us who refrain from similar judgments. But visualist phenomenology aside, there is no reason to assume that, beyond the appearance, the moon is really *in* the turbulent flux. It is not the atemporal, but its deputy, which appears in the flow of time. And just as the mirror does not in any literal sense become red when an apple is set before it, but only displays an appearance-of-red, so, although it might refract an appearance-of-atemporality, we have no reason to expect the atemporal to reside, quite literally, "in" time. If the pipe and the pencil are not *in* time—and they cannot be without contradiction—then in seeing them *revealed* in time, our gaze must be diverted from the in-itself. We cannot focus upon both original and reflection at once. The act which apprehends the object as given in time cannot be the same as that which apprehends that which is "transcendent to all temporality." And if reflection and original are not to be confused, Sartre is unwarranted in regarding the atemporal—distinguished, now, from its image or representation—as temporally given.

Time as a unitary, cohesive phenomenon is without ontological support. It "has no *raison d'être*" (Sartre 1971, 293). The second page of *Being and Nothingness* marks a vivid contrast with the Husserlian (and tacitly substantialist) analysis of transcendence. Far from a mysterious singularity (Husserl's "X") which, as the principle of the series (the manifold) of its appearances, remains aloof from the series, the transcendent, in Sartre's acceptation, *is* the infinite series of appearances itself. "The appearance refers to the total series of appearances and not to a hidden reality which would drain to itself all the *being* of the existent" (4)—an inaugural and decisive statement of Sartre's antisubstantialism. The series can be regarded as a *series* of appearances or a series *of appearances*. With the second accent, the series "itself" (if it has an "itself") drops away in favor of its elements. The serial organization of the series may vanish almost completely. Much as the *row* of chairs, as a *Gestalt* phenomenon, can give way to the row *of chairs*—so much so that we are in the presence of a loose multiplicity of chairs freed from their previous insertion in the *Gestalt*—so, the cohesion of time—the organized parade of presentation-moments—may also vanish. "If Time is considered by itself, it immediately dissolves into an absolute multiplicity of instants which considered separately lose all temporal nature and are reduced purely and simply to the total atemporality of the *this*" (293). While

Buddhism is attuned to Sartre's antisubstantialism, and welcomes the dissolution of the *itself*—the series "itself," time "itself"—it posits impermanence
as an ineluctable mark (*lakṣana*) of every *this*, and certainly, therefore, of the
instant. The instant is hopelessly temporal. And Sartre says as much in his
remarks on the constitution of the instant. The instant is "[a] beginning
which is given as the end of a prior project—such must be the instant"
(600). It is both end and beginning, and cannot be understood independently of temporal flux. The instant cannot, then, be reduced to "the total
atemporality of the *this*." In Chuang-tzu's playful dialectic, "[t]here is the
beginning; there is not as yet any beginning of the beginning; there is not as
yet beginning not to be a beginning of the beginning. There is what is, and
there is what is not, and it is not easy to say whether what is not, is not; or
whether what is, is" (1966, 15). *Śūnyatā* is the "deathless" (*amata*), and is
"beyond" the temporality of evanescent phenomena. But emptiness is not a
timeless "this." It is not an atemporal result of the dissolution of temporal
cohesion, but rather the openness which permits and frees the event of dissolution. The atemporal is not an analytic constituent of the temporal. And
the dissolution which illuminates emptiness is not an ontological reduction
displaying, in the end, what the phenomenon "really" is. It is not that the
temporal *analysandum* is "nothing but" a multiplicity of atemporal instants
(an incoherent notion). It is not "nothing but." It is *nothing*: no *thing*.
Differently nuanced, the temporal phenomenon displays its authentic *self* at
the very point at which its particularity is resolved. It displays *itself* in losing
"itself." Its *not-being-itself* is thus ontologically constitutive—not simply that
it is not *what* it is (the Sartrean accent), but rather, that it is not *itself*.
Moreover, if every *Gestalt* resolves into elements, if every "blur" resolves
into deeper-level articulate structures, and if the elements, the articulate
structures, turn out, in turn, to be further *Gestalten*, more "fuzz," then every
level is as "real" as the next—and as "unreal." "Reality" is an index of our un-
willingness to pursue the analysis at a deeper level. And the cohesion of time
is no more phantasmal than the elements into which it dissolves.

Sartre tells us that the apparent *being* of time, this "nothingness in-
itself," "is that of a particular figure which is raised on the undifferentiated
ground of time and which we call the *lapse* of time" (1971, 294). Thus,

> . . . time appears as a finite, organized form in the heart of an
> indefinite dispersion. The *lapse* of time is the result of a compres-
> sion of time at the heart of an absolute decompression, and it is the
> project of ourselves toward our possibilities which realizes the
> compression. This compression of time is certainly a form of dis-
> persion and of separation, for it expresses in the world the distance
> which separates me from myself. (294)

We find here, once again, the same deep ambiguity in the notion of the in-itself that we have alluded to in other contexts. The for-itself is the undoing of the in-itself. Consciousness is the unraveling the strands of quality which, in the in-itself, are so tightly knit as to be indiscriminable, and, indeed, ontologically fused. The question, however, remains of whether the for-itself is a Persephone unraveling in the day what it weaves in the night. If compression is an enactment of consciousness, then not only is the for-itself significantly *more* than the event of decompression, but we must thematize the dimly illuminated shade of a "being" which silently inhabits the background of Sartre's thinking. If, in other words, the "compressed" is a *Gestalt* for which *we* must assume responsibility, then the in-itself is impossible without the for-itself, and we must insist, over Sartre's disavowal, that the categorial relationship between the in-itself and the for-itself can only be that of Hegelian contrariety, not that of univectorial contradiction. If compression is a "result," if compression and decompression are reciprocal correlates, we cannot escape this conclusion. And the being, as yet unnamed in Sartre's scheme (the being which we have chosen to call the *apeiron*) can be the intrinsically unaffected subject of nihilation only if we cease to regard it as "compressed." Either compression is a brute deliverance to consciousness (thus, not a "result") or the in-itself is not compressed. If the in-itself is atemporal, the lapse of time can only be the result of an act of compression performed by the for-itself, and, like Persephone, temporal consciousness seems to have woven the fabric of time before the conscious light of day. For the temporal lapse presents itself to us in its sheer givenness. And we have here the anomaly of an unconscious enactment of consciousness—a Freudian assumption which Sartre has elsewhere dispatched (cf. 1971, 86–96). But the supposal that we could catch our Persephone at her knitting is otherwise flawed. For knitting *takes time*. And time is exactly what does not exist "prior" to the knitting. In another context, Sartre is perspicuous that the question of the existence of "[m]y place, before freedom has circumscribed my placing . . ." is "unintelligible, for it involves 'before' which has no meaning . . ." (1971, 635). Just as the cosmological "big bang" is undatable inasmuch as time unfolds only *after* the detonation, so, also, if there were a decompression of the figural lapse of time into a shower of atemporal instants, we could expect no prior "weaving." Compression cannot be a result.

Sartre is not, however, entirely unaware of this. He sees that "there exists no 'synthesis of recognition' if we mean by that a progressive operation of identification which by successive organization of the 'nows' would confer a *duration* on the thing perceived" (1971, 280). Though he comes admirably and also perilously close to admitting that compression is not a result (and thus, to contradicting himself), his purpose here is to range his position against the Husserlian theory of identity-synthesis. For Husserl, the absent, apprehended in empty intentional reference, is [re]cognized in presence through the actualization of horizonal potentiality. This [re]cognition, the identification of the present as *the same* as the formerly absent, is what Husserl calls the "synthesis of recognition" In *The Transcendence of the Ego*, Sartre accounts for the unity of lived temporal passage in virtue of "a play of 'transversal' intentionalities" (1972, 39), an evident nod to the Husserlian analysis of "retention" and "protention." Until submergence in the waters of Lēthē, the immediately elapsed phase of experience is retained within the present as a live qualitative presence, experienced *as past*, to be sure, but as a past which continues within the present. And immediately forthcoming events within the limit of that other tributary of Lēthē beyond which only speculation or calculation can probe also modify the present in protention. Our experience of temporal passage thus relies upon our ability to [re]cognize, within the present, formerly absent phases, apprehended through protention, as occurrently present, and occurrently absent phases, apprehended through retention, as formerly present. Sartre's bow to Husserl is, however, a bit stiff and ungiving. For despite its evident service, the Husserlian theory postulates, in Sartre's reading, not a temporal *Gestalt* of phases, a formation wholly subject to compromise and modification by its constituents, but a transcendent *identity*, an ideality which floats serenely above the torrent of time. Still, the lapse, whether conceived as an Husserlian identity or as a Sartrean figuration, subtends the presence of the present and the absence of past and future. As such, it is confined within the umbra of no particular temporal ekstasis, and is thus, in this sense, atemporal. It is no more (and no less) anomalous to suppose that the lapse *itself* does not elapse than to suppose that the river *itself* does not flow. There is a certain timelessness about time. And this confirms, in a sense, the resolution of the lapse into atemporal constituents. But of course, if we allow that the instants are just as atemporal as the lapse, we must also admit, by contraposition, that the lapse, in turn, is just as fluid as the instants. In Stcherbatsky's lucid and unequivocal declamation, "instantaneous being is the fundamental doctrine by which all the Buddhist system is established 'at one stroke' " (1962, 554). And Buddhism, as we have seen, would not accept the atemporality of temporal phenomena. But then, neither, in other contexts, would Sartre. The being of the instant "has the inapprehensible ambiguity of the instant, for one could not say either that it is or that it is not; in addition it no sooner appears than it is already surpassed and exterior to itself" (1971, 291). The lapse is atemporal because it subtends past, present and future. The instant might be considered "atemporal" for a very different reason: the very moment it is future, it is present; the very moment it is present, it is past. Rather than subtending, it seems to elude the temporal ekstases, and in this way is modified by none of them. But at a deeper level, its "inapprehensible ambiguity" will not allow the instant to escape temporality. And it is equally appropriate to describe it in positive terms: the instant is the conflation (not to say "compression") of the three ekstases, qualified by *all*, rather than *none*, of them. In a sense, Sartre's description of the instant as beginning and end anticipates the Derridian construal of the *now* (for Husserl, the primal upsurge of presence) as the difference between past and future. If the same moment makes ineliminable reference to *both* past (end) and future (beginning), then our apprehension of the instant requires their discrimination, and we find, at the heart of our conception of the *both* a necessary reference to the *neither* (their difference). The "ambiguity" of the instant is the inseparability of the both and the neither. If the status of the lapse parallels the status of the instants, the lapse, too, oscillates in its being between fluidity and metatemporality. And from a Buddhist standpoint, this would stand to reason. The river, after all, does flow. It can be regarded as relatively stable, and can thus anchor the scheme of reference which frames our perception of profluence. Within another frame, however, that, for example, of geologic formation, the river is no less fluid than its waters. And if there is neither a most nor a least encompassing framework, then the lapse is never more than relatively stable or fluid.

Recalling, now, that permanence "is not a purely established *given*, but a potentiality" (266), we find a clear demarcation between permanence and the figuration of moments of passage which Sartre calls the "lapse": permanence is a *potentiality*; the lapse is a *given*: "a particular figure which is raised on the undifferentiated ground of time . . ." (Sartre 1971, 294). But *is* the lapse authentically given? The distension of the lived *now* is not a lapse, not a subtension of temporal ekstases, but an enrichment of the present. In retention and protention, past and future contribute their temporally modalized "presence" to the present. The present embodies them. And in this respect, Sartre, in his idiosyncratic appropriation of Husserl, is aligned with the Buddhist view that "there is no present time (*vartāmanakāla*) apart from past and future. The present has no meaning except in relation to the past and future" (Coward 1990, 45). Indeed, "in the undecomposable synthesis of temporalization, protention is as indispensable as retention. And their two dimensions are not added up but the one implies the other in a strange fashion" (Derrida 1976, 16). But Sartre fails to draw the deconstructive/Madhyamika conclusion that, since its very being is relinquished to protention and retention, the present has no presence of its own, and thus, that "time functions as an endless deferring of presence that drives yet another paradoxical wedge into the ability to experience pure presence" (Coward, 38). Instead, for Sartre, the living-through (*Er/lebnis*) of the present is the apprehension of a quasi-substantial presence, an incarnation which claims past and future, rather than an admission of ontological indebtedness. Since the lapse "is like the *trajectory* of my act" (1971, 294), what Sartre says regarding the trajectory of a moving object is apropos: "already in the past it is no longer anything but an evanescent line, like the wake of a ship which fades away . . ." (291). The trajectory is not a concretely discernible line. There is no line "there" to discern. For once past, an elapsed moment evanesces, fades away. And the limit at which it has completely vanished, at which it ceases to contribute to the present, is the bank of the river Lēthē. Lēthē is the margin of presence. Though swollen with past and future, the ventricose present is not a lapse. Its distension is not a subtension. The potentiality which is permanence cannot, then, be actualized in an underlying form of "temporal extension" (an ungarnished oxymoron), but at best in the generation of a succeeding moment. This, however, is of no service to Sartre's conception of motion. Motion, for Sartre, is incompatible with "a radical alteration" (286) of an object's being. If there is an actual "passing" of the moment from future to present and from present to past, like a ball tossed from one person to the next (an inescapably spatializing depiction of temporal process), then actualized permanence would seem to assure an underframing continuity sprawling beneath the triune dispersions of time. But no more radical alteration of being can be conceived than the evanescence of the elapsing moment into sheer vacuity and the upsurge of a radically novel moment. If the supersession of one temporal phase by another does not represent an ontologically constitutive mutation of the object, we are confronted by the anomaly of the atemporal within the temporal. And accordingly, the lapse, as an ideality which maintains its integrity beyond the immediacy of present intuition, is not, as such, accessible to the immediacy of intuition. It overspills the lip of presence, and as such has the ideality characteristic of transcendence. It is a timeless abstraction. And the resolution into timeless elements can no longer surprise us. If, one the other hand, temporal passage rings sonorous ontological changes in the object, then motion, as Sartre conceives it, is impossible. In either case, the assumption that motion is incompatible with constitutive transmutation is exposed to serious question.

The lapse is a timeless segment of time bounded by determinate events and internally ordered by static relations of subsequence and precedence. Having once elapsed, one event will always *be* after the other (though, of course, it will no longer *come* after the other). And this tract of frozen time is an idealized segment generated by the wake of time which Bergson calls duration. Duration is thus the concrete matrix of the lapse. But the wake of a ship grows with the ship's movement. Bergson, who labored to comprehend the paradox of *la durée*, remarks that "the unrolling of our duration resembles in some of its aspects the unity of an advancing movement and in others the multiplicity of expanding states; and clearly, no metaphor can express one of these two aspects without sacrificing the other" (1955, 27). The ship's steady movement out to sea enjoys an unbroken unity. But its wake seems to be augmented at each moment by the supplantation of an ever longer figure. Or rather, the wake simply *is* the progressive series of more and more protracted figures. Bergson regards unity and multiplicity as incommensurable and yet indispensable aspects of duration. Sartre, on the other hand, regards the lapse as a "phantom," and its dissolution as displaying what it authentically *is* (in itself): namely, nothing. Like the trajectory, it is "[t]his nothing which measures and signifies exteriority-to-self . . ." (1971, 290). The wake of time is "a counterfeit which collapses immediately into the infinite multiplicity of exteriority" (290). Thus, "[t]he line vanishes at the same time as motion, and this phantom of the temporal unity of space is founded continuously in non-temporal space—that is, in the pure multiplicity of dispersion which *is* without becoming" (291). Buddhism offers here a third voice. No harm comes from acknowledging the incommensurability of motion and the dissolute multiplicity which trails it. But neither do we need to decide, with Bergson, that both conceptions are gifted with equivalent validity or, with Sartre, that the multiplicity enjoys a certain ontological privilege. Dynamism and stasis appear only within a given framework. Motion becomes phenomenally evident only with respect to some prominence which is taken as "fixed." And of course, any anchor which enables the perception of motion can abandon its iron stolidity and turn to quicksilver from an alternative vantage point—a framework with its own anchor. The Buddha's words, *sabbe dhamma anicca* (all phenomena are impermanent), overthrow at a single stroke the postulated validity of all frameworks. All assume permanence. And all are therefore inadequate. Emptiness grounds both motion and rest, and at the same time, calls their ontological postulation into question. *Śūnyatā* is no more a spatially configured multiplicity than a profluent temporal dynamic.

References

Abe Masao. 1985. *Zen and Western Thought*. Honolulu: University of Hawaii Press.

Adorno, Theodor W. 1973. *Negative Dialectics*. Translated by E. B. Ashton. New York: Continuum.

———. 1983. *Against Epistemology: A Metacritique: Studies in Husserl and the Phenomenological Antinomies*. Translated by Willis Domingo. Cambridge: MIT Press.

Agacinski, Sylviane. 1991. "Another Experience of the Question, or Experiencing the Question Other-Wise." In *Who Comes After the Subject?* edited by Eduardo Cadava, Peter Connor, and Jean-Luc Nancy. New York: Routledge.

Agamben, Giorgio. 1991. *Language and Death: The Place of Negativity*. Translated by Karen E. Pinkus and Michael Hardt. Minneapolis: University of Minnesota Press.

Bacon, Francis. 1964. *The Philosophy of Francis Bacon*. Translated by Benjamin Farrington. Chicago: University of Chicago Press.

Baier, Annette. 1985. *Postures of the Mind: Essays on Mind and Morals*. Minneapolis: University of Minnesota Press.

Barnes, Jonathan. 1983. "The Beliefs of a Pyrrhonist." *Elenchos* 4:

Barthes, Roland. 1981. *Camera Lucida*. Translated by Richard Howard. New York: Hill and Wang.

Bataille, George. 1988. *Inner Experience*. Translated by Leslie Anne Boldt. Albany: SUNY Press.

Baudrillard, Jean. 1983. *Simulations*. Translated by Paul Foss, Paul Patton, and Philip Beitchman. New York: Semiotext(e).

Belnap, Nuel D., Jr. 1963. *An Analysis of Questions*. Santa Monica: Systems Development.

Bergson, Henri. 1944. *Creative Evolution*. Translated by A. Mitchell. New York: Modern Library.

——. 1946. *The Creative Mind*. New York: Philosophical Library.

——. 1955. *An Introduction to Metaphysics*. Translated by T. E. Hulme. New York: Macmillan.

Bernasconi, Robert. 1988. "Levinas: Philosophy and Beyond." In *Philosophy and Non-Philosophy since Merleau-Ponty*, edited by Hugh J. Silverman. New York: Routledge.

Bhattacharyya, K. C. 1958. *Studies in Philosophy*. Calcutta: Progressive Publishers.

Blake, William. 1975. "The Marriage of Heaven and Hell." Edited by Sir Geoffrey Keynes. London; New York: Oxford University Press.

Blofeld, John, ed. and trans. 1958. *The Zen Teaching of Huang Po*. London: Buddhist Society.

——, trans. 1972. *The Zen Teaching of Hui Hai on Sudden Illumination*. New York: Samuel Weiser.

Blyth, R. H. 1976. *Games Zen Masters Play*. New York: New American Library.

Borradori, Giovanna, ed. 1988. *Recoding Metaphysics: The New Italian Philosophy*. Evanston: Northwestern University Press.

Bourdieu, Pierre. 1983. "The Philosophical Institution." In *Philosophy in France Today*, edited by Alan Montefiore. Cambridge: Cambridge University Press.

Brand, Gerd. [1955] 1967. "Intentionality, Reduction, and Intentional Analysis in Husserl's Later Manuscripts." In *Welt, Ich, und Zeit*, Gerd Brand. The Hague: Martinus Nijhoff. Reprinted in *Phenomenology: The Philosophy of Edmund Husserl and Its Interpretation*, edited by Joseph J. Kocklemans. Garden City: Doubleday.

Bresson, François. 1958. "Perception et indices perceptifs." In *Logique et perception*, *Études D'Épistémologie Génétique*. Vol. 6, Bruner, François Bresson, Morf, and Piaget. Paris: Presses Universitaires de France.

Brogan, Walter A. 1988. "The Original Difference." In *Derrida and Difference*, edited by David Wood and Robert Bernasconi. Evanston: Northwestern University Press.

Brown, G. Spencer. 1973. *Laws of Form*. New York: Bantam Books.

Burke, Patrick. 1990. "Listening at the Abyss." In *Ontology and Alterity in Merleau-Ponty*, edited by Galen A. Johnson and Michael B. Smith. Evanston: Northwestern University Press.

Burnyeat, Myles. 1980. "Can the Sceptic Live His Scepticism?" In *Doubt and Dogmatism: Studies in Hellenistic Epistemology*, Malcolm Schofield, Myles Burnyeat and Jonathan Barnes. Oxford: Clarendon Press.

Burnyeat, Myles, ed. 1984. *The Skeptical Tradition*. Berkeley: University of California Press.

Burtt, A. E., ed. 1955. *The Teachings of the Compassionate Buddha*. New York: New American Library.

Busch, Thomas W. 1980. "Sartre's Use of the Reduction: *Being and Nothingness* Reconsidered." In *Jean-Paul Sartre: Contemporary Approaches to His Philosophy*, Hugh J. Silverman and Frederick A. Elliston. Pittsburgh: Duquesne University Press.

Caputo, John D. 1983. "The Thought of Being and the Conversation of Mankind: The Case of Heidegger and Rorty." *Review of Metaphysics* 36:

———. 1993. *Against Ethics: Contributions to a Poetics of Obligation with Constant Reference to Deconstruction*. Bloomington: Indiana University Press.

Chang, Chung-Yuan. 1971. *Original Teachings of Ch'an Buddhism*. New York: Vintage Books.

Chuang-tzu. 1996. *The Book of Chuang Tzu*. Translated by Martin Palmer. New York: Arkana.

Conze, Edward. 1962. *Buddhist Thought in India: Three Phases of Buddhist Philosophy*. London: George Allen and Unwin.

———, trans. 1978. *Selected Sayings from the "Perfection of Wisdom."* Boulder: Prajñā Press.

Corless, Roger J. 1989. *The Vision of Buddhism: The Space Under the Tree*. New York: Paragon House.

Coward, Harold. 1990. *Derrida and Indian Philosophy*. Albany: SUNY Press.

Danto, Arthur C. 1965. *Nietzsche as Philosopher*. New York: Macmillan.

———. 1973. "Historical Language and Historical Reality." *Review of Metaphysics* 27:

———. 1980. "Analytic Philosophy." *Social Research* 47 (4).

Daumal, René. 1974. *Mount Analogue: A Novel of Symbolically Authentic Non-Euclidean Adventures in Mountain Climbing*. Translated by Roger Shattuck. Baltimore: Penguin Books.

Davidson, Donald. 1973–74. "On the Very Idea of a Conceptual Scheme." *Proceedings and Addresses of the American Philosophical Association* 47:5–20.

Demartino, Richard J. 1981. "The Zen Understanding of the Initial Nature of Man." In *Buddhist and Western Philosophy*, edited by Nathan Katz. Atlantic Highlands, N.J.: Humanities Press.

de Muralt, André. 1973. *The Idea of Phenomenology: Husserlian Exemplarism*. Translated by Garry L. Breckon. Evanston: Northwestern University Press.

Derrida, Jacques. 1972. *Positions*. Paris: Minuit.

———. 1973. *Speech and Phenomena and Other Essays on Husserl's Theory of Signs*. Translated by David B. Allison. Evanston: Northwestern University Press.

———. 1976. *Of Grammatology*. Baltimore: Johns Hopkins University Press.

———. 1978. *Writing and Difference*. Translated by Alan Bass. Chicago: University of Chicago Press.

———. 1981a. *Dissemination*. Translated by Barbara Johnson. Chicago: University of Chicago Press.

———. 1981b. *Positions*. Translated by Alan Bass. Chicago: University of Chicago Press.

———. 1982. *Margins of Philosophy*. Chicago: University of Chicago Press.

———. 1986. *Shibboleth; pour Paul Celan*. Paris: Galilée.

———. 1988. "The Deaths of Roland Barthes." In *Philosophy and Non-Philosophy since Merleau-Ponty*, edited by Hugh J. Silverman. New York: Routledge.

Dews, Peter. 1988. *Logics of Disintegration: Post-structuralist Thought and the Claims of Critical Theory*. London: Verso.

Dufrenne, Mikel. 1973. *Le Poétique*. Paris: Presses Universitaires de France.

Duméry, Henry. 1964. *The Problem of God in Philosophy of Religion*. Translated by Charles Courtney. Evanston: Northwestern University Press.

Dummett, Michael. 1978. *Truth and Other Enigmas*. Cambridge: Harvard University Press.

Dupré, Louis. 1968. "Husserl's Thought on God and Faith." *Philosophy and Phenomenological Research* 29:

Eddington, Arthur, Sir. 1935. *The Nature of the Physical World*. London: Dent.

Engelmann, Paul. 1968. *Letters from Ludwig Wittgenstein, with a Memoir*. Translated by L. Furtmeuller and edited by B. F. McGuinness. New York: Horizon Press.

Fichte, Johann Gottlieb. 1965. *The Vocation of Man*. Translated by William Smith, La Salle, IL: Open Court.

———. 1975. *Versuch einer neuen Darstellung der Wissenschaftslehre*. Hamburg: F. Meiner.

Findlay, J. N. 1970. *Ascent to the Absolute: Metaphysical Papers and Lectures*. New York: Humanities Press.

Fink, Eugen. 1970. "The Phenomenological Philosophy of Edmund Husserl and Contemporary Criticism." In *The Phenomenology of Husserl: Selected Critical Readings*, edited by R. O. Elveton. Chicago: Quadrangle Books.

Flynn, Thomas R. 1980. "Sartre-Flaubert and the Real/Unreal." In *Jean-Paul Sartre: Contemporary Approaches to His Philosophy*, Hugh J. Silverman and Frederick A. Elliston. Pittsburgh: Duquesne University Press.

Fóti, Veronique M. 1992. *Heidegger and the Poets: Poiēsis/Sophia/Technē*. Atlantic Highlands, N.J.: Humanities Press.

Foucault, Michel. 1973. *The Birth of the Clinic: An Archaeology of Medical Perception*. Translated by A. M. Sheridan Smith. New York: Pantheon Books.

———. 1977. *Language, Counter-Memory, Practice*. Edited by Donald F. Bouchard and translated by Donald F. Bouchard and Sherry Simon, Ithaca: Cornell University Press.

Fretz, Leo. 1980. "An Interview with Jean-Paul Sartre." In *Jean-Paul Sartre: Contemporary Approaches to His Philosophy*, Hugh J. Silverman and Frederick A. Elliston. Pittsburgh: Duquesne University Press.

Gadamer, Hans-Georg. 1984. *Truth and Method*. New York: Crossroad.

Gasché, Rodolphe. 1987. Introduction to *Readings in Interpretation: Hölderlin, Hegel, Heidegger, History and Theory of Literature*. Vol. 26, by Andrzej Warminski. Minneapolis: Univesity of Minnesota Press.

———. 1988. "God, For Example." In *Phenomenology and the Numinous*, edited by André Schuwer. Pittsburgh: Simon Silverman Phenomenology Center.

Genet, Jean. 1964. *The Thief's Journal*. Translated by B. Frechtman. New York: Grove Press.

Gibson, Margaret. 1991. "Making Salad." In *Beneath a Single Moon: Buddhism in Contemporary American Poetry*, edited by Kent Johnson and Craig Paulenich. Boston: Shambhala.

Gillan, Garth Jackson. 1980. "A Question of Method: History and Critical Experience." In *Jean- Paul Sartre: Contemporary Approaches to His Philosophy*, Hugh J. Silverman and Frederick A. Elliston. Pittsburgh: Duquesne University Press.

Golden, James, and David L. Jamison. 1990. "Meyer's Theory of Prolematology." *Revue Internationale de Philosophie* 44;

Guenther, Herbert V. 1983. "'Meditation' Trends in Early Tibet. In *Early Ch'an in China and Tibet*, Berkeley Buddhist Studies Series 5, Whalen Lai and Lewis R. Lancaster. Berkeley: Asian Humanities Press.

———. 1989. *From Reductionism to Creativity: rDzogs-chen and the New Sciences of Mind*. Boston: Shambhala.

Guenther, Herbert V. and Chogyam Trungpa. 1988. *The Dawn of Tantra*. Edited by Michael Kohn. Boston: Shambhala.

Gurwitsch, Aron. 1940. "On the Intentionality of Consciousness." In *Philosophical Essays in Memory of Edmund Husserl*, edited by Marvin Farber. Cambridge: Harvard University Press.

———. 1966. *Studies in Phenomenology and Psychology*. Evanston: Northwestern University Press.

Haar, Michel. 1980. "Sartre and Heidegger." In *Jean-Paul Sartre: Contemporary Approaches to His Philosophy*, Hugh J. Silverman and Frederick A. Elliston Pittsburgh: Duquesne University Press.

Hayward, Jeremy W. 1989. Forward to *From Reductionism to Creativity: rDzogs-chen and the New Sciences of Mind*, by Herbert V. Guenther. Boston: Shambhala.

Heidegger, Martin. 1950. *Holzwege*. Frankfurt am Main: Klostermann.

———. 1955. *Was ist Metaphysik?*. Frankfurt: Klostermann.

———. 1957. *Der Satz vom Grund*. Pfullingen: Neske.

——. 1962. *Being and Time*. Translated by John Macquarrie and Edward Robinson. New York: Harper and Row.

——. 1967. *Wegmarken*. Frankfurt am Main: Klostermann.

——. 1968. *What is Called Thinking?* Translated by Fred D. Wieck and J. Glenn Gray. New York: Harper & Row.

——. 1970. *Hegel's Concept of Experience*. New York: Harper & Row.

——. 1971. *Poetry, Language, Thought*. Translated by Albert Hofstadter. New York: Harper & Row.

——. 1977. *The Question Concerning Technology and Other Essays*. Translated by W. Lovitt. New York: Harper & Row.

——. 1993. "The Way to Language." In *Basic Writings*, edited by David Farrell Krell. San Francisco: Harper San Francisco.

Herrigel, Eugen. 1960. *The Method of Zen*. London: Routledge & Kegan Paul.

Hiley, David R. 1988. *Philosophy in Question: Essays on a Pyrrhonian Theme*. Chicago: University of Chicago Press.

Horkheimer, Max, and Theodor W. Adorno. 1972. *Dialectic of Enlightenment*. Translated by John Cumming. New York: Seabury Press.

Husserl, Edmund. 1982. *Ideas Pertaining to a Pure Phenomenology and to a Phenomenological Philosophy: First Book: General Introduction to a Pure Phenomenology*. Translated by F. Kersten. The Hague: Martinus Nijhoff.

Hwa Yol Jung. 1987. "Heidegger's Way with Sinitic Thinking." In *Heidegger and Asian Thought*, edited by Graham Parkes. Honolulu: University of Hawaii Press.

Inada, Kenneth K. 1970. *Nagarjuna: A Translation of his Mulamadhyamakakarika with an Introductory Essay*. Tokyo: Hokuseido Press.

Irigaray, Luce. 1991. "Love Between Us." In *Who Comes After the Subject?* edited by Eduardo Cadava, Peter Connor, and Jean-Luc Nancy. New York: Routledge.

Johnson, Galen A., and Michael B. Smith, eds. 1990. *Ontology and Alterity in Merleau-Ponty*. Evanston: Northwestern University Press.

Johnson, Kent and Craig Paulenich, eds. 1991. *Beneath a Single Moon: Buddhism in Contemporary American Poetry*. Boston: Shambhala.

Kasulis, Thomas P., ed. 1993. *Self as Body in Asian Theory and Practice*. Albany: SUNY Press.

Kern, Iso. 1964. *Kant und Husserl, Phaenomenologica* 16. (The Hague: M. Nijhoff).

Kierkegaard, Soren. 1985. *Philosophical Fragments*. Translated by H. V. Hong and E. Hong. Princeton: Princeton University Press.

Kockelmans, Joseph J. 1967. *Phenomenology: The Philosophy of Edmund Husserl and Its Interpretation*. Garden City: Doubleday.

Kohák, Erazim. 1978. *Idea and Experience: Edmund Husserl's Project of Phenomenology in IDEAS I*. Chicago: University of Chicago Press.

Kotoh, Tetsuaki. 1987. "Language and Silence: Self-Inquiry in Heidegger and Zen." In *Heidegger and Asian Thought*, edited by Graham Parkes, Honolulu: University of Hawaii Press.

Krell, David Farrell. 1979. "Analysis." In *The Will to Power as Art*. "Nietzsche," Vol. 1, Martin Heidegger. Translated by David Farrell Krell. New York: Harper & Row.

Kripke, Saul. 1972. *Naming and Necessity*. Cambridge: Harvard.

Kwant, Remy C. 1963. *The Phenomenological Philosophy of Merleau-Ponty*. Pittsburgh: Duquesne University Press.

Lacan, Jacques. 1966. *Écrits*. Paris: Éditions du Seuil.

Lai, Whalen, and Lewis R. Lancaster. 1983. *Early Ch'an in China and Tibet*, Berkeley Buddhist Studies Series 5. Berkeley: Asian Humanities Press.

Laycock, Steven W. 1994. *Mind as Mirror and the Mirroring of Mind: Buddhist Reflections on Western Phenomenology*. Albany: SUNY Press.

Levin, David Michael. 1970. *Reason and Evidence in Husserl's Phenomenology*. Evanston: Northwestern University Press.

———. 1985. *The Body's Recollection of Being: Phenomenological Psychology and the Deconstruction of Nihilism*. Boston: Routledge and Kegal Paul.

———. 1988. *The Opening of Vision: Nihilism and the Postmodern Situation*. London: Routledge & Kegan Paul.

Levine, Steve. 1982. *Who Dies?: An Investigation of Conscious Living and Conscious Dying*. New York: Anchor Books.

Lingis, Alphonso. 1991. "Imperatives." In *Merleau-Ponty Vivant*, edited by M. C. Dillon. Albany: SUNY Press.

Lispector, Clarice. 1988. *The Passion According to G. H.* Translated by Ronald W. Sousa. Minneapolis: University of Minnesota Press.

Llewelyn, John. 1988. "The Origin and End of Philosophy." In *Philosophy and Non-Philosophy since Merleau-Ponty*, edited by Hugh J. Silverman, New York: Routledge.

Loewenberg, Jacob, ed. 1929. *Hegel Selections*. New York: Charles Scribner's Sons.

Lopez, Donald S., Jr. 1988. *The Heart Sutra Explained: Indian and Tibetan Commentaries*. Albany: SUNY Press.

Loy, David. 1984. "How Not to Criticize N_g_rjuna: A Response to L. Stafford Betty." *Philosophy East and West* 34 (4).

———. 1988. *Nonduality: A Study in Comparative Philosophy*. New Haven: Yale University Press.

Lyotard, Jean-François. 1982. *La phénoménologie*. Paris: Presses Universitaires de France.

———. 1983. "Presentations." In *Philosophy in France Today*, edited by Alan Montefiore. Cambridge: Cambridge University Press.

———. 1984. *L'Assassinat de l'expérience par la peinture. Monory*. Paris: Le Castor Astral.

———. 1990. *Peregrinations: Law, Form, Event*. New York: Columbia University Press.

———. 1991a. *The Inhuman: Reflections on Time*. Translated by Geoffrey Bennington and Rachel Bowlby. Stanford: Stanford University Press.

———. 1991b. *Phenomenology*. Translated by Brian Beakley. Albany: SUNY Press.

———. 1996. "The Postmodern Condition: A Report on Knowledge." In *From Modernism to Postmodernism: An Anthology*, edited by Lawrence E. Cahoone. Cambridge: Blackwell.

Magliola, Robert. 1986. *Derrida on the Mend*. West Lafayette: Purdue University Press.

Mehta, J. L. 1987. "Heidegger and Vedanta: Reflections on a Questionable Theme." In *Heidegger and Asian Thought*, edited by Graham Parkes. Honolulu: University of Hawaii Press.

Menzan Zuiho Osho. 1988. *Jijuyu-zanmai*. Samadhi of the Self. In *Dogen Zen*, translated by Shohaku Okumura and Daitsu Tom Wright. Kyoto: Kyoto Soto-Zen Center.

Merleau-Ponty, Maurice. 1955. *Les Aventures de la dialectique*. Paris: Gallimard.

———. 1962. *Phenomenology of Perception*. Translated by Colin Smith. New York: Humanities Press.

———. 1964a. "Eye and Mind." In *The Primacy of Perception and Other Essays on Phenomenological Psychology, and the Philosophy of Art, History and Politics*, edited by James M. Edie. Evanston: Northwestern University Press.

———. 1964b. *The Primacy of Perception and Other Essays on Phenomenological Psychology, and the Philosophy of Art, History and Politics*. Edited by James M. Edie. Evanston: Northwestern University Press.

———. 1964c. *Signs*. Translated by Richard C. McLeary. Evanston: Northwestern University Press.

———. 1969. *The Visible and the Invisible*. Translated by Colin Smith. Evanston: Northwestern University Press.

———. 1974. "The Philosopher and Sociology." In *Phenomenology, Language, Sociology: Selected Essays of Maurice Merleau-Ponty*, edited by John O'Neill. London: Heinemann.

———. 1988. "Philosophy and Non-Philosophy since Hegel." In *Philosophy and Non-Philosophy since Merleau-Ponty*, edited by Hugh J. Silverman. New York: Routledge.

Merton, Thomas. 1967. *Mysticism and Zen Masters*. New York: Farrar, Strauss & Giroux.

Misra, R. S. 1971. "Interview with Dom Aelred Graham." In *The End of Religion*, Dom Aelred Graham. New York: Harcourt, Brace, & Jovanovich.

Molino, Fernando. 1962. *Existentialism as Philosophy*. Englewood Cliffs: Prentice-Hall.

Montaigne, Michel de. 1965. *The Complete Essays of Montaigne*. Translated by Donald M. Frame. Stanford: Stanford University Press.

Murdoch, Iris. 1970. *The Sovereignty of Good*. London: Routledge & Kegan Paul.

Murti, T. R. V. 1987. *The Central Philosophy of Buddhism: A Study of the Madhyamika System*. London: Allen & Unwin.

Nagao, Gadjin M. 1979. "From, Mādhyamika to Yogācarā: An Analysis of MMK XXIV.18 and MV 1.1-2." *Journal of the International Association of Buddhist Studies* 2:

Nāgārjuna. 1967. "Fundamentals of the Middle Way: Mūlamādhyamika-Karikas." Fredrick J. Streng. In *Emptiness: A Study in Religious Meaning* New York: Abingdon Press.

Nāgārjuna. 1995. *The Fundamental Wisdom of the Middle Way: Nāgārjuna's Mūlamadhyamakakarika*. Translated by Jay L. Garfield. New York: Oxford University Press.

Natanson, Maurice. 1951. *A Critique of Jean-Paul Sartre's Ontology*. Lincoln: University of Nebraska Press.

Nietzsche, Friedrich. 1954. *Thus Spake Zarathustra*. Translated by Walter Kaufmann. In *The Portable Nietzsche*, edited by Walter Kaufmann. New York: Viking Press.

———. 1964. *The Joyful Wisdom*. Translated by Thomas Common. London: Russell & Russell.

———. 1967. *The Will to Power*. Translated by Walter Kaufman and R. J. Hollingdale. New York: Vintage.

———. 1968. *The Twilight of the Idols/The Anti-Christ*. Translated by R. J. Hollingdale. Baltimore: Harmondsworth.

———. 1974. *The Gay Science*. Translated by Walter Kaufman. New York: Vintage.

———. 1980. "On Truth and Lie in the Extra-Moral Sense." In *The Portable Nietzsche*, edited by Walter Kaufmann. New York: Penguin Books.

Nishitani,Keiji. 1982. *Religion and Nothingness*. Translated by Jan Van Bragt. Berkeley: University of California Press.

Norris, Christopher. 1982. *Deconstruction: Theory and Practice*. London: Methuen.

Okumura, Shohaku, and Daitsu Tom, Wright, trans. 1988. *Dogen Zen*. Kyoto: Kyoto Soto-Zen Center.

Parkes, Graham, ed. 1987. *Heidegger and Asian Thought*. Honolulu: University of Hawaii Press.

Parsons, Howard L. 1976. *The Value of Buddhism for the Modern World*, Wheel Publication, No. 232/233. Kandy: Buddhist Publishing Society.

Pivcevic, Edo, ed. 1975. *Phenomenology and Philosophical Understanding*. London: Cambridge University Press.

Price A. F., and Mou-Lam Wong, trans. 1969. *The Sutra of Hui Neng*. Boulder: Shambhala Publications.

Prufer, Thomas. 1973. "Welt, Ich und Zeit in der Sprache." *Philosophische Rundschau* 20:

Puligandla, Ramakrishna. 1985. *Jñāna-Yoga—The Way of Knowledge. An Analytic Interpretation*. New York: University Press of America.

Quine, Willard V. 1970. *Philosophy of Logic*. Englewood Cliffs: Prentice-Hall.

Rajchman, John. 1985. "Philosophy in America." In *Post-Analytic Philosophy*, edited by John Rajchman and Cornel West. New York: Columbia University Press.

Rajchman, John, and Cornel, West, eds. 1985. *Post-Analytic Philosophy*. New York: Columbia University Press.

Rancière, Jacques. 1991. "After What." In *Who Comes After the Subject?* edited by Eduardo Cadava, Peter Connor, and Jean-Luc Nancy. New York: Routledge.

Reps, Paul, ed. 1989. *Zen Flesh, Zen Bones: A Collection of Zen and Pre-Zen Writings*. Garden City: Doubleday.

Rorty, Richard. 1979. *Philosophy and the Mirror of Nature*. Princeton: Princeton University Press.

———. 1982. *Consequences of Pragmatism*. Minneapolis: University of Minnesota Press.

Rovatti, Pier Aldo. 1988. "The Black Light." In *Recoding Metaphysics: The New Italian Philosophy*, edited by Giovanna Borradori. Evanston: Northwestern University Press.

Royce, Josiah. 1976. *The World and the Individual: Nature, Man, and the Moral Order*. Gloucester: Peter Smith.

Salis, John. 1988. "Echoes: Philosophy and Non-Philosophy after Heidegger." In *Philosophy and Non-Philosophy since Merleau-Ponty*, edited by Hugh J. Silverman. New York: Routledge.

Sangharakshita. 1987. *A Survey of Buddhism: Its Doctrines and Methods through the Ages*. London: Tharpa Publications.

Sartre, Jean-Paul. 1964. Foreword to *The Thief's Journal*, by Jean Genet. Translated by B. Frechtman. New York: Grove Press.

———. 1965. *Situations*. Translated by B. Eisler. Greenwich: Fawcett.

———. 1971. *Being and Nothingness: An Essay on Phenomenological Ontology*. Translated by Hazel E. Barnes. New York: Washington Square Press.

———. 1972. *The Transcendence of the Ego: An Existentialist Theory of Consciousness*. Translated by Forrest Williams and Robert Kirkpatrick. New York: Noonday Press.

——. 1971–72. *Idiot de la famille: Gustav Flaubert de 1821–1857.* Vol. I. Paris: Gallimard.

——. 1975. "Existentialism is a Humanism." In *Existentialism from Dostoevsky to Sartre,* edited by Walter Kaufmann. New York: Meridian, 1975.

——. 1984. *The War Diaries of Jean-Paul Sartre: November 1939/March 1940.* Translated by Quintin Hoare. New York: Pantheon.

——. 1991. *The Psychology of the Imagination.* Secaucus: Citadel Press.

——. 1993. *Quiet Moments in a War: The Letters of Jean-Paul Sartre to Simone de Beauvoir 1940–1963.* Translated by Lee Fahnestock and Norman Macafee. New York: Penguin.

Scharfstein, Ben-Ami. 1993. *Ineffability: The Failure of Words in Philosophy of Religion.* Albany: SUNY Press.

Schofield, Malcolm, Myles Burnyeat, and Jonathan Barnes. 1980. *Doubt and Dogmatism: Studies in Hellenistic Epistemology.* Oxford: Clarendon Press.

Schuwer. André, ed. 1988. *Phenomenology and the Numinous.* Pittsburgh: The Simon Silverman Phenomenology Center.

Sedley, David. 1984. "The Motivation of Greek Skepticism." In *The Skeptical Tradition,* edited by Myles Burnyeat, Berkeley: University of California Press.

Sekida, Katsuki. 1992. *Zen Training: Methods and Philosophy.* Edited by A. V. Grimstone. New York: Weatherhill.

Severino, Emanuele. 1988. "The Earth and the Essence of Man." In *Recoding Metaphysics: The New Italian Philosophy,* edited by Giovanna Borradori. Evanston: Northwestern University Press.

Sextus Empiricus. 1933. *Outlines of Pyrrhonism.* Translated by R. G. Bury. Cambridge: Harvard University Press.

Silverman, Hugh J. 1980. "Sartre's Words on the Self." In *Jean-Paul Sartre: Contemporary Approaches to His Philosophy,* Hugh J. Silverman and Frederick A. Elliston. Pittsburgh: Duquesne University Press.

Silverman, Hugh J and Elliston, Frederick A. 1980c. *Jean-Paul Sartre: Contemporary Approaches to His Philosophy.* Pittsburgh: Duquesne University Press.

——. 1988. Footnote annotations to "Philosophy and Non-Philosophy since Hegel." In Hugh J. Silverman. *Philosophy and Non-Philosophy since Merleau-Ponty,* New York: Routledge.

Silverman, Hugh J, ed. 1988b. *Philosophy and Non-Philosophy since Merleau-Ponty.* New York: Routledge.

Silverman, Hugh J. and Frederick A. Elliston. 1980. "General Introduction." In *Jean-Paul Sartre: Contemporary Approaches to His Philosophy,* Hugh J. Silverman and Frederick A. Elliston. Pittsburgh: Duquesne University Press.

Snyder, Gary. 1991. "For Nothing." In *Beneath a Single Moon: Buddhism in*

Contemporary American Poetry, edited by Kent Johnson and Craig Paulenich. Boston: Shambhala.

Sohl, Robert, and Carr, Audrey, eds. 1970. *The Gospel According to Zen: Beyond the Death of God*. New York: Mentor.

Sokolowski, Robert. 1964. *The Formation of Husserl's Concept of Constitution*. The Hague: Martinus Nijhoff.

———. 1974. *Husserlian Meditations: How Words Present Things*. Evanston: Northwestern University Press.

Solomon, Robert C. 1972. "General Introduction: What is Phenomenology?" In *Phenomenology and Existentialism*, edited by Robert C. Solomon. New York: Harper & Row.

Solomon, Robert C., ed. 1972b. *Phenomenology and Existentialism*. New York: Harper & Row.

Sprung, Mervyn, ed. 1978. *The Question of Being*. University Park: Pennsylvania University Press.

Stcherbatsky, F. Th. 1962. *Buddhist Logic*. New York: Dover.

Streng, Frederick J. 1967. *Emptiness: A Study in Religious Meaning*. Nashville: Abingdon Press.

Stryk, Lucien, and Ikemoto Takash, trans. 1963 *Zen: Poems, Prayers, Sermons, Anecdotes, Interviews*. Garden City: Doubleday.

Suzuki, Daisetz Teitaro. 1957. *Mysticism: Christian and Buddhist*. New York: Harper.

———. 1981. *The Zen Doctrine of No-Mind: The Significance of the Sutra of Hui-Neng. (Wei-Lang)*. Edited by Christmas Humphreys. New Beach: Samuel Weiser.

Takeuchi Yoshinori. 1983. *The Heart of Buddhism: In Search of the Timeless Spirit of Primitive Buddhism*. Edited and translated by James W. Heisig. New York: Crossroad.

Thiel, Rudolf. 1958. *And There Was Light: The Discovery of the Universe*. Translated by Richard and Clara Winston. New York: Knopf.

Thomas, Edward J. 1953. *The History of Buddhist Thought*. London: Routledge and Kegan Paul.

Timmermans, Benoît. 1990. "Kant et l'histoire de la philosophie: la vision problématologique." *Revue Internationale de Philosophie*, 44.

Trotignon, Pièrre. ( ) "The End and Time." In *Analecta Husserliana*, Vol. IX, edited by A.-T. Tymieniecka.

Uchiyama Kosho Roshi. 1988. *Dogen Zen As Religion*. In *Dogen Zen*, translated by Shohaku Okumura and Daitsu Tom Wright. Kyoto: Kyoto Soto-Zen Center.

Varela, Francisco J., Evan Thompson, and Eleanor Rosch. 1992. *The Embodied Mind: Cognitive Science and Human Experience*. Cambridge: MIT Press.

Wagner, Hans. 1970. "Critical Observations Concerning Husserl's Posthumous

Writings." In *The Phenomenology of Husserl: Selected Critical Readings*, edited and translated by R. O. Elveton. Chicago: Quadrangle Books.

Waldenfels, Hans. 1980. *Absolute Nothingness: Foundations for a Buddhist-Christian Dialogue*. Translated by J. W. Heisig. New York: Paulist Press.

Warminski, Andrzej. 1987. *Readings in Interpretation: Hölderlin, Hegel, Heidegger, History and Theory of Literature*. Vol. 26. Minneapolis: Univesity of Minnesota Press.

Watson, Stephen H. 1988. "The Adventures of the Narrative: Lyotard and the Passage of the Phantasm." In Hugh J. Silverman. *Philosophy and Non-Philosophy since Merleau-Ponty*. New York: Routledge.

Watts, Alan W. 1970. "Western Mythology: Its Dissolution and Transformation." In Joseph Campbell, ed., *Myths, Dreams and Religion*. New York: Dutton.

Whitehead, Alfred North. 1978. *Process and Reality*. D. R. Griffin and D. W. Sherburne, eds. New York: Free Press.

Wittgenstein, Ludwig. 1974. *Tractatus Logico-Philosophicus*. Translated by D. F. Pears and B. F. McGuinness. Atlantic Highlands, N.J.: Humanities Press.

———. 1980. *Culture and Value*. Edited by C. H. von Wright. Oxford: Blackwell.

Wood, David, and Robert Bernasconi, eds. 1988. *Derrida and Différance*. Evanston: Northwestern University Press.

Wyschogrod, Edith. 1990. *Saints and Postmodernism: Revisioning Moral Philosophy*. Chicago: University of Chicago Press.

Yampolsky, Philip B. 1967. *The Platform Sutra of the Sixth Patriarch*. New York: Columbia University Press.

Zaner, Richard M. 1975. "On the Sense of Method in Phenomenology." In *Phenomenology and Philosophical Understanding*, edited by Edo Pivcevic. London: Cambridge University Press.

Index